A Heartbeat
AND a Guitar

A Heartbeat
AND a Guitar

Johnny Cash and the
Making of *Bitter Tears*

ANTONINO D'AMBROSIO

NATION
BOOKS
New York

Books published by Nation Books are available at special discounts for bulk
purchases in the United States by corporations, institutions, and other
organizations. For more information, please contact the Special Markets
Department at the Perseus Books Group, 2300 Chestnut Street, Suite 200,
Philadelphia, PA 19103, or call (800) 810-4145, ext. 5000, or e-mail
special.markets@perseusbooks.com.

Designed by Brent Wilcox

Library of Congress Cataloging-in-Publication Data
D'Ambrosio, Antonino.
    A heartbeat and a guitar: Johnny Cash and the making of bitter tears /
Antonino D'Ambrosio.
        p.   cm.
    ISBN 978-1-56858-407-2 (alk. paper)
    1. Cash, Johnny.   2. Country musicians—United States—Biography.
I. Title.
ML420.C265D35 2009
782.421642092—dc22
                                                                    2009019825

10 9 8 7 6 5 4 3 2 1

For Franco D'Ambrosio

"*Like a buddy fallen in battle, these guys made a difference, you're hearing the truth of a man, a soul, a heart.*"

—Arlo Guthrie on Johnny Cash
and Peter La Farge

"*Gaily the Troubadour / Touched his guitar.*"

—Thomas Haynes Bayly

"*He who sings scares away his woes.*"

—Cervantes

CONTENTS

BEFORE
I Had to Fight Back

On a particularly gray, cold morning in Bowling Green, Ohio, back in February 2005, I found myself in a small, windowless room, where an undergraduate student from Bowling Green State University had just handed me a stack of records, CDs, books, and magazines. She also congratulated me on the talk I had given the night before. At the invitation of Daniel Boudreau, a Ph.D. candidate in the American Cultural Studies Department, I'd come to Bowling Green on a lecture tour to support my first book, *Let Fury Have the Hour: The Punk Rock Politics of Joe Strummer*.

The university had graciously offered to grant me access to its prestigious Music Library and Sound Recordings Archives. I soon found myself in the third-floor office of the gregarious archivist Bill Schurk, who regaled me with stories about music and the things archivists find exciting—which I happen to find exciting, too, including the documenting of materials that may seem worthless but over time provide an invaluable record of a moment that has slipped away but thankfully has been preserved forever.

For anyone who loves music, the Sound Recordings Archives is a magnificent place—every recording in human history seems to be housed there. I was excited to get into the shelves of rare LPs, music books, and other music-related media. After speaking with Schurk and his staff, I felt like Tom Hanks's character in the film *Big* when he was unleashed in FAO Schwarz and danced joyfully on the huge piano. I requested as many records as I could possibly listen to in my allotted time. The list was long and contained mostly recordings I'd never heard of, including rare albums by Woody Guthrie, The Carter Family, Django Reinhardt, Spencer Davis, Charlie Parker, and The Clash.

After thanking the student who had given me the records, I handled each one as if it were a priceless artifact. (To me they actually all *were* priceless artifacts.) I listened intently to all of them. Then, near the bottom of the stack, I came upon a Johnny Cash record that I'd checked off the list as an afterthought. I was happy, though, that the record was part of the archives; I had discovered this little-known Cash record while writing about Cash's collaboration with The Clash's former front man Joe Strummer for my previous book.

But now, as Cash's gaunt face and steely eyes stared back at me from the *Bitter Tears* album cover, I realized that there was something striking, even unsettling about this image. This wasn't the myth, the persona that has become Johnny Cash, but rather something truer, more authentically John R. Cash, the former sharecropper and cotton picker from Arkansas. In contrast to looking rock 'n' roll hip—a swaggering, pompadoured balladeer with an acoustic guitar slung over his shoulder—here his famous head of hair was cropped short and ringed by a red headband. The look in his eyes seemed troubled, as if what he was about to share was something heavy and hard.

I slid the record out of its sleeve and a piece of paper fell out, landing at my feet. Picking it up, I saw that it was a copy of a letter Cash had penned on his own letterhead, with his cursive signature at the top, and the proclamation

NOBODY BUT NOBODY
MORE ORIGINAL THAN JOHNNY CASH

at the bottom. One line jumped out at me: "D.J.'s—station managers—owners . . . where are your guts?"

The disc in my hand was not the original pressing. Bear Family Records, a German independent record label, reissued it in 1984 with lyrics, photos, quotes, commentary, and a few extra songs. It was quite clear from reading the essay-like liner notes that lots of people had lots to say about this Cash record.

The title, *Bitter Tears: Ballads of the American Indian*, prompted a question: What had Cash been up to? I looked at the recording date: 1964. Barely a year earlier, Cash had scored one of his biggest hits ever with "Ring of Fire." But the year added another layer of intrigue to the story, for it was a bellwether year in U.S. history. The headlines shouted about the Beatles, Muhammad Ali, the Vietnam War, the Newport Folk Festival, and Martin Luther King Jr.; the Johnson-Goldwater presidential election, the Civil Rights Act, Johnson's Great Society, and the early stirrings of what a few years later would become known as "Red Power"—taking its cue from the term "Black Power"—the Native movement that took hold in the 1960s and grew in the 1970s among Native people. Recorded four years before Cash's Folsom Prison performance and the American Indian Movement's takeover of Alcatraz Island, *Bitter Tears* was released smack in the middle of the roiling civil rights movement and escalating war in Vietnam. In the face of such momentous change and conflict, an album sympathetic to Native people's issues and their seemingly never-ending search for justice now seemed to me both a compelling and a daring undertaking.* At the time, Cash was a music superstar. What kind of response did he get to this album? How did the radio stations respond to a musician who was giving voice to an oppressed group fighting to be heard? A thousand

---

*Based on my discussions with various Native activists, including Dennis Banks, John Trudell, and Jose Barriero, I will use the term "Native people" in this book. As Trudell explains, "Number One, I look at us as Native people, not Native Americans, because anyone born in the nation-state of America is an American, and America, the whole concept and idea, is 530 years old. We are older than that, so when you take that American identity, obviously it isn't who we are—I mean in the real sense. It's America that tends to claim ownership of us. Number Two, we're not Indians, because we're not in India. I look at it that, whatever is going on, we are Native peoples."

more questions began swirling in my mind, but one was at the root of
them all: Why did Cash make this record?

THERE WAS only one way to start finding out, so I lifted the plastic
turntable cover, selected the proper setting, placed the record, side
2–up, on the turntable, and moved the needle over to the first song. I
pulled the earphones securely over my ears, pushed play, and listened. Soon my head filled with the sound of a flute slowly and
hauntingly playing the last bars of taps, immediately calling funeral,
wreath-laying, and memorial services to my mind. After more than
ten seconds, Cash's deep, husky voice came in, singing the name "Ira
Hayes, Ira Hayes," quivering over the second "Ira" as he strummed
the first few chords of the song on his D-28 Martin guitar. Soon,
Cash was joined by soulful backing vocals for what turned out to be
the refrain of the song:

Call him drunken Ira Hayes
He won't answer anymore
Not the whiskey-drinkin' Indian
Or the marine that went to war

These lyrics are the opening lines to "Ballad of Ira Hayes," clearly
a folksong but not in the traditional sense popularized by The Carter
Family in the 1920s and 1930s. "Ballad of Ira Hayes" is instead very
much a product of the folk revival that was occurring in the 1960s. As
the record spun on the turntable, I could sense Woody Guthrie's spirit
embedded in the grooves. I knew Cash had great feeling for Guthrie,
who himself had idolized The Carter Family. I could feel the three
distinct musical legends, each with family members who became important musicians in their own right—The Carter Family, Woody
Guthrie, and Johnny Cash—coming together to form one unique folk
family tree. The "topical folksong movement," as it was called, famously produced scores of musicians who were Guthrie disciples,
with Bob Dylan pushing the movement to the forefront of America's

consciousness. Its articulate, impassioned goodwill ambassador was Pete Seeger, but other musicians who walked the streets of Greenwich Village during the folk revival were righteous soldiers of conscience, armed with acoustic guitars and songs telling stories that sought a new America. Judy Collins, Tom Paxton, Buffy Sainte-Marie, Mark Spolestra, Guy Carawan, John Cohen, Len Chandler, and Joan Baez were some of the major voices in this growing U.S. counterculture chorus. "Ballad of Ira Hayes" is a graphic, poetic account of a Pima named Ira Hayes who goes off to war, becomes a war hero, and then returns home to eventually die an ignoble death blanketed by pain, abandonment, and humiliation. Hayes was not only a Pima who fought in World War II, but he had actually been immortalized in the famous photo of the flag-raising at Iwo Jima. But when I listened to the song that day, I didn't know Ira Hayes from Von Hayes, a second-rate baseball player on my hometown team, the Philadelphia Phillies, in the 1980s. So much for immortality.

I played the song again and again and again and again. When I looked up at the clock, I'd spent more than an hour listening to just that one song. The other songs were, if not as powerful, certainly as thought-provoking and demanding. The album was a challenge to my senses; it didn't just open my eyes, it ripped open my mind. Cash not only boldly gave voice to issues of injustice afflicting Native people but musically told the world that compassion was at the very heart of who he was as a person and a musician. He was a storyteller interested in telling the stories of real people, those ignored by the press and politicians. Johnny Cash was a folksinger.

Four hours later, I was still listening to the record, having lost count around the fifteenth time. I looked closely at all the material packed into the sleeve describing various details of what I soon realized was a tremendously controversial album. And then the name Peter La Farge caught my eye. La Farge was listed as the writer of "Ballad of Ira Hayes." A number of the other songs appearing on the record were also credited to La Farge. My mind was buzzing, eager to learn more about this record and Cash's collaboration with Peter La Farge.

I HAD come across La Farge's name once or twice before, but only in passing connection to Bob Dylan. It seemed that La Farge and Dylan were friends, maybe even close friends, during the early days of the '60s folk revival, when they moved around Greenwich Village together performing on Sundays in Washington Square Park or at venues like Gerdes Folk City or the Gaslight. "Peter La Farge, a folksinger friend of mine, had given me a couple of Colt single-shot repeater pistols," Dylan later wrote in his autobiography, *Chronicles*. Ten pages later Dylan also mentioned Cash, who "was trying to change his image, too." After admitting that he would have liked to have Mick Jones, "the quintessential guitarist" from The Clash, play in his band (a story for another time), Dylan described Cash as not only having "a piercing yell, but ten thousand years of culture fell from him. . . . He sounds like he's at the edge of the fire, or in the deep snow, or in a ghostly forest, the coolness of conscious obvious strength, full tilt and vibrant with danger." For some reason Dylan's words helped me connect these three disparate individuals to one another: La Farge, Dylan, and Cash. I realized that they shared a common bond: sometimes dark, at times bright, but always fearlessly imaginative.

DESPITE CASH'S unwavering attitude about "not mixing in politics" that usually resulted in an intentionally ambiguous stance in terms of formal politics, he often spoke with a socially aware voice on behalf of society's outcasts. His songs addressed the realities of people ignored by newspaper headlines and the nightly news. He talked about the dignity of honest work: "If you were a baker, and you baked a loaf of bread and it fed somebody, then your life has been worthwhile. And if you were a weaver, and you wove some cloth and your cloth kept somebody warm, your life has been worthwhile." Of course he sang about the prisoner. "Convicts are the best audience I've played for," Cash said when asked why he played for them so often. In Cash's voice are echoes of what Woody Guthrie once said: "I am out to sing songs that will prove to you that this is your world and that if it has hit you pretty hard and knocked you for a dozen loops, no matter what color, what size you are, how you are built, I am out to sing the songs that make you take pride in yourself and in your work. And the songs that I sing are made up for the most part by all sorts of folks just about like you."

As my senses sharpened around *Bitter Tears*, I felt that of all the personas that Johnny Cash embodied, here was the album that really embodied his true nature: the rebellious troubadour. It seemed to me that nothing in Cash's life work matched *Bitter Tears* in its scale and courage.

Throughout his career, Cash was no stranger to controversy— battling, and sometimes shaming, record industry executives when they acted with willful ignorance or prejudice against his music because it didn't fit into their comfortable, easily compartmentalized view of who he was or who he should be as a performer. As I thought about this, I was surprised to discover, among the other items stuffed inside the album's sleeve, a 1964 *Billboard* ad in the form of another letter that Cash had written on behalf of *Bitter Tears,* this one to the record industry. Appearing in the August 22, 1964, issue of the magazine, the letter was blistering, offering no less than an indictment of a music establishment that Cash deemed guilty of the worst kind of crime: censorship. As I read the letter, it seemed to breathe life into words that William Blake had written a century before: "When I tell the truth, it is not for the sake of convincing those who do not know it, but for the sake of defending those that do." Cash wrote that "'Ballad of Ira Hayes' is strong medicine." When I glanced at the last sentence, I knew that Cash was not afraid to put it all on the line. He wrote: "I had to fight back when I realized that so many stations are afraid of 'Ira Hayes.' Just one question: Why?"

Oh, my.

And so the story begins. . . .

PART ONE
A Heartbeat

Johnny Cash on stage at the Newport Folk Festival, July 24, 1964, where he performed "Ballad of Ira Hayes." *Photo by Gai Terrell/Redferns.*

The Clouds Fall

IN DECEMBER 1968, four years after the release of the record *Bitter Tears: Ballads of the American Indian*, dozens of people crammed themselves shoulder-to-shoulder inside the old trading post at the base of Cemetery Hill in South Dakota. Most had to raise themselves up on their toes to get a glimpse of the man who came to visit them. "If I had a guitar with me I'd play something for you right now," Johnny Cash said as he was pushed toward the back of the trading post. From somewhere in the crowd an old black guitar was passed forward. "Here you go," said the man who handed the guitar to the bemused music star. Cash took the guitar and glanced down at it to get a feel for the battered instrument. It certainly wasn't anything like the D-28 Martin he often played and just as often destroyed. Cash must have thought, "Yeah, I could do something with this." Moving his left hand up and down the frets, strumming the rough strings with his right hand, he tried the best he could to tune the guitar. Smiling next to him was his new wife, June Carter. Cash looked over at June to see if she was ready. He steadied himself, and then looked deep into the crowd.

FOR NEARLY eighty years the trading post on the Pine Ridge Reservation had served as a stolid witness to one of the most gruesome acts of violence committed on U.S. soil. Until Cash's visit, the sounds haunting the post were the screams of three hundred Lakota Sioux men, women, and children who were hunted down by five hundred troops of the U.S. Seventh Cavalry. "Remember Little Bighorn," some survivors heard the soldiers shout. The Seventh Cavalry had once been General George Armstrong Custer's regiment. Having taken place near the Little Bighorn River in the eastern Montana Territory on June 24 and June 26, 1876, the Battle of Little Bighorn is the most famous battle of the "Indian Wars." It remains one of the greatest victories for Native people and one of the most disastrous defeats for the U.S. Cavalry.

In an act of gross arrogance, Custer had misjudged, on the eve of battle, just how badly the U.S. Cavalry was outnumbered and therefore tactically exposed. Compounding one of the worst military mistakes in history was Custer's reckless attack plan, which was to launch a surprise assault on the Lakota, who they believed were badly outnumbered by the Cavalry. They weren't. In fact, chief Horned Horse-watching, who observed the battle from a hillside, said afterward that the Sioux camp was so big that it extended over five miles. Soon after attacking, the cavalry was completely surrounded. Custer's folly led to the death of more than two hundred troops and sixteen officers; fifty-five men were wounded. Led by Sitting Bull, the Lakota suffered the loss of only thirty-six warriors, with 168 wounded. In American popular culture, the battle is known as "Custer's Last Stand," which is a far too forgiving rewriting of the general's terrible military incompetence on that day. Native people remember it as the "Battle of the Greasy Grass."

At Pine Ridge fourteen years after, the Seventh Cavalry rode for revenge, and by way of four massive Hotchkiss guns, got it. The Lakota warriors, yelling for the women and children to run—*"Inyanka po! Inyanka po!"*—tried to resist with their bare hands. "We tried to run," Louise Weasel Bear said later, "but they shot us like we were buffalo." Ignoring Miniconjou Lakota chief Big Foot's raising of a white flag, which signaled to the cavalry that his people would not fight or resist, the U.S. troops began firing at a rate of nearly a shell per second, quickly cutting down the unarmed Lakota. Dead bodies covered the ground. Disobeying orders to load the bodies into wagons, the soldiers instead chose to leave the dead on the ground to be buried by an ensuing blizzard, hoping the expected large snowfall would conceal the atrocities they committed. Only fifty Lakota are believed to have survived what is now simply referred to as *Wounded Knee*.

The U.S. government awarded twenty-five Medals of Honor for heroism on the battlefield during what it deemed to be the last battle between the United States and Native people. Six days later, L. Frank Baum, a young editor in Aberdeen, South Dakota, wrote in the *Aberdeen Saturday Pioneer:* "The *Pioneer* has before declared that our only safety depends upon the total extermination of the Indians. Having wronged them for centuries, we had better, in order to protect our civilization, follow it up by one more wrong and wipe these untamed and untamable creatures from the face of the earth." Nine years later, in 1900, he wrote *The Wonderful Wizard of Oz*, the children's novel that became the classic film, a perennial American favorite played on television during the Christmas season. Ironically, the Wounded Knee massacre took place four days after Christmas.

The surviving Lakota found shelter in a nearby Episcopal mission after spending hours huddled and bleeding outside in wagons, exposed to the freezing cold, while an indifferent army decided what to do with them. Lying on hay once inside, some of the survivors noticed a large sign with bold letters hanging above the pulpit:

PEACE ON EARTH, GOOD WILL TO MEN

Now the old trading post was about to be filled with a different sound. The crowd became quiet, hushed by the first sounds from the stand-in guitar. The silence was broken only by Cash's deep baritone voice, balanced by the melodic voice of June Carter. Standing among the Lakota, Cash could have sung anything—he could have chanted the telephone book—and the people in that old trading post wouldn't have cared. There was something special about this moment. When Cash sang "I Walk the Line," "Jackson," and "Folsom Prison Blues," the crowd's appreciation shook the rickety trading post to its foundation.

For a short time, for those listening, Cash's music helped calm the tortured echoes of the past.

A WESTERN Union telegram dated November 24, 1968, contained two simple lines:

> "Johnny Cash show definitely willing to play
> St Francis Monday evening Dec Ninth. Please confirm."

John L. Smith, a writer who became Cash's official discographer, stared at the telegram in amazement. More than a year had passed since he first met Cash at the KRNT Theater in Des Moines, Iowa, where the musician was performing three sold-out shows. During the meeting Cash wanted Smith to listen to an "Indian song" he'd just recorded, "The Flint Arrowhead." As Cash fumbled backstage with a large reel-to-reel tape recorder, looking in vain for the song, the two discussed various aspects of Native history. "He never did manage to play the song for me," Smith recalls. But afterward, Smith received a three-page letter from Cash. The musician wanted to accompany Smith on one of his many visits to Native reservations. "If I could provide him pictures of the actual battlefield in 1890, he would give me one of his guitars," Smith explains. "I thought, 'None of this will ever happen.'"

It did happen. Smith organized a visit to the Rosebud Reservation and then the Pine Ridge Reservation in December 1968. At Rosebud, Cash played a standing-room-only benefit for the Sioux at the St. Francis Mission. The *Rapid City Journal*, publishing since 1891, the year after Wounded Knee, reported that Cash gave up a "guaranteed $10,000 concert in London scheduled for that same night."

That year marked a rebirth for Cash. In January 1968 he had performed a concert for inmates at Folsom State Prison in Folsom, California, just twenty miles from the state capital in Sacramento.

"He called me in 1968 and said, 'This is Johnny Cash,'" record producer Bob Johnston says. "I said, 'I know who you are.' He then said, 'I've always had an idea to record at a prison and Sam Phillips wouldn't let me and Columbia won't let me so I guess you won't.' I picked up the phone and got Folsom first." Columbia Records had no clue why Cash wanted to do this, but that mattered little to Cash or Johnston. "I got a call two weeks later from Cash," Johnston recalls. "He said that Columbia called and said they would fire me and drop him even if we thought about making a live album. They told him a prison record would ruin his career. Three months later I called him and said, 'We're going to Folsom on Saturday. Pack your bags.' And he did." The resulting record, *Johnny Cash at Folsom Prison*, was a huge success, climbing to the top of the *Billboard* country and pop charts. "I cut the record and it was seven million," Johnston says. "It was always an environment with Johnny, but it was the kind of environment [where] you had to fight for everything you ever did."

But at Pine Ridge, almost a year later, it was as if a century had passed since Cash appeared at Folsom Prison. Martin Luther King Jr., dead. Bobby Kennedy, dead. Both assassinated, and with them hope, or maybe peace or something still unknowable, was also dead. President Lyndon B. Johnson, facing an intense backlash against the war in Vietnam, announced in March that he would not run for reelection. In April he signed the momentous Civil Rights Act into law, but it appeared that his ambitious "Great Society" program was faltering and possibly headed for failure. Waiting in the wings was former vice president Richard M. Nixon. Once consigned to the political graveyard, the Republican had won the presidential election against Democratic candidate George McGovern by a whisker in November.

Cash found himself standing in front of a group of people that the United States had time and again tried its best to destroy. When he stepped up to the microphone on the makeshift stage of the St. Francis gymnasium of the Rosebud Reservation, the first two rows were filled with Lakota who smiled reassuringly as Cash began performing. Cash decided to play mostly songs from *Bitter Tears*. When he got around to playing "Ballad of Ira Hayes," the smiles of the chiefs, who were in full dress and seated in the front row, quickly dropped to frowns. "This happened sometimes when we played 'Ira Hayes,'" bassist Marshall Grant of the Tennessee Two said. "Its meaning was sometimes misunderstood by both white and Indian audiences."

THE MEN, those who were left, ducked for cover wherever they could find it, which was almost nowhere. They were stuck on the volcanic Japanese island of Iwo Jima. Located on the southern tip of the island the marines called the "grey pork chop," the soldiers found themselves fighting a ferocious battle with the Japanese on Mount Suribachi. It was the last days of War World II, but these men didn't know that. They were numb to any sense of time. The ending remained distant, like a slowly fading dream. All they knew was that the world—their world—was coming apart. Bombs were raining down on them.

U.S. Marine Corps corporal Ira Hayes of the Third Parachute Battalion and Second Battalion, 28th Marines—also known as "Easy Company"—never knew it could get this bad. He had joined the marines as a way to better his and his family's lot in life. This didn't seem all that much better.

Joe and Nancy Hayes brought Ira Hamilton Hayes into the world on January 12, 1923. At the time you could board the Southern Pacific Railroad and stop twenty-two miles east of Maricopa Station and sixteen miles north of Casa Grande Station and then travel down Interstate 10 (later known as the Pearl Harbor Highway) to Sacaton, on the Gila River, where the Hayes family and their fellow Akimel O'othom lived on the Gila River Indian Reservation.

A proud people known for their humility and gentleness, the Akimel O'othom were master farmers. They developed a vast system of irrigation canals to bring water to their crops. Later named the "Pima" by the Spanish, meaning "river people," they created a marvel that surpassed the engineering feats of the Roman Empire with respect to water and land use. Throughout their land, crops of corn, beans, and squash grew. The O'othom also cultivated cotton and tobacco. There was abundance.

For two thousand years the Pima lived cooperatively and peacefully within their own villages and in harmony with the land throughout

the Gila River Valley. As westward expansion came to Arizona, starting in the 1870s, the Pima were generous with their crops, allowing
those traveling to California to use the water from the Gila River. But
the Pima's openness and generosity in sharing their resources were
greatly exploited by the settlers moving through to California, trigger-
ing a series of terrible events that jeopardized their way of life. The
new settlers returned the Pima's kindness with abuse of the river,
eventually changing its flow. As more and more settlers decided to
make the Arizona Territory their home, the need for water increased.
Eventually the water was diverted upstream, and it stopped flowing to
the Pima land. In a matter of a few years, the stable, efficient irrigation system the Pima had built and sustained for many generations
was being destroyed. Neither a warring nor a hostile tribe, the Pima
decided to seek water elsewhere rather than challenge the misuse
brought on by the settlers. They migrated to the Salt River Valley,
where their misfortune only continued. Settlers were using up all the
water there as well. Then, in 1890, the United States Geological Survey found its way to Arizona and the Gila River. Ignoring two millen-
nia of time-tested sustainable irrigation that allowed water to flow
freely and easily without harming the surrounding environment, the
survey team dismantled the Pima system, replacing it with one that
turned out to be neither efficient nor structurally sound. With no recognized rights, and their treaties with the U.S. government ignored,
the Pima lost all access to the water as the government seized control
of the Gila River. The reservation literally began drying up. Seven
years after Ira Hayes was born, President Calvin Coolidge arrived to
dedicate a dam that was built by the Bureau of Indian Affairs. The
Pima were left with only their memories of a once overflowing, vibrant river, which was now hardly ever full. Soon, large sections of it
were bone dry, with blades of grass sprouting up throughout the
riverbed. Satirist Will Rogers summed up the farcical scene when he
observed, "If this were my dam, I'd mow it."

Extremely quiet and self-effacing, even among a people known for
their solemn thoughtfulness and intense rectitude, Hayes thought that

Figure 1.1. Ira Hayes, known as Chief Falling Cloud to his fellow soldiers, appears in his paratrooper gear, circa 1945. Hayes was immortalized in a World War II photograph of marines struggling to raise the American flag at Iwo Jima. *Photo by MPI/Getty Images.*

by joining the military he could bring honor to his tribe—and perhaps change the way Native people were viewed and treated throughout the country. As a child, Hayes had heard stories of Matthew Juan, a Pima who was the first soldier from Arizona killed during World War I. Even though they were not recognized as U.S. citizens, many Native people volunteered to fight in the war, Juan among them. Hayes decided to follow Juan by joining the marines. Conscious that the marines were recognized as the toughest and most respected military outfit in the country, Hayes excelled during the brutal basic training, and when he sought to join the elite, specialized unit known then as the Paramarines—soldiers trained to parachute into the most hostile conditions—he was easily accepted. "Hayes came from a poor family," Native activist Dennis Banks says. "His family just wanted Ira to be part of the American scene, do something with his life, be accepted." Dubbed "Chief Falling Cloud" by his fellow paratroopers, Hayes was big news back home. When a picture of him posing with a parachute, ready to jump out of plane, was published in the *Pima Gazette* and shown at the Phoenix Indian School, Hayes became a hero. It was not the last time that the words "Ira Hayes, hero" were said aloud.

"HERE'S AN Indian," Hayes thought to himself, "who is willing to die for this country." But would that be enough? Would anyone care? Hayes felt certain he would never find out. Although the planning for the invasion seemed well thought out, survival in this battle seemed a fantasy. The soldiers believed themselves prepared. Operation Detachment was sure to achieve its objective: destroy the airfields of Iwo Jima. Despite a force of 21,000 and a willingness to fight to the death, the Japanese were unable to stop a U.S. force that rose to 110,000. Until then, U.S. military generals had discounted one critical fact: the unyielding code of honor of the Japanese. Heavily fortifying the island, the Japanese army dug in deep. With an elaborate system of underground bunkers and caves, the Japanese left the U.S. military uncertain and off balance. They were successfully staving off the U.S. attack. Hayes must have thought that not even an additional 100,000 men would be enough.

On February 23, 1945, the fourth day of fighting, U.S. soldiers successfully planted a flag atop Suribachi—the mountain had been secured that morning. The critical turning point for the U.S. forces had come. The flag raising disgraced the Japanese, who nevertheless remained unwilling to concede the island. The U.S. military gained confidence and now believed the island theirs for the taking. Despite a battle still undecided, various high-ranking military officials began jockeying for possession of the flag. Secretary of the Navy James Forrestal wanted the flag. So did Second Battalion commander Colonel Chandler Johnson—and there was no way Johnson was going to let the secretary of the navy have the flag. Colonel Johnson dispatched Captain Dave E. Severance, commander of Easy Company, to get a team together, go back up the hill, take the old flag down, replace it with a new one, and bring him the original. "Make it a big one," Johnson told Severance, referring to the replacement flag. While they were at it, the men were ordered to lay telephone wire up the hill.

Ira Hayes, Franklin Sousley, Harlon Block, and Mike Strank were chosen by Rene Gagnon to trudge up the hill and raise the new flag. The soldiers were exhausted from battle and unsure of why they needed to go back up to the top of Suribachi. "We were certainly uneasy," Hayes said afterward. He and the others slowly climbed, laying the wire as they moved, hoping that the Japanese would not fire at them because there was nowhere to seek cover. But they never did; they were burrowed in deep, in their bunkers and caves, remaining out of sight as Hayes and the other soldiers struggled with a large drainage pipe, which the men were going to use as the new flagpole. Standing close by, Navy Pharmacist's Mate Second Class John H. Bradley decided to help out. "I saw some guys struggling with a pole," Bradley said. "I just jumped in to lend them a hand."

As the marines were attaching the flag to the old pipe, Joe Rosenthal, a thirty-three-year-old photographer, piled rocks nearby to stand on. He wanted to gain the best possible view of the flag raising. With a bushy brown mustache and a head full of tight brown curls, Rosenthal was too nearsighted for military service, but the short and athletic photographer had already distinguished himself with his camera in battles at New Guinea, Hollandia, Guam, Peleliu, and Angaur. While the soldiers were lost in the task at hand, Rosenthal placed his camera on the ground, just for a moment. With his hands busily piling rocks, Rosenthal forgot about the flag raising. The soldiers didn't give the photographer a second thought. They wanted to finish raising the flag—a task that seemed a bit ridiculous since one was already flying—and get back down the mountain.

Realizing he was about to miss the shot, Rosenthal quickly swung his camera up and snapped the photograph without using the viewfinder. Unbeknownst to all the men, their lives would be forever altered. In 1/400th of a second, with the f-stop between 8 and 16, Rosenthal immortalized Hayes and the five other soldiers. Along with Rosenthal was USMC Sergeant William Genaust, who was filming the flag raising with a 16-millimeter camera. In the short, grainy film you can see Hayes carrying a military belt rump; inside, there was a traditional Pima blanket. The film made it back home, but Genaust did not. Later in the battle he entered a darkened cave and was killed by Japanese soldiers hidden inside. His body was never recovered.

Hayes and the other soldiers finished their job and returned the flag to Johnson, who quickly locked it away in a safe. Rosenthal sent the undeveloped film back to the United States, unsure of what he had taken since he had almost missed the shot. The whole scene seemed perfunctory, unworthy of excitement. To all involved, it was just another in a long list of tasks and orders that needed to be carried out. Even the obligatory action report filed by the Second Battalion made no mention of the flag raising. As it turned out for Hayes, surviving the war was a whole lot easier than surviving the America that awaited him.

THE FOURTEEN-YEAR-OLD boy living on a 4,000-acre ranch in Fountain, Colorado, had no inkling of who Ira Hayes was. All Oliver Albee La Farge Jr. knew was that he didn't really like his stepfather, Andy Kane, much. That made two fathers who weren't fitting the bill. The Colorado ranch hand Andy Kane married Oliver's mother, Wanden Matthews, after she and writer-anthropologist Oliver La Farge divorced in 1935. "My mother was rebuilding her life," daughter Povy says. "We moved to Fountain and bought the ranch. Then she hired foreman Andy Kane to run the ranch. This was not easy for either one of us, although it was much harder for my brother. He didn't get along well in public school in Fountain. He didn't make friends in Fountain, and he didn't get along with our stepfather almost immediately, and they never did really get along."

Before long, Povy's brother was constantly in trouble. The young girl felt torn between loyalty to her parents and loyalty to her older brother. "Here I am, younger, and I would get all the questions: 'Did you know what your brother did?' and 'Did you find this?' and 'Can you tell us where he is?'" Povy recalls. When he was old enough to travel on his own, the boy made his way to Santa Fe to spend time with his biological father and his new wife, Consuelo.

Figure 1.2. Peter (left) and his sister, Pover La Farge (right), on horseback at their mother's ranch in Fountain, Colorado. Date unknown. *From the private collection of John Pen La Farge.*

A New England blue blood, Harvard-educated anthropologist Oliver La Farge Sr. won the 1930 Pulitzer Prize for the novel *Laughing Boy*, a story about the clash between American culture and that of southwestern Native people. It was one of the first books to contain entirely Native characters (with the exception of a white bartender who makes a brief appearance in the book). Oliver La Farge's achievement was not a big surprise. La Farge was the scion of a successful family boasting a lineage of artists, scientists, and intellectuals. Seymour Krim described him as a "steel spring of a man with priests and four generations of American gentlemen lining his genes." Most notably, these genes included stained-glass artist John La Farge, Oliver's grandfather, who helped design the Cathedral of St. John the Divine in New York City, and Christopher LaFarge, Oliver's brother, who wrote the novels *Hoxsie Sells His Acres* (1934) and *Each to the Other* (1939).

Oliver La Farge Sr.'s interest in the Southwest and specifically Native people became central throughout the rest of his life, as he worked

Figure 1.3. Oliver La Farge (center) writing at his home in Santa Fe, New Mexico, circa 1950s. *From the private collection of John Pen La Farge.*

with and oversaw the Association on American Indian Affairs, a Native advocacy group founded by non-Natives in New York City in 1922. Believed to have Narragansett ancestors, the elder La Farge's devotion to Native people was soon shared by his estranged son. Oliver Jr. was a sickly kid, all nerves and awkwardness. "We were both in New York City and then our parents divorced," his sister Povy explains. "Before my parents divorced they were legally separated for years, at least years in a small child's life. I never remember my father being in the apartment. We visited him on Saturdays, Sundays, and special days. This made it especially difficult when we moved to Colorado, which we did for very definite reasons. My brother was very ill with a series of ear infections, which they didn't really have antibiotics or penicillin for at the time to treat him. So the doctors told Mother that he would be deaf if he had another serious infection."

Once the family settled in the Southwest it seemed to transform them, having an almost mystical effect on both his mother and father, reshaping their sensibilities and casting them ultimately into new personas. Junior was following suit. "But take those high, frail nerves and wire them to such reality symbols as horses, water holes, rodeos, cowboys, Indians," author Seymour Krim writes, "that whole other America waiting across the mountains, and you can begin to see what Oliver Jr. was becoming." Undisciplined and frustrated, Oliver Jr. was sent to school in Tucson in an effort to keep him healthy. In a rebellious spirit of rejection, Oliver Jr. began calling himself "Pete" La Farge. "Andy Kane being a rancher, and the boys seeing cowboys and horses all around," Pete's mother later wrote, "[the two of them] decided that 'Oliver' was a sissy name and [soon Oliver Jr.] was called Pete at his request. Years later he changed his name to Peter, by which he was known the rest of his life."

Tall, lean, handsome, but already showing signs of a troubled mind, as a teen Peter tried his hand at a number of interests including painting, poetry, boxing, and bronc rodeo riding. With the latter, Peter fancied himself a skilled cowboy. It wasn't long before he was riding broncs in rodeos throughout the Southwest. Peter was intent on jumping out of his father's prominent shadow by wearing the hat of the hardscrabble rodeo people he admired. Determined to remake himself, even if it took some artful stretching of the truth, it surprised no one that the real cowboys he rode with and encountered in the Southwest believed Peter to be an "Indian." He didn't bother to correct them. It wouldn't hurt anyone if his new persona gave him an identity that made people take notice. "He could by nature play either role," Krim writes. "He had the tall, muscular, battered body of a cowboy and the straight black hair and olive-skinned face of an Indian." Playing both the "Lone Ranger and Tonto must have given him the devil chuckles for days and days," Krim adds.

Even with the excitement of the rodeo, La Farge remained restless. He wanted to escape, make a clean break. So, at eighteen he signed up with the navy and soon shipped out, as one war slowly gave way to another, in Korea. "He joined the navy to get out of graduating from Fountain Valley High school, where he was a student," Povy explains.

Figure 1.4. Peter La Farge during a rodeo competition in the Southwest, circa 1950s. On the back of the photograph, he wrote: "As a token of good faith, as a token of love. From their son (and friend), Pete (Gymkhana, Capt. 49)." *From the private collection of John Pen La Farge.*

"I use the term *student* loosely. He attended. But he wrote wonderful things while he was there, including poetry for the literary magazine." La Farge quickly came to regret joining the navy. At first, though, it was the best thing that had happened to him. "The upshot of the navy was that he was happier than he ever, ever, ever was in his life," Povy says. "He adored and really loved it. My mother and Andy went to see Peter graduate from boot camp. He looked so great all spic and span." Once through boot camp, La Farge became an undercover antinarcotics operative for the Central Intelligence division of the navy. He had entered the navy at the height of the second Red Scare, a campaign led by Wisconsin Senator Joseph McCarthy and his House Un-American Activities Committee. Wrapping themselves in Old Glory, these paranoiacs saw communists everywhere. Whether real

Figure 1.5. Peter La Farge during his time in the U.S. Navy, where he served in the Central Intelligence Division, circa 1951. *From the private collection of John Pen La Farge.*

or imagined, the witch hunt was on. "I know that people say it was hard to report on your fellow persons, but on the other hand he was in the navy and that's what he was there to do," Povy says. "It was to interdict the vast amount of drugs that no one ever heard of before [they came] into the U.S. I can't honestly say I agree with the people who say he was upset that he had to talk about his fellow serviceman because I don't see Pete even turning them in. I don't see what the contradiction was. The Pete I knew, when he got into things he didn't like, he would say 'I don't want to do this,' and he wouldn't. Anyway, he was way too young to be given that kind of responsibility." La Farge later said about his spying on his fellow servicemen: "I was very successful at what I did, but it cracked me up. One of the most difficult things to do in the world is to betray your fellow man."

Getting off the ship and out of the navy voided any ill feeling that he had about his stepfather or getting out of Fountain, Colorado. Fate intervened when, while serving on an aircraft carrier, the U.S.S. *Boxer*, a plane miscalculated the coordinates for landing and slammed into the ship, causing an explosion and a fierce fire. As the ship became engulfed in flames, ammunition began to explode. Men were burning and dying all around La Farge. The ship was nearly destroyed, and dozens of men were severely hurt, including La Farge, who suffered burns and lost some hearing in his left ear. "It was hideous," Povy says. "Pete was burned and badly hurt." Even more than the burns, the mental scars that lingered damaged La Farge deeply. He reached a breaking point. "I don't know why I was in Korea, those idiots in the White House were telling me: 'Man, you're not a soldier, you're a policeman.' Before I finally cracked up, though, the ship blew up and we fought a blaze for a couple of days before getting it out. . . . I had to walk through the fire to get out alive." Unsure about what to do next, as he convalesced in Michigan's Naval Hospital, La Farge thought maybe he'd go back to the rodeo or try his hand at something creative. Whatever. Anything was better than this. "War is a dreadful waste of human lives," La Farge later said. "That fire and the experience of betraying other people, people that I often liked, was too much for me."

While La Farge lingered in a hospital trying to get his mind and body right, a brash, broad, former Arkansas sharecropper was busily working away at becoming the worst home appliance salesman that Memphis had ever seen. Johnny Cash hoped that by day he could earn enough money to support his young family while at night he could learn enough to become successful in the music industry. He was going nowhere fast—the only thing he seemed any good at all, or liked for that matter, was playing his Martin acoustic guitar.

LIKE LA FARGE, Cash enlisted in the military with the wish of getting out of one life and discovering a new one offering some kind of future. Until then, he and his family had known nothing but struggle. The great Arkansas flood of 1927 had washed away the Cash farm; then came the Great Depression. His family managed to subsist with the help of the New Deal resettlement program, which allowed them to get back on their feet after some difficult, painful years. By enlisting,

Cash was once again putting his faith in the government. After a brief stint working in the auto plants in Pontiac, Michigan, Cash joined the air force on June 7, 1950.

Serving in the United States Air Force Security Service unit in Landsberg, Germany, Cash spent most of his time in the service intercepting Russian army Morse code transmissions. "I had such a talent for that particular line of work, and such a good left ear, that in Landsberg, where the United States Air Force Security Service ran radio operations worldwide, I was the ace," Cash later recounted. "I was the one they called when the hardest jobs came up. I copied the first news of Stalin's death." During his off time, Cash took to strumming the cheap guitar he'd picked up while stationed in Germany. Like La Farge, Cash was grateful when his military service ended, later describing it as "four long, miserable years." After his honorable discharge from the air force in 1954, Cash returned to San Antonio, Texas, where he had been stationed for basic training. He married Vivian Liberto a few weeks later, and his life changed almost in an instant. A marriage. A child. No job. No prospects. A change could be good for his young family, Cash thought.

At the time, Cash's brother Roy, an auto mechanic, was living in Memphis. Once in Memphis, Cash quickly realized the salesman game was not for him. Two of Roy's coworkers were part-time musicians. Luther Perkins played guitar, and Marshall Grant played the stand-up bass. "We decided to get together and just play a bit," Grant recalls. Playing with the mechanics gave Cash fleeting moments of peace and purpose. His mounting frustrations were gone.

They played some of the music they all loved from The Carter Family, Jimmie Rodgers, Woody Guthrie, and Merle Travis. Of course Cash mixed in a gospel song or two, his homage to the memory of his mother's sweet voice, which first stirred his own desire to play music. Out of these moments came some hope and the courage to try something on his own. Why not go over to the local record studio that had recently launched Elvis Presley into rock stardom? Maybe Sun Studio's president, Sam Phillips, could see the potential in this makeshift music group. Summoning all the nerve he could, Cash anxiously entered the studio, home also to Jerry Lee Lewis, Carl Perkins, and later Roy Orbison. The hit-making producer behind Sun Studio's success watched Cash's audition quietly.

Cash thought the best way to impress Phillips was with gospel songs, showcasing his resonant singing style. But Phillips was not impressed. He'd moved out of the gospel market—there was no money in it. He needed songs that he could get on the radio and sell in the growing music market. "Johnny was disappointed when I told him there was just really no way I could sell those darned good southern gospel songs he had written," Phillips recalled. "But I knew I had enough on my plate to try to sell him. He wasn't country, he wasn't rock, and so I thank God that I didn't try to make something out of him but what he was."

Later, Phillips explained: "Johnny basically apologized for not having more musicians. I mean Luther Perkins could really play one string at a time and I loved it. It blew me away." Cash eventually won Phillips over with his songs "Hey Porter" and "Cry, Cry, Cry."

Sensing that Cash possessed something distinctive in both his voice and spirited persona, Phillips decided to add the hopeless appliance salesman to Sun's intimidating roster of musicians. For the fledgling musician this was a major turning point, forever changing the course of his life. Phillips's instincts were right: there was something different about Cash. As a young boy picking cotton in the fields with his family, Cash had listened to his mother sing the spirituals that offered him faith. At noon he listened to Smilin' Eddie Hill's radio show, "Noontime Roundup," on WMPS out of Memphis. A mix of hillbilly and traditional music wafted out of the radio into the fields like a soothing breeze, a cool wind giving Cash much-needed relief on those hot Arkansas afternoons in the fields. There was the King of Country Music, Roy Acuff; the Texas Troubadour, Ernest Tubb; of course The Carter Family; and his favorite, the Singing Brakeman, Jimmie Rodgers. This music moved and inspired him. With this as his foundation, Cash soon understood the power of music as a spiritual force, helping people transcend the hardships of life and giving comfort or hope to those who needed it, just as his mother's singing and the songs coming through the radio had done for him.

WITHIN DAYS of the flag raising, Joe Rosenthal's photo became a national sensation. The Associated Press staff photographer on assignment with the wartime picture pool, who wore glasses with thick lenses and nearly missed the shot, was now hailed by editors all across the United States as capturing the "greatest picture of the Pacific war." Rosenthal told the *New York Times*, "They won't let me carry a gun but I can pack my camera right with the boys in the front lines and show they're fighting." In March, a *San Francisco Chronicle* editorial called for a memorial based on the photograph. A few days later, Postmaster General Walker announced the reproduction of the photograph as a postage stamp. Then, the federal government saw gold. Why not use Rosenthal's picture to help raise money for the war effort? The Treasury Department used the photo as the official insignia of the Seventh War Loan, a war bond that attempted to seize on the patriotic fervor generated by Rosenthal's photo. Almost as fast as the snap of the shot, three and a half million copies of the poster featuring the insignia were printed and distributed throughout the United States.

Rosenthal's good fortune continued when the trustees for the Pulitzer Prize decided to lift the deadline rule and present him with the award, calling it an "outstanding example of news photography." Still, Rosenthal's good fortune did not rub off on some of the soldiers now forever immortalized in the photo. For them, the picture became simply "the photograph." By the time the battle of Iwo Jima was over, only three of the men in the photo were still alive, and not all in one piece: John Bradley had lost a leg. Following the flag raising, the third surviving soldier, Rene Gagnon, was unharmed, and on April 27, 1946, was promoted to corporal.

For Ira Hayes, the lasting effects of war, blending with a life of hardship on the Pima reservation, created a piercing sense of loss. Hayes traveled to the island with a battalion of 250 men and returned to the United States as one of only twenty-seven who had managed to survive. All told, 6,821 U.S. soldiers died in the battle, 5,931 of them marines—almost one-third of all the marines lost in World War II. The excitement and praise for the photo meant that the surviving men in the picture had to face the glare of the U.S. spotlight. Hayes had gotten what he wished for, which was to make his people proud by becoming a hero, but now he didn't want any of it as the public attention and scrutiny surrounding the photograph made him relive the horrors of war over and over again. The guilt of surviving while so many died haunted him. When he closed his eyes at night, the faces of the dead soldiers stared back at him. He returned to the United States not a hero but a sad man, his spirit a faint flicker—not the fierce flame it had been when he first joined the marines, so full of promise.

The picture became ubiquitous, appearing on every newsstand, hanging in every storefront and front porch window. Rapidly it was ingrained into U.S. popular culture, at one time or other gracing the cover of nearly every American magazine and newspaper. The image created an emotional frenzy, as thousands of grieving parents of dead and missing soldiers flooded the War Department with letters and phones calls demanding "a picture of my son." On April 1, 1945, the *New York Times* reported that thousands of mothers, fathers, and wives wanted a copy of the photo as proof that their loved ones were still alive. It soon became a problem for the military, which was faced with telling heartbroken parents the painful truth: "It is the parents, the mothers especially, who have touched the hearts of the authorities . . . everything is being done to convince them they are wrong" [that the photo did not contain their son].

At first, Hayes didn't want his identity revealed, going so far as to threaten Rene Gagnon not to tell anyone that he was one of the men in the photo while the identities were still unknown to the press and military officials. But from the moment Hayes and the other surviving soldiers in the photograph set foot on U.S. soil, they were paraded around the country—even invited to shake the president's hand. The

New York Stock Exchange halted trading to salute the men with a banner that read:

WELCOME IWO JIMA HEROES

They were now enlisted in a new campaign: selling U.S. war bonds. After somehow making it through one of the bloodiest battles of the war, was this what they had come home to? On April 6, 1945, Gagnon, the only soldier who really tried to capitalize on his notoriety, told the Associated Press that he would "rather face another operation than make a bond tour."

Hayes couldn't have agreed more. The crowds, the adulation were nice, and for a while he tried his best to accept the celebrity. But the tour was taking a terrible toll. Going to the White House and meeting the president of United States? That was okay. But being celebrated as a hero? The demons began to stir. The cheers from the people lining the streets to get a glimpse of Hayes as he was carried in an open car from small town to big city did little to silence the voice in Hayes's head that reminded him nearly every second of the soldiers, the friends, he had left behind on the island in the Pacific.

He wanted to stop the madness. The parades and the cameras and the crowds: it was all just a dizzying, confusing spectacle made all the more unsettling because the soldiers repeatedly told the press that theirs was the *second* flag raising, with a *replacement* flag. The press chose to ignore this part of the story, seeking instead to drain every sentimental, sensational drop—whether true or not. Hayes just wanted to live his life, but he was slowly losing any idea of how to do that, let alone deal with his increasing sense of guilt about surviving the war. With every appearance, every radio, TV, or newspaper interview, and every parade, Hayes and the other men were forced to relive what they experienced. There was nothing glorious about war. So Hayes drank, and drank— and drank some more to wash away the sorrow. His behavior became erratic, and his despair, oftentimes, was palpable. Hayes broke down on more than one occasion when he met a dead soldier's family.

Hayes was kicked off the tour and sent back overseas when his behavior and drinking became difficult to handle. In some ways, he was relieved to be sent back overseas; being a soldier was all he was any good at, giving him a strange sense of peace that he couldn't find at home or in the white-hot intensity of the bond tour spotlight. He missed the camaraderie of the battalion, the order and routine of military life. In more ways than he could even say, the marines were his family. It was a community he felt safe in. Yet Hayes was now on a terrible path that he didn't have the strength to turn back from. Chief Falling Cloud was plunging from the sky to the ground.

Honorably discharged with the rank of corporal in 1946, Hayes had a chest full of medals to bring home, including the World War II Victory Medal, the Naval Commendation Medal, and the Presidential Unit Citation. Yet when Hayes drifted back to the Pima Reservation, nothing seemed to have changed, even with hundreds of people seeking him out on the res to ask if he was "the Indian who raised the flag." It was as if time had stood still and he'd never left—as if the war had not happened, he had not been on Iwo Jima, he had not planted the flag. All of it was a dream gone wrong. If anything, the living conditions were becoming increasingly worse for his tribe. There was a separate United States that his people were not welcome in, one that was reaping the rewards of newfound prosperity and a sense of superiority following World War II. But the America that Hayes saw all around him was fading away, drying up, invisible. Hayes was slipping away too. Trying to grasp for something, Hayes thought he'd once again leave the reservation. Chicago sounded good. But it wasn't. His depression deepened after he moved to Chicago in 1952, and the need to numb the pain grew. Alcohol's grip on Hayes led to trouble with the police.

After a fifth arrest for drunkenness and loitering in a park on July 26, 1953, Hayes spent the weekend in jail. Once, his name had appeared in the headlines of the front-page stories of every major newspaper in the country, his picture broadcast everywhere. But in the July 27, 1953, edition of the *New York Times*, it took just three short lines to report Hayes's sad fall from grace: "One of the Marines who participated in the historic flag raising on Iwo Jima's Mount Suribachi was released today after spending the weekend in jail on a drunk charge." When Betty Martin, the former wife of singer-actor Dean Martin, read of Hayes's recent troubles in Chicago, she contacted him with an offer to come to Los Angeles and serve as the family chauffer and handyman. In the hopes of making a fresh start, Hayes eagerly accepted the offer.

On October 29, 1953, the *Chicago Tribune Daily* ran a photo of Hayes seated at a piano surrounded by Martin's four children under the headline "New Job for Iwo Hero." The short paragraph told readers that Hayes was "starting a new life in Los Angeles" and that in the photo "he tries choral singing with the Martin children." Only eleven days after Martin brought Hayes out to Los Angeles, the former marine was once again arrested on a public drunkenness charge after police found him "sitting on a curb counting a wad of bills over and over again." This time he was placed in a sanitarium. His time in Los Angeles had gone much differently four years prior when he, John Bradley, and Rene Gagnon appeared as themselves in the film *Sands of Iwo Jima*, with Hayes appearing in a scene with the film's star, John Wayne, who rose to fame by "killing" thousands of Native people on screen.

Hayes was running out of options, struggling and failing everywhere he tried to make a fresh start—until he finally returned to Arizona and the Sacaton Indian Reservation, where he began each day by raising the flag. Far from seeing it as an honor, he found the act humiliating, an ironic twist of events after the famous Iwo Jima flag raising. Liquor sapped whatever spirit was left in him. Destitute and despondent, he filled his days with drinking. Still only in his early thirties, Hayes felt defeated. With his mind muddled, he often got into arguments that led to fights. There was nothing left of the man; what war and the embarrassing removal from the war bond effort didn't take from him, despair and alcohol did.

DURING THAT same summer, the U.S. Congress turned its attention to Native people. A feeling was growing in the Eisenhower administration that the federal government should cut off support to the tribes, believing that the appropriate course for Native people was to assimilate into mainstream American life. In 1950, the head of the Bureau of Indian Affairs, Dillon S. Myers, loudly called for termination—meaning that all federal aid, services, and protection for Native people living on reservations would end. "The ultimate answer is the assumption of full jurisdiction by the state." It's interesting to note that, before joining the BIA, Myers had been in charge of the War Relocation Authority, where he was responsible for the internment of Japanese-Americans during World War II. The administrative war Myers waged against Native people forced BIA Tribal Relations Chief D'Arcy McNickle, a Native anthropologist who had spent more than two decades at BIA, to resign in protest. Soon after, McNickle joined the American Indian Development Corporation with the aim of doing grassroots community work with tribes across the country. The thinking behind the policy of termination, McNickle said, "goes back to mutton-chop whiskers and high button shoes," referring to the dress of the men who colonized the country while buying and selling slaves. Oliver La Farge Sr. soon added his voice to those opposing termination, calling it "a crisis more acute than any that has faced Indians in our time."

Among those leading the administration's efforts were Secretary of the Interior Douglas McKay and Assistant Interior Secretary Orme Lewis. BIA Commissioner Glenn Emmons quickly joined the campaign. Yet the Eisenhower administration found its most willing and vocal proponent of the policy in Utah Senator Arthur Watkins. Senator Watkins rolled up his sleeves and went about the business of doing the administration's dirty work. In return, control of Native affairs was essentially handed over to the senior senator, a devout Mormon who made his political mark as a fierce isolationist and an aggressive opponent of organized labor in a congressional career that began in 1946.

Even though Senator Watkins publicly stated that when he visited reservations he "had the same experience [as] visiting Europe [and] the refugee camps of the Near East," he believed that termination was a "final solution" (the term he actually used). He therefore bullied and battered his way toward ensuring that the policy was enacted by Congress. With the exception of Lyndon B. Johnson, then the brazen senator from Texas, no one in either the House or the Senate was as determined and forceful as Watkins. Facing little opposition, Watkins did whatever he pleased to get the termination bill passed. Senator Watkins "had an unbending faith in the rightness of his cause," and "he did not hesitate to use pressure," author Charles Wilkerson later explained. Not above intimidation and undermining the rule of law, Watkins framed termination as a critical step in Native self-determination. The tactic camouflaged the measure's true purpose, which was nothing more than a land grab. With vocal support from Senator Karl Mundt, Watkins withheld tribal funds, provided congressional witnesses with misleading information, and used whatever anti–big government or racist rhetoric would sway people to side with the policy.

Watkins's ignorant view of Native life in the United States was made fantastical when he used his own personal story as a comparison—he was a staunch Mormon from Utah, which was as far removed from the reality of Native people as possible. He insisted that Native people could make it just as he had if they just pulled themselves up by their own bootstraps. If he could succeed, coming from nothing and struggling to rise in American society, then so could Native people. "They want all the benefit of the things we have," Watkins rationalized, "highways, schools, hospitals, everything that civilization furnishes, but they don't want to help pay their share of it." Oliver La Farge countered that such thinking was a "profound misunderstanding of the true condition, status, and needs of American Indians."

Former BIA commissioner John Collier called termination nothing more than "Indian takeaway." Years before the termination struggle, Collier had successfully led a protest against another piece of federal legislation that had attempted to take away Native land. The Bursum Bill allowed non-Indians to claim Pueblo land in New Mexico. Three Indian advocacy groups joined together to block the passage of the Bursum Bill: the Eastern Association on Indian Affairs, the New Mexico Association on Indian Affairs, and the American Indian Defense Association. Collier led the latter group. After defeating the Bursum Bill, the coalition recognized the need to organize in order to fight similar types of legislation that might arise. La Farge had been EAIA's president back in 1933, later merging with the NAIA and the American Indian Defense Association. Based in New York, the new group became the American Association on Indian Affairs.

"My father first traveled to the Southwest with Elsie Parson, a famous anthropologist, and then did illustrations on a book of hers," Peter La Farge's half brother Jon Pen La Farge says. "He became committed to the Indian cause partly through anthropology as a student at Harvard, when he would come out to New Mexico and the Four Corners area in the summer, fascinated by the Navajo as a living anthropological record. He became more involved in a political fashion over the Bursum Bill, which would have legalized all the non-Indian squatters on Indian land in New Mexico—and there were quite a lot of squatters. It galvanized all the different Indian rights groups into one national effort called the Association of American Indian Affairs. My father was president for thirty years."

The U.S. government's view that federal guardianship had prevented Native people from standing on their own feet and living successfully in the United States spelled nothing but disaster. Although it was certainly true that something needed to be done to redress the problems afflicting reservations—"the most complete colonial system in the world that I know about," according to D'Arcy McNickle—nothing the federal government intended to do was going to help in any way.

Survey upon survey unequivocally detailed the desperate living conditions faced on reservations. Through neglect, acute mismanagement, and racism, the BIA and the larger federal bureaucracy were revealed as the main culprits. Watkins and his fellow committee members knew all this because they had commissioned these very reports and surveys. Nonetheless, Watkins remained undaunted. He fervently argued that Native tribes no longer needed federal protection and that joining the American mainstream could easily solve the problems rampant in reservation life. Watkins puffed out his chest, and with little sense of irony declared that he was doing for Native people what Abraham Lincoln had done for blacks: "Following in the footsteps of the Emancipation Proclamation ninety-four years ago I see the following words emblazoned in letters of fire above the heads of the Indians—'These People Shall Be Free!'" The ironies of Watkins statement were not lost on many Native people. "Lincoln—the great emancipator?" Red Lake Chippewa Roger Jourdain asked. "He emancipated the slaves and emancipated 10 million acres of our land at the same time."

Congress adopted House Concurrent Resolution 108 on August 1, 1953: "Whereas it is the policy of Congress, as rapidly as possible, to make the Indians within the territorial limits of the United States subject to the same laws and entitled to the same privileges and responsibilities as are applicable to other citizens of the United States, to end their status as wards of the United States, and to grant them all of the rights and prerogatives pertaining to American citizenship." A young senator from Massachusetts, John F. Kennedy, voted in support of termination. A rising senator from Arizona, Barry Goldwater, was one of its vocal supporters, as was the Senate minority leader, Lyndon Johnson. Each of these politicians possessed ambitions greater than the U.S. Senate, none of which included pursuing justice for Native people.

Immediately following the passage of the act, D'Arcy McNickle's tribe, the Flathead, together with the Klamath, Menominee, Pottowatomie, and Turtle Mountain Chippewa were terminated. Tribes throughout the states of California, New York, Florida, and Texas were slated for termination. Perhaps no other piece of legislation in recent memory aimed to really do what its name so plainly implied: for now, without any federal support, "by terminating the government's trusteeship of Indian reservations and making Indians assume all the responsibilities of full citizenship," Native people, Watkins contended, must "pull themselves up by their bootstraps," whether they even had boots or not.

The passage of termination was a complete 180-degree turn from the Fourteenth Amendment adopted in 1868 that granted full citizenship to all people born in the United States—but made a clear exception when it came to Native people, the rationale at the time being that in some parts of the country, like Colorado, Native people would outnumber whites. Citizenship guaranteed the right to bear arms, which congressional leaders certainly did not want to confer on people the federal government had so grossly wronged since it wrested that privilege from the British. Consequently, with the passage of Public Law 280 in 1953, the 1823 Supreme Court ruling in *Worcester v. Georgia* was nullified, allowing the states to enforce U.S. law on Native land. The new federal policies' aim to grant citizenship was more of a convenient cover masking their true intent: to open up long protected Native land in what amounted to a free-for-all land grab campaign. Upon passage of Public Law 280, Wisconsin, California, Oregon, Minnesota, and Nebraska had state criminal and civil jurisdiction over Native lands, where the objective was to usurp the land for profitable public works projects including power plants and dams.

IN THE early morning of January 24, 1955, a frozen body in Sacaton, Arizona, lay next to a broken-down truck, long ago discarded and now rusting through. How that body got there still remains shrouded in mystery. Here are what few facts are known. Kenny and Vernon Hayes joined their brother Ira for an all-night card game. Sitting in an abandoned hut some three hundred yards from where Ira lived, the brothers were joined by Harry and Mark White and Henry Setoyant. A huge amount of drinking followed. Soon, Kenny and Vernon decided to leave and asked their brother to go with them. Ira was on a winning streak, and he begged off. The drinking continued into the early morning. An argument broke out among those that remained, first shouting, then pushing. Soon, Harry and Mark decided to leave. Henry and Ira were the last two remaining in the hut.

It was no surprise that the dead body next to the trash heap of a truck was indeed Captain Ira Hamilton Hayes, formerly of the United States Marine Corps. Frozen in time as one of six soldiers deemed the "immortal heroes" in the photo known as "Flag Raising at Iwo Jima," and cast in bronze in a monument in the U.S. capital by the artist Felix DeWeldon—which had been unveiled on November 10, 1954, just a few months earlier—it turned out that Hayes was not immortal. It was Henry Setoyant who went to the Hayes' home to tell them something was wrong with Ira. Ira's father, Joe, his mother, Nancy, and brother Vernon ran in a panic to where the body lay. In their hearts they hoped, but in their heads they knew that their son and brother's troubles had finally caught up with him. What the war could not do, sadness, drink, and a lifetime filled with despair did. Just one month shy of the tenth anniversary of the flag raising, Ira was gone. He had turned thirty-two just two weeks earlier.

Dr. John Parks listed the official cause of death as exposure to the cold and overconsumption of alcohol. On January 25, 1955, the *New York Times* concluded its brief news item on Hayes's death with these words: "The post-war years were not kind to Hayes. He wandered from his home in southern Arizona and tried vainly to find a place for himself in the white man's peacetime world." There was so much left out of the piece—a life, really—that it only added to the tragedy. No one cared any longer that Hayes was a once a war hero. That was old news from a time that seemed not a decade past but a century. A BIA caseworker remarked that Hayes's "attitude was not bitterness but some hurt that I couldn't sort out." Echoing the standard practice of newspapers throughout the country, the *New York Times* made sure to point out how Hayes died rather than how he had tried to live. The article ended simply, coldly: "He was arrested many times for intoxication." John Bradley more aptly described Hayes's death when he remarked, "This makes him truly a casualty of war."

IN THE summer of 1955, the first integrated school in the South since Reconstruction, the Highlander Folk Center in Monteagle, Tennessee, had just admitted a diminutive forty-two-year-old department store seamstress from Montgomery, Alabama. Rosa Parks, a descendant of Indian slaves on her father's side, was going to participate in a workshop on school desegregation. Parks heard nothing but good things about the school's civil rights organizing workshops, with their emphasis on nonviolence and racial unity. Led by progressive educator Myles Horton, Highlander was a hub for teaching and training aimed at supporting the growing civil rights movement throughout the South.

Primarily a school for adults who were labor and civil rights organizers, Highlander was a place where white and black people lived and worked together. They provided literacy classes for blacks who were denied the right to vote due to the literacy requirement. A young minister from Alabama named Martin Luther King Jr. found their teachings on nonviolence critical in the course he was charting to end segregation and second-class citizenship for Blacks in the United States.

A year earlier, the U.S. Supreme Court's landmark decision on school desegregation, known as *Brown vs. Board of Education*, seemed to open the door for the civil rights movement. Parks enrolled in Highlander's race relations class, which centered on nonviolent civil disobedience as a tactic for confronting segregation. Parks listened, learned, and for the first time felt that she lived in "an atmosphere of equality with members of the other race." Inspired by her time at Highlander, but still deeply uncertain that people in her community would stick together to fight segregation when things got hot, she returned to Montgomery not knowing what awaited her but willing to do what was necessary.

Months passed, and Parks remained committed to what she learned at Highlander, trying to help change a system that kept her locked in as a second-class citizen. Then, on December 1, 1955, she was thrust into the heart of the movement. After she boarded a public bus, tired from many hours of standing on her feet, she refused to give her seat up to a white passenger. The white passengers got angry; the black passengers watched quietly, their hearts racing with support for Parks. After several

angry attempts by the bus driver to make Parks give up her seat, the police were called. Rosa Parks was promptly arrested.

News of Parks's arrest quickly spread throughout Montgomery. Jo
Ann Robinson, head of the Women's Political Council, outraged by
another show of racial injustice, dashed off and circulated a flyer
throughout Montgomery's black community. "Another woman has
been arrested and thrown in jail because she refused to get up out of
her seat on the bus for a white person to sit down," Robinson's flyer
said. "This has to be stopped. Negroes have rights too, for if Negroes
did not ride the buses, they could not operate."

The charming young pastor of the Dexter Avenue Baptist Church,
Dr. Martin Luther King Jr. helped put a fine, eloquent point on the
matter when he said that Rosa Parks provided a good example for the
desegregation struggle because she was recognized as "one of the finest
citizens of Montgomery—not one of the finest Negro citizens—but
one of the finest citizens of Montgomery." King was chosen as president of the Montgomery Improvement Association after activists
formed the group to lead the boycott following Parks's arrest. In what
was just a hint of the type of speaker King was to become, his speech
to the group promised resolute strength for the hard work ahead. "We
have no alternative but to protest. For many years we have shown an
amazing patience," King said. "We have sometimes given our white
brothers the feeling that we liked the way we were being treated. But
we come here tonight to be saved from that patience that makes us patient with anything less than freedom and justice."

WHILE PARKS prepared to attend Highlander, Johnny Cash and the
Tennessee Two (Perkins and Grant) released their first record for Sam
Phillips under the Sun Studios label. Cash, who until then had been
known as "John" or "J. R.," was now called "Johnny" by Phillips. On
the front side of the record was a song titled "Hey Porter," and the flip
side was the song "Cry, Cry, Cry." Cash wrote the former tune—which
expressed the voice of a homesick young man—while stationed in
Landsberg, Germany, where he played with fellow southerners in a

group called the Landsberg Barbarians. It became Johnny Cash's first hit, reaching number six on the *Billboard* country charts. Just like that, Johnny Cash was a music star.

On December 7, 1956, the *Memphis Press-Scimitar* ran a story by the newspaper's entertainment editor, Bob Johnson, called "Million Dollar Quartet." There was really no need to read Johnson's article. The photo taken by United Press International photographer Leo Soroca that appeared under the headline told the whole story. Elvis Presley sat at a piano looking up at Jerry Lee Lewis, who was farthest to his right. Next to Lewis stood Carl Perkins, acoustic guitar in hand. Standing over Elvis's left shoulder was Johnny Cash. The four came together for an impromptu jam session at Sun Studios after Elvis, no longer with Sun and now with RCA, paid an unexpected visit to the label that made him a star. Only four months prior, Elvis had appeared on the *Ed Sullivan Show*, where an estimated 83 percent of the television audience—55 million people— tuned in to watch him perform. Supposedly someone among the gathered musicians asked, "Y'all know 'Will the Circle Be Unbroken' by The Carter Family?" which led the musicians to crowd around the piano. Cash later wrote of the session, "No one wanted to follow Jerry Lee, not even Elvis."

ONE HUNDRED days into the bus boycott, Rosa Parks returned to the Highlander School to attend a special event held in her honor. This outwardly timid, uncertain woman had accomplished more with her simple gesture in a moment of exhaustion than had decades of tireless work. Highlander director Myles Horton—later called the "father of civil rights movement" by James Bevel, the director of Direct Action and Nonviolent Education of the Southern Christian Leadership Conference—put a simple question to Parks: "What was on your mind, Rosa?" Parks responded, "Well, in the first place, I had been working all day on the job, not feeling too well after spending a hard day working. The job required I handle and work on clothing that white people would wear and that accidentally came into my mind. And this was what I wanted to know—when and how would we ever determine our rights as human beings?"

Parks's words stirred all who came to meet and listen to her that day at Highlander. The words spoken on that day seemed to travel back in time, connecting to the eulogy delivered more than a year earlier in a small church in Sacaton, Arizona. On that day, January 25, 1955, some two thousand people crowded into Cook Presbyterian Church to hear Pastor Esau Joseph praise U.S. Marine Corporal Ira Hamilton Hayes. "He was a good man: he wished harm to no human being," Pastor Joseph said. "On foreign soil he fought that men may inherit peace . . . a peace which he himself has found only now." In his own way, Hayes fought for the very same thing as Parks. "Let's just say he had a little dream in his heart that someday the Indian would be like the white man and be able to walk all over the United States," said fellow marine Rene Gagnon. Dennis Banks, a young Anishinaabe who had served in the Army in the early 1950s, said, "Ira Hayes was let down by a society trying to get out from being very segregationist. When Hayes came back of course it was even worse. Yes they honored Ira Hayes the marine, but Ira Hayes the Indian, they didn't. They ignored him."

FRESHLY DISCHARGED from the navy following a stay in a mental institution in Michigan, Peter La Farge set about rewriting his whole life. La Farge got back to the rodeo, but since his skills really weren't very good, he found himself often hurt—sometimes seriously. "The fact that he could even do the bronc stuff was kinda unusual, because he didn't ride that much or that well," his sister Povy explains. "He wasn't that good a basic horseman, and you can't ride broncs casually. It's just too dangerous and doesn't make any sense. Of course, that would not have stopped him. I always thought that he did whatever came up and was handy." At one point, La Farge's leg was crushed when a Brahma bull fell on it. "There's a saying in rodeo," he later said. "It's not an occupation, it's a disease." There were other terrible accidents as well. "He had so many bad accidents, Povy recalls. "I remember he wrecked at least four cars."

Once both physically and mentally healthy, La Farge still was unsure of what was next. One idea he had was to make his way to a city, like Chicago or New York. Now that he felt strong enough, maybe he could start out on a new path in life. "He may have started acting because someone offered him a job," Povy says. "I never remember Pete sitting down and thinking, 'Well, I need a little change of career here.'" Nothing in La Farge's life was predictable or ordinary. He'd already tried painting, poetry, the rodeo—he even gave the navy a shot. Why not acting, or maybe writing a play or two? This could be the fresh start La Farge needed. So, as 1956 drew to a close, La Farge was closing the door on his past life. "He never got on with his Great White father," Seymour Krim writes. "And Jim Nash [a writer and friend of Neal Cassady] tells me that he was practically a non-son after the old man birthed him . . . and somewhere along those hot deserts of the southwest . . . Oliver Jr. threw away his given name and thumbed his nose at his birthright and became Peter La Farge." The terrible navy accident, the car accidents, the rodeo, and his broken relationship with his father, Oliver—all of it was gone.

AROUND THAT same time, on November 13, 1956, the U.S. Supreme Court upheld the earlier ruling of a federal district court: Alabama's racial segregation laws for buses were unconstitutional. On December 20, 1956, the Montgomery bus boycott officially ended.

All Passes—
Only Art Endures

FROM THE MOMENT Carnegie Hall opened in 1891 it was something special, new, and exciting in a city renowned for its dis-
tinctiveness. Walter Damrosch, son of New York Philharmonic
conductor Leopold Damrosch, was the person who convinced Andrew Carnegie that New York needed a world-class music hall of its
own. Without one, the city stood no chance in competition with the
great cultural centers of Berlin, London, and Paris. The Scottish-
born industrial titan, who had made his fortune first in Pittsburgh at
Carnegie Steel Company and later with U.S. Steel after a merger
with Federal Steel Company, agreed to fund the venture. As the old
century gave way to the new one, Carnegie Hall quickly became the
hallowed performance ground for classical and popular music in the
United States, helping to cement New York's place among the world's
most vibrant cultural cities. Designed by architect William Burnet
Tuthill in the style of the Italian Renaissance, America's most prestigious rental hall was the place where many aspired to perform.
Once they arrived on the stage at Carnegie Hall they could say, "Yes,
I've made it."

A list of just a handful of the musicians who have premiered
work there reads like a who's who of twentieth century music. An-
tonín Dvořák, with Anton Seidl conducting, world-premiered his

now-famous Symphony no. 9 in E minor, opus 95, known as the *New World Symphony,* on December 13, 1893. Richard Strauss did the same on March 21, 1904, with his *Sinfonia Domestica.* George Gershwin debuted *An American in Paris* there on December 13, 1928, and Edward Kennedy Ellington, known as "Duke," unveiled *New World A-Comin'* on December 11, 1943. Ellington, in fact, made Carnegie Hall his annual holiday performance venue, deciding to premiere something new there every year from 1943 to1948. It was at Carnegie Hall that he offered perhaps his most ambitious and certainly longest composition, *Black, Brown, Beige.* Ellington introduced the song as "a parallel to the story of the American Negro." In a career with many triumphs, it stands as a major achievement.

The building that runs southeast from the corner of Seventh Avenue between West Fifty-sixth and West Fifty-seventh streets in Midtown Manhattan and sitting a few blocks south of the world's most famous public space, Central Park, Carnegie Hall also housed one of the world's best orchestras, the New York Philharmonic. The two made history when the Philharmonic became the first major orchestra to broadcast live on the radio. With Erich Kleiber on the podium, CBS Radio carried the performance on Sunday, October 5, 1930, from Carnegie Hall. But under the direction of Leonard Bernstein, the first U.S.–born and –educated conductor to earn international praise, the orchestra decided to leave Carnegie Hall in 1962 for its younger rival on the west side of Manhattan, Lincoln Center for the Performing Arts. For the devoted patrons of Carnegie Hall, losing the Philharmonic was tantamount to sacrilege. For Lincoln Center, which had opened just three years earlier on May 14, 1959, with a groundbreaking ceremony that brought out President Dwight D. Eisenhower, getting Bernstein and the Philharmonic was a major coup.

But Carnegie Hall is a resilient place, even managing to survive a possible shuttering after it was sold to a developer back in 1960. Losing the Philharmonic two years later—although extremely disappointing—

didn't break Carnegie Hall. Even today, it remains one of the premiere concert halls in the United States.

When Johnny Cash and his bandmates, the Tennessee Two, began booking dates in 1961 for their 1962 tour, Carnegie Hall was at the top of their list. The music star and his troupe of musicians, which included The Carter Family, Johnny Western, Sonny Terry, and George Jones, had never performed there before. Cash's manager Saul Holiff believed that now was the time to do it. At this point in Cash's career, Holiff was a trusted member of his inner circle. It had been Holiff who orchestrated the new record contract with Columbia that would prove both lucrative and creatively liberating for Johnny Cash.

On December 4, 1961, Holiff made the call to Carnegie Hall's booking manager. For decades, Gilda Weissberger kept a meticulous booking ledger detailing who would play in which part of the hall and for how much. When she received the call from Holiff, she noted all the relevant information without as much as a slight acknowledgment of who Johnny Cash was. The discussion was a typical back-and-forth with an artist's manager or agent, so routine that Weissberger must have done it a thousand times before. A look at the ledger reveals that the conversation unfolded like this:

"Which hall do you prefer?" Weissberger asks Holiff.
"The Main Hall," Holiff responds.
"Afternoon or evening?"
"Evening."
"What kind of act is it?"
"Folksinger," Holiff said.

Next to Johnny Cash's name Weissberger dutifully wrote "folksinger."

For the rental fee of $825, Johnny Cash and the Tennessee Two were going to realize a dream. They, along with The Carter Family and The Glaser Brothers, were scheduled to perform in Carnegie

Figure 1.6. Ledger dated May 10, 1962, identifying Johnny Cash as "Folksinger" for his Carnegie Hall debut. *Courtesy of Carnegie Hall archives.*

Hall's magnificent Main Hall on May 10, 1962, at 8:00 p.m. "Playing Carnegie Hall was a dream come true," Marshall Grant says. "We were just so proud and excited to play there. Everyone had their families come to New York City with them for this moment." Cash's bandmates and fellow performers were excited about the Carnegie Hall performance, but Cash appeared to be elsewhere, lost in his head.

The actor, singer, and radio host Johnny Western was the emcee for the scheduled performance. Western joined Cash in 1958, a few months after fiddle player Gordon Terry, previously with Bill Monroe's group, joined the troupe. "When I traveled with John, my roommate was Gordon Terry." Western says. "We just became closer than Saturday is to Sunday." Since the beginning, Cash possessed an uncanny ability to attract the best musicians around. Record producer Bob Johnston described Cash's unique ability to pull together great musicians for his cause as "one in a billion." Western and Terry are two of the many examples. Cash could call on Western's many talents as a guitarist and vocalist. Terry was acknowledged as the finest bluegrass fiddle player in the country. "The Carnegie Hall show was going to be a big one for us," Western recalls.

"We had a big problem on our hands," Grant says. "John was nowhere to be found before the show. We were all ready to go and minutes away from going on stage and John disappeared somewhere in New York City." The last time Grant and the other performers had seen Cash was when they did their final rehearsal. "I never knew who he ran with when he was in New York," Grant continued. "At the

Figure 1.7. Publicity photo of musician and longtime Johnny Cash emcee Johnny Western at the time of Cash's Carnegie Hall debut, circa 1962. *Courtesy of Carnegie Hall archives.*

Carnegie Hall show, one of the biggest of our career to that point, John was who knows where doing who knows what."

WHILE CASH was somewhere out in the city, seemingly interested in pursuits other than performing at Carnegie Hall, Pete Seeger was at his home in Beacon, New York, preparing himself for the worst. In a few days he was going to learn whether he was going to prison after being found guilty of contempt of court over a year before in a federal jury trial. Free on $2,000 bail, the forty-three-year-old folksinger had performed many times at Carnegie Hall. The venue never shut its doors to him, even when he was smeared by the House Un-American Activities Committee seven years prior. Subpoenaed to testify before HUAC, Seeger's appearance and refusal to cooperate on August 18, 1955, enhanced the musician's reputation as an individual of uncompromising integrity and character.

Appearing before HUAC, Seeger wore a tweed jacket over a dark plaid shirt and yellow tie and told the committee that he was just a "banjo picker." He refused to invoke the Fifth Amendment in order to protect himself against self-incrimination and instead declared that the committee had no right to question him regarding his political beliefs or associations.

Reporting on the hearing, the *New York Times* chronicled HUAC lawyer Frank E. Tavenner's useless and often laughable attempts to get Seeger to admit he was a communist or was ever connected to the Communist Party. "Sir, I'd refuse to answer that question whether it was a quote from the *New York Times* or the *Vegetarian Journal*," the lanky folk musician answered at one point. "I resent the suggestion that just because my opinion may be different than yours, that I'm any less American than you."

Seeger's love of his country was evident in all of his work. In 1942, while he was in The Almanac Singers, the group scored a major hit with "Round and Round Hitler's Grave"; the lyrics had been contributed by Woody Guthrie, who was writing about Mussolini. Performed to the tune of "Old Joe Clark," the song sold more than a million copies, helping to galvanize support for the war effort.

Other members of the committee, determined to trap Seeger, jumped in with accusations that Seeger "used his talent" to entertain at communist events. Pounding his fist on the table, Democratic Representative Edwin Edward Willis from Louisiana took aim at specific Seeger songs, including "Wasn't That a Time?" Leaning across the rail separating the committee from Seeger, Willis pointed at the bemused musician and accusingly asked, "Was that the same . . . a slimy satire on the Constitution and the Bill of Rights?" Seeger simply replied, "I have sung for Americans of every political persuasion, and I am proud that I never refuse to sing to an audience, no matter what religion or color of their skin, or situation in life. I have sung in hobo jungles, and I have sung for the Rockefellers, and I am proud that I have never refused to sing for anybody."

What began on February 6, 1952, when stage and radio actor Harvey Matusow testified in front of HUAC, naming names and informing the committee that "yes, indeed" Seeger was a member of the Communist Party, rose to a jingoistic crescendo on July 26, 1956, when the House of Representatives voted 373 to 9 to cite Seeger, playwright Arthur Miller, and six others for contempt. The successful American folksinger, founder of the influential folk groups The Almanac Singers and The Weavers, could now add "federally indicted enemy of the state" to the list of his accomplishments. The fallout led to mainstream media outlets, including television, to blacklist Seeger.

Later, it was revealed that Matusow turned over false evidence in order to protect himself against HUAC. Matusow himself, the trusted HUAC informer, told all in his book, *False Witness*, published in 1955. In it, he admitted that he was an FBI agent paid to lie about who belonged to the American Communist Party. And beyond that, he revealed that Senator Joseph McCarthy and his chief counsel, Roy Cohn, asked him to lie. Going from patriot to rat, Matusow was found guilty of perjury, jailed for nearly three years, and was ultimately blacklisted himself.

The obvious target of HUAC was not just Seeger but folk music. The members of the committee and other radical right-wing politicians were already in a panic over rock 'n' roll. The committee was even more paranoid about folk, declaring it at one point to be the "subversion of American culture." It wanted Seeger because of his success with The Weavers, which coincided with the post–World War II Red Scare and the eventual rise of HUAC. The committee's targeting of one of folk's icons was an attempt to stop the revival of the genre and diminish its popularity and influence on a new generation of American youth. Seeger's fingerprints were all over the growing movement. In the 1930s, he traveled with his father, Charles, the pioneering musicologist, throughout the South, where he first became captivated by traditional folk. Already an avid music lover, thanks in part to his mother, who was an accomplished concert violinist, Seeger believed early on that music, folk in particular, is a social force, that a "guitar could be mightier than the bomb."

Seeger worked alongside another key figure in the folk revival, Alan Lomax, at the Library of Congress's Archive of American Folk Song. While there, Seeger met Woody Guthrie. Taken with Guthrie's

Figure 1.8. Pete Seeger (left) and Woody Guthrie in Oklahoma City, circa 1940. Both musicians would influence the life and music of Johnny Cash and Peter La Farge. *Courtesy of Guy Logsdon/ Library of Congress, American Folklife Center.*

wayward spirit, Seeger joined the musician in his travels around the country, hopping railroad trains and busking along the way. Later, Seeger helped Lomax put together *Hard Hitting Songs for Hard-Hit People*, a compilation of Guthrie songs. Seeger decided that music would allow him to engage with and highlight issues that were important to him, including racial justice, crosscultural communication, and international peace. He still considers his role as a musician as being a "planter of seeds," hopeful that some seeds "land on good ground, grow, and then multiply."

The Almanac Singers presented an amazing opportunity to plant seeds far and wide. The group consisted of Bess Lomax Hawes, Baldwin "Butch" Hawes, Sis Cunningham, Josh White, Sam Gary, and later Woody Guthrie. All were major influences on the folk revival movement. Still, it wasn't until 1950, when the group re-formed as The Weavers, that Seeger achieved a greater level of popular success with a string of major hits, including a cover of Leadbelly's "Good-night, Irene," Woody Guthrie's "So Long, It's Been Good to Know You," and the group's own "Kisses Sweeter Than Wine." A few weeks following his HUAC appearance, Seeger performed in New York. Quickly surrounded by reporters, he was asked for an explanation about his decision to challenge the committee's right to question his political beliefs. Producing a banjo, he played "Wasn't That a Time?" The gathered reporters tapped their toes as Seeger played. The song is about the American Revolution. The committee never bothered to ask about that.

PETER LA FARGE'S stay in Chicago was brief, a momentary layover on his way to New York in 1958. While there, he joined the Goodman Theater and began acting in regional plays.

When the decade had begun, there were only seven theaters in Chicago. But by the time La Farge arrived in the city, the theater scene was beginning to explode. New theaters with ambitious creative aspirations were mushrooming everywhere. La Farge must have tried his luck at more than a few of these grand new theaters, starting with the cultural center in the Fine Arts Building at 410 South Michigan Avenue. This magnificent structure was designed by architect Solon S. Berman and built by the Studebaker Company in 1885 for the assembly and display of its carriages and wagons. In 1898 the building was converted into a 1,000-seat theater and a 500-seat playhouse. Anyone who entered the building couldn't help noticing the inscription over the doors:

ALL PASSES—ART ALONE ENDURES

At the time in his mid-twenties, La Farge was not giving that much serious thought to his next move. Alone and once again facing an uncertain future, he was invited to perform in an off-Broadway play. Seeing it as a move in the right direction, La Farge jumped at the chance, quickly packing his bags and leaving Chicago behind. New York was alive, hot with thrilling possibilities. For La Farge, a decade filled with fits and starts was ending.

JUST AS La Farge was finding his way to New York, Guy Carawan landed at the Highlander Folk Center. Carawan grew up in California but had roots in the South. With a father from North Carolina and a mother from South Carolina, he says he has always considered himself "half southern." Carawan told writer Bob Reiser, "I always itched to know about my roots. Every time I'd hear a recording of a five-string banjo, something inside me stirred." After a chance encounter with Pete Seeger in 1952, Carawan decided to wander out in search of his roots. Performing folk music throughout the United States, Europe, and China, he gained not only a clearer perspective but also a mission. After hearing Martin Luther King Jr. speak in 1958, Carawan called Myles Horton. "I'd met him before, and he said Highlander needed a musical director. My job would be to help get people singing and sharing their songs."

After the Montgomery bus boycott, Highlander was visited by people from all around the country. With success came increased opposition, some of it violent; the Ku Klux Klan tried to scare the center into ceasing its civil rights activity. Highlander was contributing to a movement that was growing in strength and power daily. An opportunity to dramatically alter American culture and politics was within its grasp. It was important for the center to continue establishing new methods that brought people into the movement while building unity and creating a situation in which fundamental change was not just possible but impossible to stop. Understanding how important singing was in southern culture, Highlander invited Pete Seeger to conduct a few music workshops, an offer Seeger was glad to accept. Seeger, ever the folksong stalwart, was flooded with requests and invitations to perform throughout the United States and abroad. His touring schedule was impressive, and enviable. Whatever small measure of success the hatchet men of the House Un-American Activities Committee had against Seeger appeared to be outweighed by the significance folk music was gaining in U.S. popular culture. Seeger's principled stance may have cost him lucrative television appearances, but it opened up other avenues of exposure and support. As Carnegie Hall associate archivist Rob Hudson explains,

"Carnegie Hall would never close its doors to Pete Seeger no matter if he was blacklisted or not." A whole new world was being born, one in which music—folk, traditional, hillbilly—could play a key role in shaping. Johnny Cash was watching and listening.

"ARMED INDIANS Break Up Klan Meeting," screamed the headline of the *Greensboro Daily News* on January 19, 1958. On the same day, the *New York Times'* front-page story led with "Raid by 500 Indians Balks North Carolina Klan Rally." In 1956, Congress had passed a bill officially recognizing the Lumbee Indians, the largest tribe in North Carolina and one of the largest tribes in the United States, with more than forty thousand members. The Lumbee reside primarily in Robeson, Hoke, Cumberland, and Scotland Counties in western North Carolina. They take their name from the Lumbee River. The threat arose for the Lumbee in 1957 when Klan wizard and Free Will Baptist minister Reverend James W. "Catfish" Cole of South Carolina launched a campaign of terror targeting the tribe. "The Lumbee are mongrels," Cole told the *Greensboro Daily News*. "There's about 30,000 half-breeds up in Robeson County and we are going to have some cross burnings and scare them up."

With the start of a new year, Cole and the Klan increased the number of their terrorist actions. "Trouble began . . . when two crosses were burned on Indian property following what the Klan considered relaxations in the race barriers," the *New York Times* reported. Then Cole took his campaign on the road, speaking throughout the country against the "mongrelization" of the races. Feeling confident that no one would resist the Klan's activity against the Lumbee, Cole decided to stage a large rally on January 18, 1958, in the small town of Maxton, North Carolina. If the rally was successful, the Lumbee would capitulate and "take their place," and Cole would realize one of his greatest ambitions: control of the Klan in both North and South Carolina.

Maxton sheriff Malcolm McLeod met with Cole and explained that "his life would be in danger if he came to Maxton and made the same speech he'd been making." Inflated with his own misguided sense of power, Cole believed that the show of force by the white supremacists would trump any potential opposition by the Lumbee, or anyone else for that matter. The days of "race mixing" in Robeson County were over, Cole told Sheriff McLeod. But the Klan wizard's hubris and ignorance would prove dangerously foolish.

Once Cole arrived at the designated spot—a cornfield in Maxton—he realized that attendance at the rally would fall short of the hoped-for five thousand; it was going to be no more than fifty. Five hundred armed Lumbee, however, soon encircled the Klansmen and others who had gathered to hear Cole speak. The Lumbee opened fire on the Klansman, a majority of whom had run into the nearby brush trying to escape. Next, the Lumbee destroyed the amplifiers and dared the few remaining Klansmen to fight. Suddenly, tear gas spread throughout the field, dispersing both the Lumbee and the Klansmen. Sheriff McLeod had placed two plainclothes deputies in the crowd with the intention of preventing a "riot" or "fatalities." Cole, one of the first to panic and run away, left his wife behind to hide in Hayes Pond, a nearby swamp.

The Lumbee called their attack of the Klan the "Battle of Hayes Pond." Their show of unity and defiance was covered prominently in other national publications as well, including *Newsweek* ("North Carolina: Indian Raid"), *Life* ("Bad Medicine for the Klan: North Carolina Indians Break Up Kluxers' Anti-Indian Meeting"), and *U.S. News and World Report* ("When Carolina Indians Went on the Warpath"). On March 13, Cole was convicted of inciting a riot and sentenced to two years in prison. A few months later, in another positive turn of events for Native people, Secretary of the Interior Fred Seaton delivered a radio speech in which he stated, "It is absolutely unthinkable to me as your secretary of the interior that consideration be given to forcing upon an Indian a so-called termination plan which did not have the understanding and acceptance of a clear majority of the members affected."

MARTIN LUTHER King Jr. stands to the right in a grainy black-and-white photo, smiling and looking toward the camera, with his suit jacket draped over his right arm. His left arm is half raised, his hand in the air, perhaps waving to someone outside of the photograph. Over his left shoulder, a whole head and shoulders taller, stands Pete Seeger, offering the young minister a wide smile. Also in the photo is Rosa Parks, her head turned slightly down and to the right, deep in conversation with two others in the photo. Seeger met King only a few times, but in this photo you can see that, as Seeger later recalled, those few times were worth a lifetime of meetings.

The photo was taken at Highlander Folk School in 1958. King, Seeger, and Parks were there together for the twenty-fifth anniversary of Highlander's opening. Zilphia Horton, one of the school's cofounders, had recently passed away, and Myles Horton had asked Seeger to come lead everyone in song. At the end of the festivities, Seeger decided to play an old gospel hymn traditionally sung in black churches throughout the South. The tune, originally called "I'll Overcome" (often referred to as "I'll Be Alright"), was Zilphia's favorite song. She had taught it to Seeger in New York around 1946 after learning it herself from tobacco worker Lucille Simmons, who sang the hymn while on strike in Charleston, South Carolina. The lyrics were changed by Horton from "I'll be alright" to "we will" first in 1948 when the song was used in support of Henry A. Wallace's presidential campaign. Seeger then put his own twist on the song, changing "will" to "shall." With King and Parks clapping along, Seeger quickly had everyone join in the joyful singing. Afterward, the song's refrain stayed with King, who later mentioned it to a friend of Seeger's who drove the civil rights leader to the airport. "That song, 'We Shall Overcome'—it sticks with you, doesn't it?"

For young Guy Carawan, Highlander's new music director, music was a lifeline. He knew the power music had in the old labor movements; workers and organizers used traditional songs to speak directly to a particular issue and moment by just simply changing a tune's lyrics. "The IWW was a singing union," folklorist and shipbuilder Archie Green says. "They published songs that they sung in a book called 'The Little Red Songbook,' and from 1909 until today it's remained in print." Some of the songs became major hits, such as Henry McClintock's "Hallelujah, I'm a Bum." Singing together offered a way to diffuse hostile and potentially violent encounters between workers, bosses, and company guards. "Old Wobbly, dock worker Fred Hansen, was one of the best at using music to lower the heat in confrontations and raise the spirit of peacefulness. He was a peacemaker and when there was a strike on the dock, tempers start to rub raw—you don't know how you're going to feed your kids," musician Utah Phillips explains. "Someone picks up a brick to throw at a goon or a company guard, Fred Hansen would jump in with a song and get everybody singing, because everybody singing together meant they weren't throwing punches or throwing rocks."

One of these keys songs was "Solidarity Forever," written by Ralph Chaplin, who composed new lyrics over the melody of an old marching song, "The Battle Hymn of the Republic," which itself took the melody from "John Brown's Body." These songs carry all the weight and power of every person who ever sang them. They are filled with wit and humor, sadness and hope, purpose and salvation. That's why they have endured. It's also why they resonated so much with the musicians exploring folk and traditional music in the 1950s. The group at Highlander understood this music's power. With Carawan as music director, Highlander possessed someone with intimate experience of just how transformative and inspirational music could be.

In the South, the relationship between most people and music was a bit different from that of people active in labor and other movements. There, people connected with song through their time in the church, singing hymns and spirituals. Carawan explains: "So, my job as music director at Highlander was to create workshops where we could take these songs and make them appropriate for the civil rights movement." It wasn't easy at first. Many were uncomfortable with changing religious songs about salvation or redemption into songs calling for confrontation and action, albeit nonviolent action. They believed they were slighting God somehow. Perhaps changing the words of an old spiritual from "over my head I see trouble in the air" to "over my head I see freedom in the air," as Bernice Johnson Reagon had done, would be seen as a sin. But Carawan was able to convince them that in fact they might be slighting God by *not* using the music, since the pursuit of justice, of human rights, is the pursuit of the highest of Christian ideals.

The approach began to work; people realized that this was indeed their music: people's songs and freedom songs. There was nothing wrong with changing the words in a way that expressed what they were feeling, their yearning for a better future. Carawan described this approach later to Reiser: "The songs could take on so many meanings. They could be jubilant, or they could be a lament because someone got killed. They could help people gather their determination, or they could be funny and satirical. You could dance to some of the songs, anything to help people get through all this. The music became a part of everything. You couldn't tell who was the singer and who was an organizer, because the organizers sang and the singers organized."

When Guy Carawan first arrived at Highlander, he often sang "Keep Your Hand on the Plow, Hold On," a song that was a key part of the 1930s labor movement. While traveling the country throughout the 1950s, he witnessed Seeger perform the song a number of times at various labor meetings and rallies. It wasn't long before it became a signature song in Carawan's repertoire. A participant in the Highlander Citizenship School program, Alice Wine from John's Island, South Carolina, liked the song and told Carawan, "I know a different echo. We sing 'Keep your eyes on the prize.'" Wine, who also participated in the literacy program at Highlander, then performed her own version, "Keep Your Eyes on the Prize," for Carawan. He was drawn to this version and began singing it at community meetings and gatherings, asking people to join in and sing with him.

"Wine's song is a great example," Carawan says. "She just captured the spirit, the energy of the moment. I had to help spread that song around." The moment when he first performed "We Shall Overcome" to a group of civil rights activists changed his life, and it gave King and the other civil rights leaders what they needed to help move

Figure 1.9. Guy Carawan (left), Bernard Lafayette (center), and James Bevel (right). Lafayette and Bevel were among the leaders of the Nashville Student Movement and the Student Nonviolent Coordinating Committee. A turning point in Carawan's life and the civil rights movement took place when he performed "We Shall Overcome" at a SNCC meeting in 1960. *Photo by Thorsten Horton, courtesy of Guy and Candie Carawan.*

people throughout the South and beyond. "I just started teaching people, everyone, 'We Shall Overcome,'" Carawan says. "It took hold of people as it did me when Seeger first taught the song to me in 1950. It was the Student Nonviolent Coordinating Committee meeting where I first performed it." The late Walter Stafford, a member of SNCC, told me of that moment: "It just fit. It said everything we needed to say, and it inspired and moved people to action." The soundtrack to the movement had been born, and it was quickly growing.

FIVE YEARS had passed since Ira Hayes's tragic death. In that time, the plight of Native people worsened. According to a report by the Ponca Tribe of Nebraska, since 1953, when the Indian termination policy was forced upon Native people, over one hundred tribes had been terminated; 1,365,801 acres of Native land were removed from protected status; 13,263 Native people lost tribal affiliation. In the government's attempt to "Americanize" Native people and make them full citizens, they further degraded their already precarious living conditions. Resolution 108, the one Senator Watkins called the "final solution" and the "Indian emancipation proclamation," was a disaster. "It's clear that the termination policy had devastating effects on tribal autonomy, culture, and economic welfare," Native activist John Trudell says. "The lands belonging to the Native people, rich in resources, were taken over by the federal government for exploitation." The *New York Times* reported that "these bills halt the Bureau's extension services, services that have been a vital factor, along with the Bureau's soil conservation and credit programs, in recent Indian progress toward economic independence." Native tribes across the United States reported the same stark reality: the termination policy had little to do with improving the quality of life of Native people. Far from emancipating them, the policy seemed to be literally terminating Native people.

Already poor on most reservations, education was now to be funded by the states, which had little interest in doing so. The funding dried up, causing many tribal schools to close their doors. The ones that remained open were worse off than before. Many Native children were forced to attend public schools, where they were not accepted and encountered harsh discrimination. Healthcare was deteriorating even more rapidly. Tribes were no longer eligible for the federal Indian Health Service. Hospitals and clinics closed, and with them the means to get basic, preventive healthcare. The story of the Menominee people in Wisconsin provides a sobering example of the effects of termination on Native people.

The Menominee people had been hit hard by tuberculosis just as termination was enacted. The epidemic grew quickly, and in a matter of months over 25 percent of the Menonimee people were afflicted. Because treatment was no longer available, the only thing they could do was give in to the affliction. Nearly a third of the tribe ended up terribly ill or dead. If there was any kind of emancipation taking place, it was the thousands of Native people who were forced to move off the reservations. Lacking healthcare, housing, jobs, and a good education, they found a coarse, intolerant America awaiting them in the towns and cities they relocated to.

PRESIDENT EISENHOWER and General John Bragdon of the Army Corp of Engineers were eager to expand their public works projects, which included building highways, dams, and power plants throughout the country. On December 28, 1954, Robert Moses, the imposing chairman of the New York State Power Authority, had proposed a plan to build a huge power plant in Niagara, New York, but to do so he would have to take over hundreds of acres of land belonging to the Tuscarora. The Moses proposal was a clear violation of two treaties, the Stanwix Treaty of 1784 and the Pickering Treaty of 1794.

Tuscarora Chief Elton Greene wrote a letter to Moses, reminding him that the treaties must be respected and "protest[ing] the attempt by the New York State Power Authority to take a few hundred acres of our Tuscarora Indian lands for a storage reservoir." The Tuscarora were in the same position as the Allegany Seneca, who were facing the removal of hundreds of acres of land and the flooding of their reservation. Moses angrily answered, "The treaties you talk about have nothing to do with your reservation in Niagara County." Willfully lying with the intention of misleading the public about the situation, Moses wished to stimulate angry public opposition to the Tuscarora's legal claim to the land.

Moses also offered what he believed was fair financial compensation for the land, nearly $1,000 an acre. "We will keep our land and the Power Authority can keep their money," Chief Greene said in rejecting the offer. When William Rickard of the Tuscarora General Tribal Council testified in front of the Federal Power Commission on November 8, 1957, he eloquently summed up the cultural chasm that existed between Native and non-Native people: "In the first place, we do not feel that we own the land. It is only loaned to us to save for the ever coming faces of the next generation of Tuscarora." Rickard was the son of Chief Clinton Rickard, a respected Native leader and strong voice of resistance to what he regarded as the movement to mold Native people "into imitation whites."

At first, Moses and the Power Authority wanted 600 acres of Native land. Then it was 960, and soon 1,383, or about one-fifth of reservation land. Chief Greene was right to complain: "We do not know what they will want when they are through." Moses argued that only 640 acres was protected by federal treaty and therefore any efforts by the Tuscarora to block the Power Authority's efforts were criminal. The Tuscarora remained determined to resist, and they blocked a number of attempts at surveying the land. But the power project was dragging on and much money was being lost. Then, on April 1, 1959, in a public display of unity, a Native delegation representing 180,000 people met in Miami to protest white encroachment on Native land. The Tuscarora were represented, as were the Mohawk, Seneca, Oneida, Cayuga, and Chippewa. Mad Bear of the Tuscarora denounced President Eisenhower as "not a man to honor treaties." In the end, thirty-six tribal representatives signed thirty-six buckskins to form the United Indian Nation, emphatically rejecting a current bill that would force U.S. citizenship upon Native people. Again Chief Rickard put a fine point on the issue: "We were all aware of the unfortunate circumstances of the Western Indians who had this dubious blessing imposed upon them in the nineteenth and early twentieth centuries and had had their lands taken away in the process, leaving them homeless, paupers begging the government for support."

"THE PROBLEM Pete had was one that pops up in our family throughout the generations," says Povy La Farge. "It's the multiplicity of real genius—it makes a difficult life. Not many people can do all these different things. I know at one point he was riding broncs in Madison Square Garden and then playing the lead in an off-Broadway production of *King Lear*. He was only thirty-one or thirty-two at the time, which is amazing for that role." Somehow, through his short time acting in Chicago and then touring with a theater company, La Farge got a part in an off-Broadway production of *Dark of the Moon*, a play by cousins Howard Richardson and William Berney that is based on the legend of Barbara Allen, who marries a witch boy.

Produced by Temple Productions and directed by Norman Roland, *Dark of the Moon* opened at Carnegie Hall Playhouse on February 26, 1958. La Farge played the role of Burt Atkins. The playbill's actor biography lists him as a "product of the Goodman Theatre in Chicago" and the "son of Oliver La Farge, Pulitzer Prize–winning novelist." *Players* magazine described the play as "a powerful fantasy in a setting of the Smoky Mountains. It achieves that rare combination of being spectacular and at the same time intimate and intense." The *New York Herald Tribune* called it "a show of magical appeal," and the *London Daily Herald* labeled it "an astonishing play, a fearsome legend." Arthur Gelb of the *New York Times* wrote on February 27, 1958, that the play "is a provocative mixture of fantasy and earthiness. In this oddly piquant production, the color of folklore and the pathos of human yearning are effectively combined. . . . The cast is too large to permit singling out more than a few for special praise." Gelb cited actors John Brachita, Maude Greer, Conrad Bain, Ann Hillary, and Norman Roland, but not La Farge.

Playing the role of Miss Metcalf in the February 1958 production of *Dark of the Moon* was the actress Susan Becker. She and La Farge were in love and soon married. At first, everything seemed to click for La Farge and his new wife. "He and his very shy, very plain first wife finally found a nice, roomy apartment on Christopher Street [in the West Village]," Krim explains. "Not very far from where the Lion's Head and the 55 Club now are, near Sheridan Square, and it was from this headquarters that Pete began to make his downtown play as a new kind of bohemian personality-pitcher." But there was trouble not long after. "They were both not very well mentally," Povy says. Their love affair and marriage quickly fell apart while each of them continued to struggle with mental illness. Susan finally broke. Completely. The two split. Susan was later institutionalized at a Michigan hospital and never recovered.

By 1959, it didn't take La Farge long to discover the new music scene in Greenwich Village. The area was already well known for its rich countercultural history. Back in 1916, the French surrealist and Dadaist Marcel Duchamp, accompanied by fellow artists, set off balloons from atop the Washington Square Arch, celebrating the founding of the "Independent Republic of Greenwich Village." The internationally acclaimed dancer Isadora Duncan had once made "the Village" her home, as did playwright Eugene O'Neill. O'Neill's friend, the radical journalist John Reed, also lived nearby for a time. The seeds of democratic dissent and creative wonder sprouted wildly, shaping a bohemian society that clearly challenged the U.S. system. When La Farge discovered it, Washington Square Park had become an outdoor stage filled with live performances open to anyone who happened to wander by. Dada. Surrealism. Writers. Artists. Political radicals. Bohemians. They all helped breathe life into a small section of Manhattan that gave life to a ripening counterculture. All these movements helped shape an era of "new bohemians," who took a bit of what the Beat poets offered in the 1950s, mixed it with the rebellious spirit of rock 'n' roll, and then layered it with a new brand of U.S. folksong.

A decade before, in the 1950s, the coffee houses had given way to the rush of young men and women who migrated to the Village from all over the country with acoustic guitars slung over their shoulders, ready to sing you a song. The performance by Seeger's old folk group, The Weavers, at the Village Vanguard on Christmas Day in 1949 foreshadowed a folk revival that would soon pour into the American conscience and popular culture.

In the midst of this shining historical moment, Peter La Farge could at once feed off its energy and contribute to its heat. It was more than he got from acting and riding broncs. Even though La Farge managed to secure a few starring roles, the daily pursuit of them became tiresome. The electricity of the Village music scene was more of what he needed.

One day, simply ducking his head under a low archway and entering the basement performance space located at 116 MacDougal Street, he was home. Opened in 1958 by John Mitchell, the Gaslight was originally a "basket house," where performers were paid the proceeds of a passed-around basket. Beat poets including Allen Ginsburg and Gregory Corso performed there. With its twin entrances at the bottom of a pair of stone stairways, located on either side of the flight of steps leading to the shops above, the Gaslight didn't seem to be much at all, almost hidden from view. Yet the cavernous café's effect on American popular culture was exciting and distinct. Standing in front of a brick wall that framed the stage, a new breed of comedians, including Woody Allen, Dick Gregory, and Bill Cosby, made audiences think and laugh with biting, socially conscious commentary. Once inside, with the eyes of the hushed crowd focused on the stage where a lone musician sat playing a guitar or a comedian addressed a crowd, La Farge's troubles seemed to disappear.

Gilbert Vandine "Cisco" Houston could tell right away that there was something different about La Farge. He just couldn't tell what. With his full baritone voice and smooth guitar sound and his fabled relationship with Woody Guthrie, Houston was already considered a music legend by the time he met La Farge. "Houston's another one of these unadorned," folksinger Tom Paxton says. "He had a beautiful voice and played very simple guitar. I met him one time at Folk City. Just one of these simple, direct singers. Not a lot of flash or fire but straight from the shoulder." Of course La Farge already knew who Cisco was; he'd seen him perform and listened to his records. Cisco's interest in La Farge made the younger musician forget all about acting. "Cisco was always with Woody," radio host Oscar Brand says. "He also got along better with Peter better than anybody I knew. He wanted to help him as much as he could, even while being so bound to Woody." In their own way, La Farge and Guthrie were both "unadorned."

As THE battle between Robert Moses and the Tuscarora intensified, the story began to attract national attention. Eleanor Roosevelt, Marlon Brando, and Edmund Wilson were just some of the people who started speaking out publicly about the government's treaty violations. Wilson, considered the finest literary critic of the time, decided to travel to the Tuscarora Reservation in an effort to write about the situation, which resulted in a four-part series for the *New Yorker* magazine, appearing in 1959. The following year it was published as a book titled *Apologies to the Iroquois*. "He made his apologies to the Indian tribes that his family, among others had displaced," Gore Vidal wrote in the essay "Edmund Wilson: Nineteenth-Century Man." Although Wilson's work was well intentioned, the Tuscarora did not take it "at all seriously because he was not among us long enough to know our people or our situation," Chief Clinton Rickard wrote. "There are a number of errors and misinterpretations . . . some of which are laughable. Everywhere he went on different reservations, he was unable to understand or represent the Indian situation properly."

But despite all the mistakes Wilson committed, he got one important thing right. As Chief Rickard conceded, Wilson accurately captured the "low tricks that had been used against us by Robert Moses and the SPA," which included wiretapping. Unhappy with Wilson's book, in 1960 Moses published a pamphlet titled *Tuscarora: Fiction and Fact* in which he denied the "false canards that Indians' telephones were wiretapped." And after holding the Power Authority at bay for some time, the Supreme Court ruled against the Tuscarora, using an extremely narrow definition of what constitutes a Native reservation under the Federal Power Act. "Injustice had triumphed," Chief Clinton later wrote. "A large portion of the land we had so carefully accumulated 180 years earlier to compensate us for the loss of our North Carolina lands and to provide a homeland for our people forever had been wrenched from us by a government that was supposed to protect us."

Although the U.S. government's relationship with Native people continued to be one based on duplicity and cruel shortsightedness, the resurrection of the figure of Ira Hayes was underway. This time it was the Hollywood director Delbert Mann who placed a spotlight on Hayes. Mann's debut feature film, *Marty*, which was based on a teleplay by Paddy Chayefsky, had won Oscars for Best Actor, Best Picture, Best Screenplay, and Best Director in 1955. A script about Ira Hayes titled *The Outsider* appealed to his social sensibilities and creative vision. It seemed right for him. Once Mann agreed to make the film, actor Tony Curtis actively and passionately lobbied to be cast as Ira Hayes.

Curtis's perspective on the Ira Hayes story was vastly different from John Wayne's. Fourteen years earlier, Wayne used Iwo Jima (and Hayes) to promote his fiercely anticommunist views in the film *The Sands of Iwo Jima*. Curtis didn't see it as a metaphor for an America that was invulnerable, righteous, and above criticism. Instead, he empathized with the tragic story of Hayes, believing he could provide a nuanced, thoughtful portrayal of the tormented Hayes, the one few people knew. The harsh, sad reality of Hayes's story provided a counternarrative to the one that had become almost legend. Curtis and Mann felt it must be told.

William Bradford Huie and Stewart Stern wrote the screenplay with this idea in mind, and when Universal Pictures agreed to make the film, all involved felt the picture should find an audience in the rapidly shifting cultural climate of the 1960s. The studio and the director felt the final film was excellent and that Curtis's performance was even better. On October 5, 1961, the *New York Times* reported that the studio was releasing the film early in the hope that the Academy would consider Curtis as a contender for Best Actor. The Academy didn't, and the film quickly faded from theaters.* "People tell me I should have won an Oscar for my portrayal of Ira," Curtis said. "There wasn't enough buzz about it to move the Academy voters. But I loved playing the

---

*A more striking cinematic portrayal of the plight of Native people in America came out a year earlier with the release of Kent Mackenzie's *The Exiles*. The film follows the first wave of Native people relocated by the Bureau of Indian Affairs in the 1950s. The particular group of Natives featured in the film lived on the edge of downtown Los Angeles.

Struggles similar to Hayes's can easily be seen in any of the people presented in the film. "The desolate image of modern man cut off from any meaningful tradition, preserving identity only through group difference and hostility toward the patterns of environment, is, as people used to say, an 'eye-opener,'" film critic Pauline Kael wrote. "Instead of recreating a culture that has disappeared, MacKenzie shows us the living ruins. . . . In the future, those who are interested in the American motion picture are likely to refer to 1961 not in terms of the big Hollywood productions, but as the year of *The Exiles*."

role—I felt a special empathy for anyone in pain, especially the pain of being shunted aside or treated poorly."

As the memory of Ira Hayes was receding again, the career of Johnny Cash was ascending like a rocket. Starting from the cotton fields of Arkansas, surviving the shaky audition at Sun Studio, and arriving at the premier performance venue in the country, Cash was on a foot-to-the-floor, full-throttle ride. He continued to form a reputation as a musician who was not afraid to take chances, redefining American popular music along the way.

Cash's band now included drummer W. S. Holland. Nicknamed "Fluke," Holland sat in on the impromptu meeting of Elvis, Cash, Carl Perkins, and Jerry Lee Lewis at Sun Studios—dubbed the Million Dollar Quartet sessions—and played drums on Carl Perkins's original version of "Blue Suede Shoes." After hearing him play drums, Cash told Holland, "I want you to work with me every show I play for as long as I'm in the business." From that moment forward, Holland toured with Cash everywhere he went. Many credit Holland with pioneering the use of drums in rock 'n' roll.

Even though Cash's recordings with Sun Records were very successful, he was unhappy with his contract, which he felt was unfair and constricting. Of the twelve records Sun released following Elvis's departure from the label, eleven were Cash records. But Cash was frustrated because Sam Phillips's interest was locked into promoting the fiery piano player Jerry Lee Lewis. Cash could plainly see that Lewis was a key musician in the success of rock 'n' roll, but he too had gained an important place in music, and on top of that he was selling tens of thousands of records and producing hit songs. "Folsom Prison Blues" reached number 5 on the country charts, while "I Walk the Line" doubled its success by crossing over into the pop charts and climbing to number 13. Cash knew he could do more. He needed to do more. Although he had done a lot for Cash, Phillips was preventing him from going further. "Cash told me that he went to Sun Records and Sam Phillips time and again to do a live record in a prison or a concept album," record producer Bob Johnston says. "He told Cash he would drop him from the label, fire him, and ruin his career, and that as long as he was with Sun he would never be allowed to do an album at a prison or any of these other albums he had in mind."

Cash was restless and determined to move ahead with or without Phillips. In the short time he was at Sun, Cash proved the enigmatic producer right about one thing: that he was much more than just a country singer. Bucking hard against what he perceived to be a situation that was limiting him both financially and creatively, he signed with Columbia Records in 1958. "[Phillips] had me on a beginner's rate after three years," he later told *Rolling Stone*'s Robert Hilburn. "I didn't feel right about it." Bob Johnston observes that "Phillips didn't really get Cash. He wanted him only to do what [Phillips] wanted. Cash was never allowed to do what he wanted. Cash had to leave Sun. It was the only choice and the right choice." Phillips had sold the rights to Elvis Presley, and now he was losing Cash to a bigger label. He was bitter when he learned that Cash had lied to him about his Columbia negotiations, but the producer thought he would be all right without Cash. Let Cash go and he'll see. Cash did see.

Columbia, the giant New York–based label, was home to some of the best producers in the music business, including John Hammond, Don Law, Tom Wilson, and Bob Johnston. Coming from England didn't prevent Don Law from becoming one of the best country music producers on the scene. Revered in music circles for producing Robert Johnson, he produced his share of top-selling artists such as rockabilly singer Johnny Horton, honky-tonk musician Lefty Frizzell, western swing player Ray Price, and "Mister Country" Carl Smith. "Law lets an artist be an artist," Price remarked. Perfect. Law was just the type of producer Cash needed: someone who would let him be an artist. Learning from his tenure at Sun, Cash made sure that the freedom to explore and record different kinds of music—not just country or gospel, but rock, traditional, and folk—was included in his new deal with Columbia.

The first song Cash recorded with Law and Columbia was "Don't Take Your Guns to Town." It became one of Cash's biggest hits and put to rest any uncertainty surrounding his decision to leave Phillips. The album it appears on, *The Fabulous Johnny Cash*, captures the freshly liberated musician at his best. Law and Cash made a fine team, the producer adding some sparkle to Cash's minimalist, austere sound. The record hit 19 on the *Billboard* pop chart and produced two top-ten hits on the country charts. Working with Law, Cash found the perfect production partner to try his hand at the gospel, folk, and Americana albums he'd wanted to record. With *Ride This Train* in 1960, Cash achieved his goal. Recorded at "The Singing Cowboy" Gene Autry's ranch, Cash almost accidentally made one of the first concept albums in pop music history. Largely comprising traditional folk ballads, the album is, of course, about railroads: how they developed, and how they changed America. The album changed Cash—it made him feel like the kind of musician he always thought himself to be: a storyteller unafraid to sing about what was happening in the world around him.

The record's opening track, "Loading Coal," is a Merle Travis song. Cash felt connected to Travis's authenticity and sincerity, and with his newfound creative freedom, he was eager to record something by the country star. Cash wanted to put his own spin on the music, letting Travis know that he honored those who came before him and that he was going to be a musician who would push the music they loved further ahead. When Travis sang about coal miners, he knew what he was talking about—innately. These were not songs written by a studio composer tucked away in a Los Angeles or New York studio after reading a book about the plight of miners. Travis's music was something he felt, part of the air he breathed and the blood that ran through his veins. The songs Travis made famous when they were played on the radio in 1937 dealt with issues that he saw people struggle with every day.

Cash heard Travis's music on the radio while living in the Dyess Colony Resettlement Area in Mississippi County, Arkansas. Folklorist Archie Green says, "You can't help but think that when Travis sings 'Sixteen Tons,' with the lyric based on something Travis's father said in reply to a question about his health—'I can't afford to die, I owe my soul to the company store'—would have an impact on anyone listening who could relate to that struggle."

The musician Tennessee Ernie Ford agreed with Green. Ford hosted a successful television show on NBC. When the ratings started to flag, he turned to Travis's music, specifically "Sixteen Tons," to kick-start it. In 1955, Ford recorded his own version of the Travis tune, selling 2.5 million copies and topping the charts for more than ten weeks. On January 8, 1956, Ford told the *New York Times*' Oscar Godbout, "Finding good material is tough. . . . Then I remembered the songs of Merle Travis."

Merle Travis was born and raised in Muhlenberg County, Kentucky, a company-owned coal mining town. His father was a miner, pressed down by the thumb of the company that kept the workers and their families tied together like cattle. As a kid, using a guitar his brother made for him, Travis began to develop a style of guitar playing that later became known as "Travis picking." The finger-picking style was native to Travis's region of western Kentucky, but the young musician took it to another level, forever influencing guitar playing. By introducing jazz chords and melodies, he went beyond the simple three-chord foundation of country and traditional hillbilly music. Cash revered it.

Cash first met Travis in the mid-1950s while he was climbing the ladder of music stardom. At the time, Travis was already a legend in country music and a successful studio musician in Hollywood, where he recorded tons of music and even appeared in the popular film *From Here to Eternity* singing "Reinstatement Blues" alongside Frank Sinatra, who won an Academy Award for Best Supporting Actor for his role as smart aleck Angelo Maggio. Travis saw something in Cash from the start and the two formed a bond. "Nothing goes by him," Travis said of Cash. "Nothing gets near him. Nothing is not of interest to Johnny Cash. Every kind of people is in our audience." Travis later told writer Christopher S. Wren that the music he and Cash wanted to play "had been twisted, braided and finally welded together until it's a piece of music that's Americana." Bingo! "Cash and Travis represent something genuine and real," Archie Green says. So it was no surprise that when Cash got his chance with his new label he would look to a voice that helped him find his own: Merle Travis.

If only it were really that easy. *Ride This Train* may have been one of the first pop music concept albums, but Columbia Records wasn't in the least bit happy. From here on out, the label said it would not support Cash's efforts to stretch creatively. "He was encountering the same kind of stuff at Columbia [as he had at Sun]," Johnston says. "As before, the suits couldn't see what he was doing and just wanted to tightly control the direction of his music. Cash never gave in to that shallow thinking." They wanted hits, hits, and more hits. After all, this is why Columbia invested so heavily in him.

Not to be outdone, Phillips took to releasing repackaged Johnny Cash records, such as *Now Here's Johnny Cash*, to take advantage of the musician's increasing popularity. Cash was not pleased. He was set to release his next concept album for Columbia and wanted to present himself in own his way to his audience.

Cash's *Lure of the Grand Canyon* (1961) features spoken narration by Cash over a recording of Ferde Grofé's *Grand Canyon Suite*. An American pianist, arranger, and composer, Grofé had worked for some time with the Paul Whiteman Orchestra and taught orchestration at the Juilliard School of Music. Cash's decision to produce an album using Grofé's music was extremely daring. The concept album was essentially unheard of at the time in popular music. Working with Don Law once again, Cash didn't stop there. He brought in popular arranger Andre Kostelanetz to conduct. As Cash describes a day visiting the Grand Canyon, any lingering doubt that Cash made the right decision to leave Sun Records is silenced. Albeit with mixed results, Cash reached a higher level of creativity and self-expression that would not have been permitted under his first label.

ON THE day of his performance at Carnegie Hall in May 1962, Johnny Cash left rehearsals in a surly mood, frustrated. "His voice was just in terrible shape," Western explains. "It was essentially gone.

The whole day rehearsing he had his secretary taking notes to pass on to us to tell us what to do. He was trying to save his voice. But it was too late." As the musicians waited nervously for Cash to arrive, they girded themselves against what had they experienced often before.

Walking around the surrounding New York neighborhood, filled with spiring buildings and bright lights, must have felt like a hallucination. When he was interviewed earlier that day by television journalist Mike Wallace, Cash was fidgety and high-strung. Wallace did not help matters when he asked Cash absurd questions like "Country music at Carnegie Hall. Why?" In no frame of mind to deal with such thoughtless, stereotypical questioning, Cash responded irritably, "Why not?"

Cash had planned the Carnegie Hall show as a tribute to one of his musical heroes, Jimmie Rodgers. Famously known as the Singing Brakeman and the Mississippi Blue Yodeler, Rodgers is considered by many, including the Country Music Hall of Fame, to be the father of country music. Following his death at the age of thirty-five after a career that lasted only six years, Rodgers's story developed an allure of tragedy similar to that of James Dean's. The inscription on Rodgers's statue in Meridian, Tennessee, best describes his music: "His is the music of America. He sang the songs of the people he loved, of a young nation growing strong. His was an America of glistening rails, thundering boxcars, and rain-swept nights, of lonesome prairies, great mountains and a high blue sky. He sang of the bayous and the cornfields, the wheated plains, of the little towns, the cities, and of the winding rivers of America."

A former railroad brakeman, Rodgers's songs moved Cash as a young boy and held a special place in his heart. Railroads connected the people to the country, moving them from place to place, and sometimes even saving them. Cash learned this early on when a flood forced his family and the residents of the Dyess Colony Resettlement Area to leave their land. "Down near Stuttgart, Arkansas, we weren't moving over five miles an hour," Cash recalled, "because the water was clear over the tracks. They were afraid they might hit a big log across the tracks if they went faster. I remember a lot of women and children were crying because they were so worried and upset." He wrote a song about the experience, "Five Feet High and Rising." "It was late at night, and everybody on the train was sleeping," Cash said. "My mother, I remember, had dressed me in my new suit. I kept running up and down the aisles."

Moving agitatedly through the rear entrance of Carnegie Hall, Cash finally made his way backstage. The impressive group of musicians gathered there must have collectively thought, "This is not the way you want your Carnegie Hall debut to begin." There were The Carter Family with the legendary Mother Maybelle. There was Western, Gordon Terry, the Tennessee Two, George Jones, and The Glaser Brothers. Now at Carnegie Hall, on a night when he should have been filled with a sense of tremendous pride and achievement, Cash instead was on the verge of catastrophe. "It was literally a minute before we had to go on and John finally shows up," Grant says. "He was just downright filthy, dirty, really nasty. It was embarrassing for all of us. I knew that this was going to be a bad night for us." The show was sold-out, "Sold-out to the rafters with great anticipation," Western recalls. "Everybody was able to really go and do it, but John was just suffering."

Somehow the other musicians kept it together, performing at a high level—perhaps used to this from Cash, as Western, Grant, and others explain. "I was introducing everybody—George Jones, The Glaser Brothers, The Carter Family, Mac Weisman," Western says. "We had a surprise walk-on from Merle Kilgore." Cash had asked Kilgore, at the last minute, to stop at a New York costume shop and get a Civil War rebel uniform before heading to Carnegie Hall to perform the hit "Johnny Reb," a song he'd written for his good friend Johnny Horton, who had died in car crash less than two years before. Cash thought this would be a nice addition to a show.

Cash had opted to imitate Rodgers in his tribute, dressing as Rodgers had appeared in the widely seen picture of him wearing his actual railroad engineer uniform and posing with two thumbs up over a guitar. He had contacted Rodgers's widow, and she had agreed to let Cash wear her husband's old railroad hat and one of his jackets, and to use one of his railroad lanterns. But since Rodgers was a great deal smaller than Cash, the clothes wouldn't fit. "He had starved himself," Western explains. "He was a big man, but at this point he weighed 158 pounds or so." He had been taking pills to help him lose weight, but they also dried out his throat. Cash's pallor was made even more disturbing by his clothes, which were a mess. The blue scarf tucked in around his neck was grimy. The black and white checkered conductor's hat with the long, floppy bill was rumpled and cocked to one side. His shirt was half untucked and smudged with dirt, and his pants seemed to be falling off. "He looked like he had just hopped off a freight train after taking it all the way across the country to get there for the show," Grant remembers.

The other musicians knew why he looked the way he did and why he was acting frenzied and out of control. The members of his band had had some experience—too much experience now—of Cash falling deep into his own soul, aided by those "damn pills" as Grant angrily calls them.

Western was the emcee and the first performer of the night. Dressed in a skinny tie and a brand-new Italian suit with skinny lapels that Cash asked him to have made specifically for the show, he had the unenviable task of trying to hold it all together. The anxiety and tension were high. When the show started, Western still had no idea where Cash was, but then, out of the corner of his eye, he saw Cash stage left, ready to come on. "There were many times that I never saw John until he had to walk on the stage," Western says, "I could see him in the wings over there when I introduced him. It was a terrible sight. I was dreading it." Gaunt, hollow-eyed, and incoherent, the star of the show asked for the house lights to be turned off. He wanted the lantern he was carrying to light his entrance.

Cash intended to play nothing but Rodgers's songs, in the same way the former brakeman had performed them: standing with the guitar straddling one knee. He started with "Waiting on a Train." Cash later recalled that he "waited for the roar of recognition" but "no one recognized" the song, instead they "yell[ed] for 'Folsom Prison Blues.'" But on this night, this was the least of Cash's problems. When he opened his mouth, nothing came out. The audience at first thought he was joking and laughed. He tried to continue playing, but the effect of the pills brought him down low—too low. If only for the sake of the performance, Cash had always found a way to pull it together before. "We tried to move around the stage a bit more than usual," Grant says. "Most of the time when he was like that we could cover up and take the edge down a bit and hope he could get to another level. It didn't work." The only level Cash could reach was one further down. "I kept hoping the pills I'd taken would boost me up to where I didn't care anymore, but they didn't," Cash said afterward.

Cash had assembled a great number of old, traditional instruments to be placed on the stage for the performance. When he got around to grabbing any of these instruments, Cash suddenly dropped to his knees and began to crawl around the stage while trying to play the chosen instrument. At one point he knocked over a microphone, sending it crashing to the stage floor and causing feedback to screech through the PA system. The spectacular Main Hall had seen many performers take the stage, but none quite like this. The standing-room-only crowd that filled the five-level auditorium could only watch as Cash fell apart. "The whole show was a disaster," Grant says, as though it just happened last week. "It was a big, big mistake."

Cash was just lost that night. "He sunk as low as you can go," Grant says. "I still think it was the worst show we ever played. We didn't play very many songs." Western adds, "We had a stage full of great performers. Everybody else was in top shape performing, and the headliner of the show, John, was just having one of the most miserable nights of his life." In some way, Cash managed to perform for half an hour or so. "Let's put it this way," Western says. "Had John been able to perform to the same level that everybody else was performing, it probably would have been one of the greatest performances of his entire career." Grant agrees, but unfortunately it was miles away from even a decent performance. "You could see how troubled he was." Grant says. "There was just nothing we could say to him."

Cash's first appearance at Carnegie Hall was nothing short of a nightmare. The audience knew it and still offered Cash a polite, warm round of applause. Yet the damage was done and a significant opportunity squandered. Don Law was there with others from Columbia with hopes of producing a live album from Cash's first-ever Carnegie Hall performance. "Ya know, Columbia was set up to record a live album," Western sadly recounts. "They never even turned on the machines."

Cash stumbled off the stage, looking through everyone he passed. They stood aside silently, too embarrassed for the music star to say anything. Cash walked up the stairs to the makeshift backstage area that had been set up for him. Still in a manic state but sapped of the spirit that compelled him to perform, he sat alone, slumped in a corner. The other musicians began clearing out around him. "John virtually did a disappearing act," Western says. "No one knew where he went. He was just gone."

All Causes May
Here Find a Place

T HE NIGHT BEFORE the Carnegie Hall performance, Johnny
Western, Cash's trusted emcee, went down to Greenwich Village with Tompall Glaser of Tompall and the Glaser Brothers to check out the local music scene so they could see for themselves what the new breed of folk was really about. The two men made their way to 147 Bleecker Street, between LaGuardia and Thompson. There the musicians slipped into a popular music venue known as the Bitter End. Western and Glaser were soon asked to come up on stage, invited to join in and perform. The tall, handsome man leading the open mic night had recognized the two men and was thrilled to have the musicians there. For Ed McCurdy, already performing folksongs for close to a decade, Western and Glaser were revered members of the timeless alliance of musicians who briefly encounter one another as they crisscross the country to perform. At the time, Western boasted a hit television theme song, "Ballad of Paladin," played at the end of each episode of the popular CBS program *Have Gun—Will Travel* starring Richard Boone. Likewise, Tompall and the Glaser Brothers had earned much respect within the new circle of folk musicians for their creative blending of folk with rock 'n' roll. And the group's many public appearances with Johnny Cash didn't hurt either.

"It wasn't quite an open mic type thing," Western remembers. "It was a deal where we were set to do that as a little bit of a plug for the Carnegie Hall show the next night." The two musicians charmed the crowd, and by the end of the night, Western and McCurdy were friends who would develop a lifelong bond. McCurdy had been anticipating Cash's visit to New York since seeing the show's bold concert bill throughout the city weeks before:

Proclamation!!! THE ROYAL MAJESTY KING COTTON and
SUPPORTING HIS MAJESTY'S SUBJECT HIS SELECTED BARD
JOHNNY CASH—STORYTELLER—and singer of the sad,
the beautiful, the important stories, songs, color,
heritage of his Majesty's Realm—Dixieland.

The concept behind the concert seemed strange, out of step with the time. While the country was in the midst of a tense civil rights showdown, Cash brought his traveling band of "knights and ladies of folk-western bluegrass" to New York City in satirical support of "King Cotton."

It's hard to escape the troubling historical connotations the term *King Cotton* conjures in one's mind. After all, a century before, the phrase was used as a rallying cry throughout the South by politicians for two purposes: to stress the importance of the cotton crop to the Southern economy and to deter the North from continuing efforts to abolish slavery. The Southern states were confident that King Cotton was powerful enough to win the brewing war, believing that if cotton were withheld from the North the U.S. economy would collapse and that their European trading partners, heavily dependent on cotton imported from the United States, would quickly come to their aid. South Carolina Senator James Henry Hammond summed it up best in 1858: "Without firing a gun, without drawing a sword, should they make war on us, we could bring the whole world to our feet. . . . What would happen if no cotton was furnished for three years? . . . England would topple headlong and carry the whole civilized world with her

Figure 1.10. Publicity still of Johnny Cash at the time of his Carnegie Hall debut, May 10, 1962. *Courtesy of Carnegie Hall archives.*

[except for] the South. No, you dare not to make war on cotton. No power on the earth dares to make war upon it. Cotton is King."

Perhaps Cash, with this sharp display of his biting, ironic sense of humor, thought it funny to pay homage to the soft, staple fiber that grows around the seeds of the cotton plant that his family depended on for survival for most of his early life. Whatever the reason, it remained a strange choice to debut the show in a place that was becoming the counterculture support center of the civil rights movement, thanks in large part to the music Cash held dear and was there to share: folk.

None of this was of concern to McCurdy at the moment. The ribald musician thought of Cash as one of America's foremost singing storytellers, and he had gone to the Carnegie Hall show, where he was shocked to find himself bearing witness to a man coming apart. After the show, McCurdy made his way backstage. Looking for Cash, he found the music star alone. McCurdy fixed his eyes on him. He knew what the troubled music star was going through. He believed he could help, offer a word of support and understanding. When the opportunity presented itself, he walked over to Cash.

"It's called Dexedrine, isn't it," McCurdy said.
"What is?" Cash derisively answered.
"What you're taking," McCurdy responded. "I just kinda of recognized it myself. I'm a kindred spirit. I've been into all that stuff myself. I'm in a program right now and don't do anything, but I recognize Dexedrine."

Cash was in no mood to be diagnosed or analyzed, especially following the fiasco on the Carnegie Hall stage, the reality of which still hadn't fully sunken in. He was too far away in his own head and still hadn't recognized McCurdy, whom he tried to discourage from continuing—he sure wasn't going to take unsolicited advice from someone who just walked up to him and started spouting off about how he should change his ways. McCurdy refused to stop until he was heard, or at the very least until he had said everything he wanted to say. At last, Cash's unease fell away when he realized that McCurdy was the singer of the Scottish and Irish folksongs he loved so much. Cash knew McCurdy's music well. He began to understand that McCurdy knew what he was talking about and then opened himself up a little more. The haze of pills, made murkier by the let-down of his performance, lifted for a moment. The two men continued to speak.

Ed McCurdy is one of the indefatigable figures of the postwar American music scene. When he started his career in 1937 in New York, McCurdy first studied operatic voice in the hope of becoming a professional singer. It didn't pan out. "Blessed with a booming baritone voice and an adventurous spirit, he left home in the middle of the Great Depression for New York City to study operatic voice, begin his life's great adventure, and make a career as a professional singer," McCurdy's manager, Doug Yeager, says. "With little money in his pocket, he stayed at the YMCA or at friends' apartments, often went days with little food, and put every penny he saved towards his voice lessons. Within the year he headed west and landed a job as a gospel singer and announcer for WKY Radio in Oklahoma City." His gospel-singing career took him then to WFMD in Frederick, Maryland, and later to Niagara Falls. Never losing sight of his dream to hit it big as a popular singer, McCurdy again turned left when he hoped to go straight, ending up in the wild, unpredictable world of vaudeville. He toured with the popular A. B. Marcus Show, performing with the likes of Danny Kaye and Fat Jack Leonard. While his time with A. B. Marcus was exciting, McCurdy never gave up his dream of becoming a solo singing star. Yeager best sums up the musician's long, winding journey to folksong: "Ed's penchant to take to the barroom pulpit to talk about the lives of folk, to protest against war, or the infringement of anyone's civil rights, finally led him to singing folksongs."

After successful stints performing in Vancouver's Palomar Supper Club, serving as emcee at San Francisco's Club Lido, and working as the tuxedoed baritone singer at Sally Rand's, the famed burlesque club, McCurdy moved to Toronto in 1948 to host a folk program for CBS Radio. In 1949 McCurdy wrote "(Last Night) I Had the Strangest Dream," and the song changed his life forever. Musicians such as Pete Seeger and Guy Carawan connected to its stirring antiwar message and began performing it often themselves. "It was 1950, and to speak out directly against war was not a popular stance," Carawan says. "It never is." Johnny Cash loved the song as well and hoped to record his own version one day. McCurdy became close friends with Seeger, Lee Hays, Oscar Brand, and Richard Dyer-Bennett. He returned to New York and quickly landed a six-week gig at the Village Vanguard.

His provocative musical sensibility and resonant vocals allowed him to connect with the growing folk audience. It wasn't long before he signed a recording contract with Elektra Records. With Oscar Brand and Ramblin' Jack Elliott, McCurdy recorded *Bad Men and Heroes*. He was now firmly installed as one of the key musicians of the burgeoning folk revival movement. On February 17, 1957, the *New York Times* described McCurdy as having "a better voice than most folksingers" and being "a pleasure to hear." And after he performed at Town Hall in 1959, the paper singled him out, writing that he "has a disarmingly diffident manner" that reveals "the real depths of his artistry in a sensitive and moving performance of as well-worn a piece as 'Frankie and Johnny.'"

As the critical acclaim grew, so did his stature among his fellow musicians. By the end of the 1950s he was one of the most popular folk musicians around.

McCurdy's love of folk music was not the only thing he shared with Cash. Cash had hoped to be a gospel singer, but history interceded and swept him along, placing him at the intersection of rock, country, and folk. It's quite possible that Cash heard McCurdy in one of those radio broadcasts coming out of Okalahoma City in the 1940s.

The musical traits that set McCurdy apart from most other musicians were the ones that connected him to Cash. "Like Cash sorta did, McCurdy started as a rocker in the '50s," observes Yeager. "Then he expanded and became enamored with the folk boom. He really felt a connection to all those folksingers." The two had singing voices that gave their music a rich, resonant quality, one that made it unmistakably their own. They also had an inclination toward carousing, rabble-rousing, and risk-taking. "Ed was a big drinker," Yeager says. "When he met Cash, who was also a big drinker at the time, it was just another thing that connected them."

Toward the end of the 1950s, the new folk sound was moving deeper into the American mainstream thanks in large part to the more commercial, scrubbed-clean groups like The Kingston Trio. McCurdy had gone in the other direction, producing a series of records—*The Ballad Record*, *Barroom Ballads*, and *A Ballad Singer's Choice*—that incorporated elements of traditional folk music, cowboy songs, and Irish ballads, carrying them off with a bravado and bawdiness unlike anything out there. If Seeger was the diplomat of folk, arguing its case to the public, McCurdy was its resident provocateur. "He partied hard, drank hard, fought hard, and lived life to the fullest," Yeager says. "He was an irrepressible rascal, but with a lovable heart of gold." Touching upon serious issues of the day, mixing various folk sounds, and exhibiting a persona that was as audacious as they came, McCurdy's popularity soared as he toured college campuses around the country.

McCurdy's sexually provocative music soon trumped his more serious work, most significantly with the release of 1957's *When Dalliance Was in Flower*. Considering its overheated themes of lust and desire, it was no surprise that the album was a major success. Young people around the country were playing the record in dorm rooms and dance halls. Many were taking the first steps toward freeing themselves from the dull, prudish ideals of the 1950s. In 1958 McCurdy recorded a second volume, followed by a third, *Son of Dalliance*, in 1959. "Ed went to the library and went through all these Elizabethan stories. That's how he came up with the *Dalliance* albums," Yeager explains. "People always called him 'dirty Ed McCurdy.' He would bark back, 'I do not sing dirty songs. Oscar Brand sings dirty songs. I sing erotic songs.'"

On the heels of the success of the *Dalliance* series, McCurdy appeared at the first ever Newport Folk Festival in 1959, where his performance attracted such positive notice that Vanguard included four of his songs on the record *Vanguard Records' Folk Festival at Newport*. Started by jazz promoter and producer George Wein, who was behind the successful Newport Jazz Festival, the Newport Folk Festival was originally intended to occupy just one afternoon. "In '59, I approached Pete Seeger and saw what was going on with The Kingston Trio and other groups," Wein says. "There was such a demand for it. I thought that there was enough here to have a full festival. So I cancelled the folk afternoon and created a whole festival. I loved Pete. If you are Diogenes looking for an honest man you just find Pete Seeger."

Wein invited Chicago music promoter Albert Grossman to come out and produce the festival with him. At the time, Grossman operated the Gate of Horn in the basement of Chicago's Rice Hotel, a venue that showcased folk music. "I got Albert Grossman, who was managing Odetta," Wein explains. "He helped produce this event with me because he knew all these folksingers better than I did. Albert was a genius but wasn't well liked, and fairly ruthless. He was our artistic director, and he used the festival to connect to artists." Soon after the festival, Grossman sold the Gate of Horn and formed a production company with Wein. "He lived with me for two years," Wein says. "My wife couldn't take it. He'd come home and smoke pot, and he owed money to everybody so people would be calling at all hours of the day and night. He would have broken up the partnership regardless because he would have screwed his mother if it could gain him something." Wein and Grossman ended the partnership; the latter decided that his interests lay in managing the new crop of folk musicians, and the former wanted to continue producing the Newport Jazz Festival and Newport Folk Festival, while promoting the numerous musical artists and events he was deeply committed to.

Studs Terkel, the renowned Chicago-based oral historian and blacklist victim, was the opening-day emcee. Terkel was very familiar with many of the festival's artists, owing to his time hosting the radio show *The Wax Museum* on WNER in Chicago. Pete Seeger had been a guest on the show in 1945, and Terkel had used it to promote other musicians such as Mahalia Jackson, Woody Guthrie, and Big Bill Broonzy. At the festival, Terkel introduced Seeger, the first performer, as "America's tuning fork."

In spite of the impressive array of traditional, country, blues, and folk musicians—including John Jacob Niles, Sonny Terry, Brownie McGhee, Odetta, Frank Hamilton, and Frank Warner—young people clamored for The Kingston Trio. The folk pop group's performance was surrounded by controversy because Wein had bowed to crowd pressure and moved it ahead of five-string banjo virtuoso Earl Scruggs. By the time The Kingston Trio made way for Scruggs, the crowd's unrelenting calls for the immensely popular folk-pop group to continue made it nearly impossible for the bluegrass legend to perform. Scruggs, a bit stunned and more than a little upset, cut his set short. Slighting the revered Scruggs ended up haunting Wein, particularly following the crowd's loud demands for The Kingston Trio to continue before Scruggs could even take the stage. "They refused to quiet down, despite the considerable efforts of emcee Oscar Brand," Wein says. "Earl Scruggs played a brief set before the return of The Kingston Trio. . . . I lost a lot of friends in the folk world because of that slip-up."

Following the success of the '59 Festival, where an eighteen-year-old Mexican-American folksinger named Joan Baez emerged as a star, Grossman told the New York Times' Robert Shelton: "The American public is like Sleeping Beauty, waiting to be kissed awake by the prince of Folk music."

As the 1960s were fast approaching, McCurdy, now the respected elder statesman of folk music following a decade-plus career, served as respected mentor and cool guide for the fresh new faces flooding into Greenwich Village from all around the country. One of those bright young hopefuls was Peter La Farge, who McCurdy befriended while hanging out at the Gaslight in 1960. The meeting changed both of their lives. For La Farge, the one-time boxer, actor, rodeo star, and naval intelligence operative, Greenwich Village was now home. La Farge surrendered completely to folk music, quickly becoming one of the more popular musicians in topical songwriting. "He was very emotional," folksinger Tom Paxton says. "He would spill it out." Like McCurdy, La Farge had an outsized persona that made him extremely attractive to many of the young, aspiring musicians. It was hard for him not to be.

When he was a young writer working with Sing Out!, Josh Dunson came across La Farge quite a bit in Greenwich Village. "He always wore a cowboy hat and boots," Dunson says. "He was always asking us to review his records." Founded by outspoken journalist, editor, publisher, radio show host, and political activist Irwin Sibler, Sing Out! aimed "to preserve and support the cultural diversity and heritage of all traditional and contemporary folk mosaics, and to encourage making folk music a part of our everyday lives." Getting a song published or mentioned in Sing Out! was a goal of many folk musicians. Soon Sibler was receiving many letters praising La Farge's

Figure 1.11. Outspoken journalist, editor, publisher, radio show host, and political activist Irwin Sibler was the founder of the influential folk magazine *Sing Out!* *Photo by Diana Davies, courtesy of the Ralph Rinzler Folklife Archives and Collections, Smithsonian Institution.*

work, such as this one from 1962: "Seems to me he's one of the rarer authentic guys to come out of the West in sometime; and what I like especially is that he swings with the juke, rodeo, and youth crowd; not with the anthropological boys on a Ford Foundation binge." The letters were a stamp of approval and a validation that La Farge had touched people with his work and even more could be counted among the rising performers in the new folk circle.

From head to toe La Farge was a walking contradiction: at once cowboy and Indian. "He walked confidently through the crowded Village streets, like a determined high priest," Seymour Krim recalled. "Except he was dressed like Tom Mix" (a famous silent film actor in Westerns) while many "thought he was an Indian and not a white man at all." He chose to boldly present the two competing sides of himself. "I do remember when Peter first arrived on MacDougal Street," the New Lost City Ramblers' John Cohen says. "I spent very little time with him. I was always curious about the relationship between his 'story,' his cowboy/Indian appearance, and his family history. I had just read *Laughing Boy* before I met him." Dick Weissman of the Journeymen tells about meeting La Farge in 1960 or 1961: "I saw him in some social situations. He was a very intense character and seemed clearly a bit out of his mind. But here's another interesting thing about the folk revival: while I knew who Oliver La Farge was and had read *Laughing Boy*, most people didn't have a clue who he was. Indian issues were not hot issues." There was no doubt that La Farge was quite a character: he lumbered around New York, according to Seymour Krim and others, dressed in a full "black Phantom of the Opera cape" while holding "a small club or cane under its fold," wearing rodeo clothes and a cowboy hat and sometimes brandishing a rope or lasso at parties.

"He was a striking and strong presence," according to Suzie Rotolo, who would know because her then-boyfriend, Bob Dylan (who also created a persona largely based on myth), counted La Farge as a good friend. The two made quite a pair: one small and slight, the other tall and muscular, each hiding a true part of who he was in hopes of finding his new "real" self. "I often saw him, Dylan, and Gil Turner together," Dunson says. "They were part of the *Broadside* group."

Dylan and La Farge also lived in the same building, the Hotel Earle at 163 Waverly Place, across from Washington Square Park. (La Farge also lived for a time at the Buckingham Hotel, joining the ranks of several celebrated artists who lived at the Midtown Manhattan institution, including painter Georgia O'Keeffe, Dadaist George Groz, and lithographer Marc Chagall.) They lived next door to each other, Dylan in room 305 and La Farge in room 306. When Ramblin' Jack Elliott returned to Greenwich Village after six years performing abroad, he moved into room 312, just down the hall. "I had known Peter from the rodeo circuit," Elliott says. "We shared some good times, and I remember then that he had an interest in music." Ramblin' Jack's arrival gave Dylan and La Farge a new sense of legitimacy in the folk scene, Elliott having been Woody Guthrie's sidekick for a time, traveling and performing with him throughout the country. Like Cash, he loved Jimmie Rodgers, and like Dylan and La Farge, he had reinvented himself completely, transforming himself from Brooklyn-born Elliott Charles Adnopoz, son of a doctor, into cowboy and folksinger Jack Elliott. (Odetta claims her mother gave Jack the nickname "Ramblin'" because of his incessant talking.)

It was around 1961 that a skinny, mop-haired thirteen-year-old boy began sneaking into the Kettle of Fish, a hangout for so many folk musicians. From the moment it opened in 1950 on MacDougal Street, the bar drew a heady crowd of artists, intellectuals, and newly college graduated white middle-class youths seeking to reinvent themselves. A 1950s picture of Jack Kerouac—standing in front of the bar's glowing neon sign, head cocked upward, looking full of the bravado and vigor that defined his writing during those years—one senses the energy and spirit that swirled inside the bar. The teenager came seeking this energy; he wanted to be in the midst of it all, soaking in as much of the spirit as he possibly could. Observing the myriad folk musicians who made the bar their nightly haunt was exciting. An aspiring musician, he possessed a pedigree that linked him to folk royalty, and, try as he might, he couldn't conceal himself for long. Anyone who knew anything about folk music could see who he was because it was his father that they had all listened to early on, who had inspired them to pick up a guitar and write a song or two.

Arlo Guthrie already possessed the keen sense of humor that so many loved in his father, Woody. "From the moment we met Arlo, we just liked him," musician Tom Paxton says. "When Arlo would come into the Gaslight we would make him get up and sing. He was just a high school kid or something." Guthrie remembers going down to the Village when he was eleven or twelve to see Cisco Houston perform. Houston was his father's best friend, and he had looked out for Arlo during the elder Guthrie's more than decade-long battle with the degenerative neurological affliction Huntington's disease. So when Arlo appeared backstage with his guitar, Houston couldn't resist inviting him to come out and perform with him during the show. "It was so thrilling," Guthrie remembers. "I was shaking like a leaf in a hurri-

Figures 1.12a and 1.12b. Cisco Houston's last performance at Gerdes Folk City in New York, February 1961. A teenage Arlo Guthrie was there to see the final performance of Peter La Farge's mentor and Woody Guthrie's best friend. *Photo by Robert Malone, courtesy of the Ralph Rinzler Folklife Archives and Collections, Smithsonian Institution.*

cane." Nervous, but not nervous enough to keep off the stage, the young Guthrie got up and performed. Houston was battling terminal cancer, which he concealed from both the public and his close friends, and this show was his last at Gerde's Folk City. On April 29, 1961, at the age of forty-two, Houston died. The *Chicago Tribune*'s Robert Cromie wrote, "This is a short time in which to have become a legend, but Cisco made it, as *900 Miles: The Ballads, Blues and Folksongs of Cisco Houston* shows." The bass singer of The Weavers, Lee Hays, wrote an obituary titled "Cisco's Legacy" in *Sing Out!* "Houston walked with grace through an imperfect world, and the world will be better because of the lives he touched." Arlo Guthrie says his performance with Houston was the dying musician's passing of the torch to him.

Peter La Farge was deeply affected by Houston's death. Houston had taken an interest in La Farge when the younger musician first appeared in the Village and started playing the coffee houses, and he served as a mentor to the younger musician. Houston saw a little bit of himself in La Farge, having traveled a somewhat similar path. "Houston sampled the world in all its variety," Cromie writes. "He was an actor, a union organizer, a cowhand, a roustabout, and radio entertainer." As Hays recounts, Houston was something like a father to La Farge, someone who "gave advice, kidded him, encouraged him to do all he could to fight the evils of injustice, like Jim Crow, prejudice, fall-out, apathy and dishonesty. Everybody wants to live well. Fight for education, clean clothes." La Farge was paying attention, and with guidance from the likes of musicians Josh White and Big Bill Broonzy, started to display a real knack for songwriting.

When La Farge appeared in the play *Dark of the Moon*, his cast biography stated that he had been a "concert folksinger since the age of fourteen." Whether this was true or not didn't matter; again La Farge was seemingly stretching the truth to create his own myth. It didn't seem much different than the fantastical rewriting of one's personal history that some artists tended to indulge in, not only the folk scene but throughout American music. It's true that when La Farge was a teenager, some time around 1944, he did indeed meet Josh White. "A key thing in me and Pete's life was when our mother became the mayor of Fountain—the first woman to become mayor in Colorado," La Farge's sister Povy says. "As mayor, she invited people to come and speak. Among them, strangely enough, were the great blues singer Josh White and his brother Bill. They were our houseguests." Oliver La Farge later wrote that "when Josh White came through town, the boy, still a teenager, his hands rough from handling cement sacks, introduced himself. White was interested in him." "Pete had a guitar and Josh wanted to hear him play," Povy continues. "He was just a kid—thirteen, fourteen—and his voice was changing a little bit. Josh White sat down with him and worked and worked and worked with him. He sat there with this gawky kid and treated him like an adult and a real person. He would say, 'Yes, that's good' or 'Let me hear that note' or 'Sing it again.' That's where Pete's

Figure 1.13. Josh White performing in 1955. White mentored Peter La Farge early on and continued to have a tremendous influence on the musician when he appeared in the folk revival scene in the early 1960s. *Courtesy of Doug Yeager.*

guitar [style of playing] came from, and you can see Josh White's guitar [style] in Pete's playing."

Josh White was a controversial figure because of his decision to cooperate with the House Un-American Activities Committee. Pete Seeger, in particular, was very upset about White's HUAC appearance. Many others in the folk music community shared Seeger's feelings. "Some people, especially on the left, didn't like Josh White," musician Dick Weissman says. "He didn't name names, but he cooperated with HUAC, telling them he was a young boy and didn't know what he was doing and that he joined the party because there were a lot of white chicks there. La Farge was a cowboy anarchist type guy, and I don't think he cared about that whole left-wing thing about White." While White served as his guitar teacher, La Farge's songwriting mentor was Cisco Houston. "I don't know if I would have started writing songs if it hadn't been for Cisco Houston, who read my poetry and insisted

Figure 1.14. Arlo Guthrie performing at the Newport Folk Festival in 1967. *Photo by Diana Davies, courtesy of the Ralph Rinzler Folklife Archives and Collections, Smithsonian Institution.*

that I write songs," La Farge explained. Channeling his grief over Houston's death, he penned a stirring tribute:

Cisco Houston passed this way,
Sang a song and was gone next day.
We loved and we mourned him,
But he's gone away.
And the morning rises
On the people who stay.

Standing behind a column in the middle of the barroom, teenage Arlo Guthrie peered over to a table where two men sat together, locked in an intense conversation. He had seen them before doing the same thing. He'd also heard many people talking about the music both were producing. Guthrie recognized both men from the Sunday

Figure 1.15. Musicians playing in New York's Washington Square Park in the 1960s. Peter La Farge spent Sundays performing in the park, a gathering place for aspiring folksingers. *Photo by Diana Davies, courtesy of the Ralph Rinzler Folklife Archives and Collections, Smithsonian Institution.*

gatherings in Washington Square Park, where scores of musicians set up and busked for the numerous students and tourists who strolled through. "I was at boarding school at the time," Guthrie says. "When summertime came around I'd go to Washington Park every Sunday and watch all these musicians perform. Music was shared and friendships were made. I remember Dylan and La Farge. La Farge was an intense and emotional performer and person." Guthrie met La Farge on one of the nights he had sneaked into the Kettle of Fish. From the moment they met, Guthrie felt something unique and powerful coming from the older man. Just by the sheer force of his personality and the controversial issues he was addressing in his music, he could tell that La Farge "was part of the transition from the more traditional folksinger to the style that changed the face of what a folksinger could be because they told stories that seemed more immediate and were a departure."

Columbia Records producer John Hammond would have agreed with Guthrie's description. An heir to the Vanderbilt fortune, Hammond blazed a path in music that was profound. Although very supportive of blues, gospel, and jazz, Hammond was unimpressed with bebop, and for a time left music. To Hammond, the new music had become so elitist that only a fringe group of people he referred to as "hipsters" could follow or participate in it. Instead, Hammond wanted to find something fresh, inclusive, and expansive. He had always possessed a strong instinct for work that at its core appealed to the most sought-after record-buying market: American youth.

When Columbia head Goddard Lieberson invited Hammond to return to the label that he had helped build into an entertainment powerhouse, the veteran producer eagerly accepted, agreeing to work for only $10,000. The low salary added another layer to Hammond's legend and fueled his famous self-importance. "John Hammond is one of the deans of America's recording industry," Lieberson said. "We are happy to welcome him back to Columbia, where he made his first discs twenty-seven years ago." Badly out of step with the times, Lieberson and the other Columbia executives were desperate to capture the emerging 1960s youth market. Under pressure from their parent company, CBS, they turned to Hammond in hopes that he still had the golden touch that at one time brought Billie Holiday, Count Basie, Teddy Wilson, and Charlie Christian to the label.

Through the late 1950s Hammond kept a close watch on the rising folk tide in pop culture. Folk groups such as The Chad Mitchell Trio, The Brandywine Singers, and The Kingston Trio were selling hundreds of thousands of records. He started scouting around, trying to uncover potential artists who could be the right fit for Columbia. Hammond tapped directly into the counterculture movement at hand, even if that meant signing a musician who was still blacklisted and facing charges for contempt of Congress. "I felt [Pete Seeger] would give Columbia a better image with the kids," Hammond later explained. "We were willing to take a chance on a controversial artist because he was obviously a great artist." But there was a problem: the entities responsible for Seeger's blacklisting included CBS.

"John went right to the top," Seeger recalls. "He was told 'Seeger is persona non grata.'" Hammond was unfazed. He knew that Seeger would sell a lot of records for Columbia and understood that at the very end of it all, that's what really mattered to the record executives. CBS relented and let Hammond offer Seeger a record contract. He pushed and pleaded and successfully signed Pete Seeger—one of his first efforts to profit from the popular success of folk music—demonstrating that he hadn't lost any of the alertness that turned more than one of his discoveries into chart-topping big sellers. Lieberson's faith in him was rewarded, albeit at the cost of some consternation and hand-wringing.

At first, Seeger himself had strong reservations. He wanted no part of being on a major label, which could impose all kinds of creative obstacles, including censorship, or require groveling for approval from corporate lawyers. "I never had a desire to be a pop success," Seeger says. "I'm not sure it's a good thing." At that point in his career, a relentless touring and public performance schedule generated Seeger's primary income. When the opportunity presented itself, he would record a few things for Moe Asch's Folkways Records. Surprisingly, when Seeger spoke to him about Hammond's proposal, Asch felt that Seeger should seize the opportunity. A big label like Columbia offered a significant platform for Seeger to get his music and message out to many, many more people than Folkways could ever dream of reaching.

With Seeger's move to Columbia, Hammond made a statement to the young folksingers and musicians who saw the former Weaver and Almanac Singer as something like a father figure, nearly as important in music as Woody Guthrie. With Seeger firmly onboard, Hammond now could train his experienced eye—or, more appropriately, his ear—on finding a new music star. "I always thought of him as a great, great example that age really doesn't mean a goddamned thing so long as you really have ears and you have enthusiasm," Columbia executive Bruce Lundvall said. "John's credo really had nothing to do

Figure 1.16. Publicity portrait
of Peter La Farge taken by
Jim Marshall in New York's
Central Park, circa 1962–1963.
Jim Marshall.

with commercial or pop records or anything like that. What John was always excited about was the original voice."

When the *New York Times*' Robert Shelton wrote about one of those original voices on September 29, 1961, Hammond's instincts as a scout were validated again. "Although only 20 years old, Bob Dylan is one of the most distinctive stylists to play a Manhattan cabaret in months," Shelton wrote. "His music making has the mark of originality and inspiration," According to the greatly respected folk manager Harold Leventhal, who counted both Guthrie and Seeger as clients, Dylan was already in Hammond's sight because Seeger had invited the young musician to his Columbia recording sessions. Not too soon after, Leventhal was representing Dylan and another folksinger in the new circle he hung around with: Peter La Farge.

The counterculture inspired La Farge, exciting and challenging his creative sensibilities. He moved closer and closer to a life in music that would allow him to give voice to the plight of Native people. Thanks to his upbringing, La Farge was already sharply attuned to the issues. The significance of the black civil rights movement offered a glimpse of what could happen for Native people if a movement addressing their marginalization were to take root. While the force of the civil rights movement indirectly informed other organizing efforts, including those in the Native community, the objectives of integration and full citizenship were in stark contrast to what many Native activists believed was needed for their people. The new decade of change brought just as much uncertainty as it did hope.

IN 1960, John F. Kennedy, the former senator from Massachusetts, became the youngest person elected president in the country's history. His record as a supporter of civil rights was mixed. But once elected, Kennedy had to decide between ignoring the problems facing blacks, Native people, and others encountering harsh discrimination and substandard living or delivering on his campaign promises.

In spite of those promises, the new president failed to do much of anything in regards to civil rights. Gary Wills, who had been a young journalist during the Kennedy administration, later wrote that the threat of public exposure of Kennedy's past affairs and relationships, including one with a suspected Nazi named Inga Arvad, "made him acquiesce to [FBI director J. Edgar] Hoover's campaign to destroy King." As one year slipped into the next, Kennedy seemed to be hoping the issues would simply fade away.

IN JUNE 1961, Native people staged a nationwide conference in Chicago. According to conference records, "Representatives at the large conference presented a cross-section of the American Indian community and included urban Indians, traditional Indians, modern Indians, and Indians from both recognized and non-recognized tribes. Several hundred people attended the meeting with over four hundred of attendees registered representing seventy-nine tribes." The conference, of course, addressed the termination issue and the havoc it

Figure 1.17. Photo from 1961 of the newly formed National Indian Youth Council. *Courtesy of the National Indian Youth Council Photograph Collection, Center for Southwest Research, University Libraries, University of New Mexico.*

continued to inflict on Native self-determination. At the conference, Native youth took center stage, forcefully yet thoughtfully declaring that a new path needed to be taken. Even though the Native population had grown from 300,000 at the turn of the century to 800,000 by 1960, the future of Native people depended on doing something to change their current situation. Led by such strong young activists as Herbert Blatchford and Clyde Warrior, the National Indian Youth Council was formed. The NIYC's first president, Paiute Mel Thom, described its perspective: "We decided that what we needed was a movement. Not an organization, but a movement. Organizations rearrange history, movements make history." If there had been any uncertainty about the new group's commitment to self-determination, Clyde Warrior removed it: "This is all I have to offer. The sewage of

Europe does not flow through these veins." Explaining the significance of the NIYC and strong statements like this, Native activist
Dennis Banks says, "The NIYC is probably the first activist type of an
organization, certainly not the first to do some kind of activity or action, but there was a lot of work that NIYC did that was pioneering
from an organizational standpoint for Native people. Clyde Warrior
was a major, major player and spokesperson in this regard."

Arising from the conference, prominent anthropologist, writer,
and Native activist D'Arcy McNickle, who was a Salish Kootenai
from the Flathead Reservation, helped compose a document listing
NIYC's grievances and presenting a statement of beliefs. Calling it
the Declaration of Indian Purpose, a not too subtle allusion to the
Declaration of Independence, it asked for a redirection of "the responsibility of the United States toward the Indian people in terms of
a positive national obligation to modify or remove the conditions
which produce the poverty and lack of social justice, as these prevail
as the outstanding attributes of Indian life today." It also emphatically stated, "We, the Indian people, must be governed by high principles and laws in a democratic manner, with a right to choose our
own way of life. . . . What we ask of America is not charity, not pa-
ternalism, even when benevolent."

The document was a bold step, making it clear that the NIYC
aimed to do more than just deliberate. Self-determination was one of
the main themes of its discussions about strategies for addressing economic development, education, employment, healthcare, housing,
legal services, public relations, and delivery of social services. Another
main issue of the conference was redressing the century-long injustice
of broken treaties. More than four hundred treaties were signed between the U.S. government and Native peoples, but by the 1960s nearly
all had been violated or broken. The Tuscarora's ongoing fight with
the New York State Power Authority was just one example. Kennedy
continued the well-worn tradition of breaking or ignoring these
treaties. In the case of the Seneca, Kennedy betrayed a statement made
by George Washington himself, that "the United States acknowledges

all the land within the aforementioned boundaries to be property of the Seneca nation."

Indeed, during his campaign, Kennedy had stridently pledged that he would chart a new course of action in relation to Native people. He did so on October 28, 1960, when the senator sent a letter to Oliver La Farge, who was still president of the Association of the American Indian:

> My administration, as you can see, would make a sharp break with the policies of the Republican Party. I am sure Indians know that in 1953 and 1954 a Republican administration and a Republican Congress joined in what became known as a "termination program." That headlong drive to break faith with our first Americans was fortunately slowed down when the Democratic Party regained control of Congress in 1955. Since then, the Congress has been a protective shield for Indians against bureaucratic attacks. Indians have heard fine words and promises long enough. They are right in asking for deeds. The program to which my party has pledged itself will be a program of deeds, not merely of words.

In excerpts released to the press by the Democratic National Committee, Kennedy stated: "There will be no change in treaty and contractual relationships without the consent of the tribes concerned." At the National Congress of American Indians on November 16, Dr. Karl Menninger told the *New York Times* that Kennedy's statement "was one of the greatest documents of the whole campaign. We are hopeful for a new horizon. The hopeless years may be past." Not long after his election, however, Kennedy broke his promise by approving the construction of the Kinzua Dam project on the Allegany Seneca Reservation. It forced the Senecas, the last of Pennsylvania's Native people, to flee their land when catastrophic flooding made it unlivable. In December 1960, the *New York Times* reported that the American Civil Liberties Union attempted to halt the Kinzua Dam project by sending a letter to President Kennedy showing that he had reneged on his campaign promise to respect treaty rights, which could result in the "reservation being destroyed. Notwithstanding the treaty between President George Washington and Chief Cornplanter of the Senecas." But its protests were ignored.

The more Peter La Farge learned, the angrier he got. With his father in the mix of things, he felt privy to what was happening to the Seneca. His distress began manifesting itself in his songwriting, and disturbingly in erratic behavior that was sometimes downright frightening to people around him. Especially when he was drunk or stoned, he would get aggressive, threatening those he encountered. Cisco Houston and other musicians helped encourage him to incorporate his social awareness into his music, spurring him to write a slew of topical songs in a short time.

La Farge had become a regular at Sis Cunningham and Gordon Friesen's apartment gatherings. The couple founded *Broadside* magazine, a small mimeographed publication that asserted a strong presence in the folk community. Its contributors, the people who made up what Josh Dunson calls the *"Broadside* gang," indicate the magazine's influence: Eric Andersen, Len Chandler Jr., Bob Dylan, Richard Fariña, Tuli Kupferberg, Peter La Farge, Julius Lester, Ewan MacColl, Matt McGinn, Bernice Reagon, Pat Skye, and Mark Spoelstra. "I only attended a couple of these meetings," Happy Traum says. "They were, as I remember, pretty free-form, with a bunch of singer-songwriters sitting around and singing songs they thought should be in *Broadside* magazine. I remember Tom Paxton, Phil Ochs, Gil Turner, Bob Cohen, and others being there."

Once assembled in the apartment, the musicians sat together, listening to each other perform new works and hoping to get their songs published in the magazine. La Farge captured the group's attention when he introduced a new song about a Pima who joined the marines, went to war, became a war hero, returned home to encounter prejudice and despair, and met a tragic end. As he began to play early versions of "Ballad of Ira Hayes" at these sessions, it became evident to all who watched that La Farge had penned one of the best topical songs of the moment. "He had a great head start on everybody. If he sang 'Ira Hayes,' he was

Figure 1.18. *Broadside* magazine founder Sis Cunningham emcees a concert in her New York apartment, date unknown. Many folksingers including Bob Dylan, Ramblin' Jack Elliott, and Peter La Farge spent time at the Cunningham and Friesen's developing new songs. *Photo by Diana Davies, courtesy of the Ralph Rinzler Folklife Archives and Collections, Smithsonian Institution.*

Ira Hayes. The way Ira Hayes was treated was the way Peter felt he had been treated," Oscar Brand explains. "I thought when he performed he carried the whole weight of the Indian nation with him." Bob Dylan later said, "Nobody ever said 'Well here's another protest song.' The guy who was best at [protest songs] was Peter La Farge. He wrote 'Ira Hayes,' 'Iron Mountain,' 'Johnny Half-Breed,' 'White Girl,' and about a hundred other things." (It was "Cisco Houston that convinced me to write 'Ira Hayes,'" La Farge was quick to point out.)

Looking through La Farge's notes from that time, it is clear that he was very aware of Hayes from the moment the Pima Indian was identified as a hero upon his return from World War II until his sad death in 1954. Immersing himself in Hayes's story, La Farge masterfully crafted a song that serves as a moving allegory for what happens to

America's outcasts once their usefulness passes. La Farge must have come across the story of Hayes during La Farge's short time in Chicago, where the war hero had tried in vain to make a life for himself. The press clippings tell a tragic story: There's the sad face of Ira Hayes staring back at the reader in a May 19, 1953, *Chicago Tribune* photograph showing him being welcomed at LaSalle Station by a group of Native people dressed in traditional clothing but none were representatives of Hayes's own tribe. The gathering seems pathetic, almost minstrel-like. The article reports that Hayes was brought to Chicago "under a federal relocation and placement program for Indians." La Farge dug deeper and learned that Hayes had tremendous difficulty adjusting to life in Chicago: He was arrested a number of times for public drunkenness. The pressure of trying to adapt to city life and trying to make his own way with nothing while facing prejudice was breaking him. His tragic life moved La Farge, who was angered by the sneering tone that seemed to surface whenever Hayes's name was mentioned in the newspaper. La Farge must have been infuriated by this painful truth when it was decided that Hayes was to be buried at Arlington Memorial Cemetery. On January 26, 1955, the *New York Times* concluded an article titled "Arlington Burial Set" with an amateurish example of journalism in the condescending line, "He tried to work in some of the big cities but liquor always tripped him up."

La Farge completed "Ballad of Ira Hayes" in 1960 and performed it everywhere in New York City and throughout the folk festival circuit. "I remember him at certain festivals," Dunson recalls. "He would do well at festivals because it was not a full concert; it was a twenty-minute set. He would be on a workshop and be absolutely marvelous in his energy, enlivening the workshop." His time spent working out his material at Cunningham and Friesen's apartment gatherings helped him develop as a songwriter. Dunson remarks that "he was very, very considerate of the both of them, thanking them profusely for their support."

Tom Paxton was one of the musicians who attended the *Broadside* gatherings. Friesen described him as a "good, flat, straight-forward guitar picker, unafraid of 'controversial' ideas and determined that what he says shall be heard." He was a rising star in the folksong movement with deeply thoughtful songs, including "Ramblin' Boy," "What Did I Learn in School," and "The Willing Conscript." He encountered La Farge early and often. "I first I saw him on the street all the time," Paxton says. "Then I saw him all the time at the Gaslight, where I performed often. We became friends." Paxton liked La Farge very much and felt that he was different from most of the musicians in the folk circle. "He was real. I remember seeing a photograph of Peter on a buckin' bronco with a cast on his leg for chrissakes." The two sensed a shared kinship and ended up doing a few songs together. "He was from Colorado and New Mexico," Paxton explains, "I was from Oklahoma. The backgrounds seemed to connect. I understood where he was coming from, and he understood me even though I was from a small town in Oklahoma and not a cowboy. I valued him."

Pete Seeger took an interest in La Farge at this time as well. "Pete was doing something special and important," Seeger said. "His heart was so devoted to the Native American cause at a time that no one was really saying anything about it. I think he went deeper than anyone before or since." Seeger invited La Farge to his home in Beacon, New York, where "Pete helped me build the fireplace." La Farge was now one of the key musicians at the forefront of the "topical song movement." Or was it something else? "Actually, a new term may be needed since many of the songs of this kind being written nowadays stand, musically and poetically, considerably above what have previously been classed as 'topical songs,'" Friesen reflected in *Broadside*. "Inspired by the folksongs of the past, these writers are going to original folk approaches and are trying to write and sing about modern times in the same direct way their predecessors wrote and sang about things in former times." In truth, La Farge, Paxton, Dylan, and the other members of the core group of new musicians were "true folksingers," Friesen concluded.

La Farge was continually singled out as one of the brightest examples. "Peter was very, very dedicated not just to Native American issues but to all social issues, movements," Dunson says. "He was outraged at the killings of African Americans in the South, and he expressed it in songs about that as well." When Seeger performed at Carnegie Hall in 1961, he invited La Farge to join him on stage. "Seeger was good for La Farge," Dunson explains. "He gave him a more disciplined musical framework that was very helpful." La Farge was now playing everywhere and becoming more and more popular. "I saw him at the Gaslight and Gerdes, but where he was best was at Town Hall," Dunson recalls. "They did a 5:00 show on Mondays called 'The 99-Cent Hootenanny' at Town Hall. It was just a beautiful sound and a great setting."

ON FEBRUARY 5, 1961, a letter to the editor written by acclaimed cultural anthropologist Margaret Mead appeared in the *New York Times*. In it she wrote, "Alan Lomax's outstanding contribution—a genuine integration between cultural theory, geographical specificity and folklore style—is on the very growing edge of our knowledge." Indeed, Alan Lomax was quite a force in the folk world. He had it in his blood and his bones. His father was John A. Lomax, a pioneering folklorist and musicologist who founded the Texas Folklore Society at the University of Texas–Austin and went on to reshape and expand the Archive of American Folk Song at the Library of Congress. Father and son worked tirelessly to preserve and promote American folk music, in large part by recording songs of sharecroppers and prisoners throughout Mississippi, Texas, and Louisiana. They ultimately gathered more than ten thousand field recordings from all around the world for the Archive.

Folk and Americana music were Alan Lomax's passion and life's work, which led him to seek out oral histories and interviews from an array of legendary musicians from Woody Guthrie to Muddy Waters to Leadbelly to Jelly Roll Morton, among hundreds of others. He produced records, concerts, and radio shows in the United States and in England, and helped kick-start the folk revival with his concerts at New York's Town and Carnegie Halls. Lomax seemed to be everywhere doing everything to promote folk. While in England he worked with the BBC's home service to produce a radio show on folk; organized a "skiffle" group, Alan Lomax and the Ramblers—with Shirley Collins, Ewan MacColl, and Peggy Seeger—that appeared on British television; and created a ballad opera, *Big Rock Candy Mountain*. When the opera premiered in December 1955 at Joan Littlewood's Theater Workshop in Stratford, East London, it featured an American cowboy musician from Brooklyn named Ramblin' Jack Elliott.

In a word, Lomax was folk's impresario; he was single-minded in his determination to orchestrate and conduct its rise in American popular culture. It was no surprise, then, that Lomax attracted some of the best and the brightest of folk's new breed. Like the *Broadside*'s Cunningham and Friesen, Lomax invited musicians to join him at his apartment. Many of them came: Dylan, Paxton, Ramblin' Jack Elliott, Memphis Slim, Guy Carawan, and The New Lost City Ramblers. The list is a veritable who's who of the folk scene. And of course Peter La Farge was right there too. "One of the first times I met Peter was at Alan Lomax's house," Paxton says. "Lomax held Peter in great, great esteem."

It was at this time that Paxton spotted La Farge's darker side. "It was obvious that he'd been drinking," Paxton recalls. "There was a little menace to him." Oscar Brand says, "I wanted him to be a hundred times happier than he was. I respected Peter very, very highly. He was always welcome in my house. But I was really sorry that I couldn't do more for him or spend more time with him. I don't know if I could have been of real service or help. I never know if I'm any good, but I would like to have done more to make him feel better about himself and his work."

Being the dedicated documentarian that he was, Lomax decided to film and record these gatherings. The result was a film shot mostly in 1961 called *Ballads, Blues, and Bluegrass*. The grainy footage shows the musicians sitting in Lomax's cramped New York City apartment on West Third Street. As Todd Harvey of the Library of Congress explains, "The film is clearly meant to emulate a house party." It seems

that Lomax assembled the musicians he enjoyed the most to participate in these good old-fashioned jam sessions: The New Lost City
Ramblers and Roscoe Holcomb, Clarence Ashley with Doc Boggs,
Ramblin' Jack Elliott, Memphis Slim and Willie Dixon, Ernie Mars,
Guy Carawan, Jean Ritchie, and Peter La Farge. At one point, Lomax
addresses the camera directly: "Well, you're in Greenwich Village now,
where people come to get away from America. It's not jazz around
here anymore—it's folk music. Jazz is high-hat and aging. Young people have gone mad over ballads, blues, guitar playin', and banjo
pickin'." Lomax places the performers in one of the corners of his
apartment, where they perform one, sometimes two songs. The camera cuts to those listening, who oblige the camera with looks of fasci-
nation and delight. During Jean Ritchie's performance, La Farge
appears, broadly smiling and sitting next to a young woman.

The high point of the film, both emotionally and musically, is La
Farge's performance of "Ballad of Ira Hayes." He stands with one
foot propped up on a chair, like Jimmie Rodgers, and Lomax films
him from the waist up. Over his right shoulder we see Lomax's floor-
to-ceiling bookshelf. Over his left shoulder there are various photos
taped to the wall. (According to Harvey, these are prints of Alan's
photography from his 1952–1953 Spanish fieldwork.) A bit further to
the left we see some open-reel recording equipment, the tools that
made Lomax famous. La Farge's hair is slicked back; he is wearing a
button-down Western shirt with no print and something like a bolo
tie, a pack of smokes in the pocket. La Farge says, "All this moved
west, and as it came, it incorporated the white man and the Indian,
the old songs and the new songs. And even today there are things to
write about, for a cowboy [La Farge begins strumming his guitar], and
I'm a cowboy, an Indian, and I'm part Indian, or a human being. This
is a song about a human being who was also an Indian, and if you
don't remember his name, I think you may after this song. It's called
'Ira Hayes'." The footage and performance are literally spectacular.
"In my view it is the most compelling performance of the film," Harvey says.

Ramblin' Jack Elliott agrees. He was there that night, sitting right in front, watching closely, and what he saw was something special and transformative. "La Farge just brought this incredible intensity when he performed," Elliott says. "He had this poetry that is 'Ira Hayes'—you couldn't help but be riveted and moved." Seeing La Farge playing the guitar almost violently, nearly spitting the words out as he looks into the camera, one senses that he not only believed every word but that he somehow lived the terrible story every time he sang it. The image created by just the sounds of Lomax's raw, unedited audio recording of La Farge's performance is even more powerful because the anguish and fury in his voice create a searing image in one's imagination. The words ring true as La Farge hands down an indictment, a scorched-earth, take-no-prisoners telling from a point of view that is often unwelcome and concealed.

Coming in at 16:40 on Lomax's recording, La Farge patiently strums his guitar, almost as though he's tuning it, and then quietly yet forcefully he sings, "Iiiira Hayes." It trails off; there is murmuring in the background. Once again La Farge sings, "Iiiira Hayes." The buildup has those gathered hushed but restless, tense with anticipation. He continues with a wistful, soulful "Ira Hayes," and then he builds into "Call him drunken Ira Hayes . . ."; someone offers a backing sound by shaking maracas. Next there is a break in the tape, but then La Farge continues, " . . . a tribe of Pima Indians . . ." By the time he gets to the chorus excitement is stirring in the background.

Then, dramatically, La Farge sings about the flag raising, stops playing the guitar, and sings, almost shouting, " . . . the Indian Ira Hayes" and again starts playing the guitar, singing more of the chorus "no water, no . . ." He stops. Then, singing in almost a whisper but one that's tinged with anger " . . . and when do the Indians dance? . . ." He pounds his hand against the guitar, hammering the notes out, singing, "Call him drunken Ira Hayes / He won't answer anymore . . ."

The performance is theatrical; the actor in La Farge responds to the energy of the crowd, giving the singer the courage to get deeper into the song. When he arrives at the chorus for the second time, he sings softly, almost whispering, as if to acknowledge that what comes next is too painful to say out loud. Finally, La Farge seems to burst with fury as he hammers the notes on the guitar, singing " . . . and when do the Indians dance? . . ." then screaming "Call him drunken Ira Hayes . . ." Those listening remain silent. The recording fades out.

La Farge is followed by Ramblin' Jack Elliott. Lomax quickly cuts to La Farge, who is listening to his one-time rodeo buddy and now fellow musician. Elliott does what he does best: tell stories and add a sense of humor to an event. "This is my favorite song right now. That song got me all over Europe," he says. "What I really like to play are some of Woody Guthrie's songs. Woody is about the best singer, guitar picker, composer, songwriter that I've ever heard, come against, or heard about. This is a song that Woody wrote while in the Merchant Marines during the war. He used to have a fiddle with his name carved on it that said 'Woody Guthrie SS William B. Floyd 1944, drunk once, sunk twice.'"

Lomax ends the recording with a rendition of "We Shall Overcome," at which point all the gathered musicians join together to sing. As the musicians continue to hum the tune, Lomax speaks directly to the camera and says, "Well, we spent an evening of folksong together here in Greenwich Village five flights up to listen to Memphis Slim and Willie Dixon from Chicago, great bluesman. You've heard one of the finest of all Kentucky banjo players, Roscoe Holcomb. You heard The New Lost City Ramblers and the Green Briar Boys—young singers from New York City who try and believe in singing like folksingers from the mountains. You heard many wonderful people tonight. We hope you've enjoyed it. It's just a little sample of the great strength, vitality, and beauty that there is in American folksong. We hope you'll join us again. Now, let's all join in one of the great songs of the South, the freedom song of the integration movement with Guy Carawan."

The performance was a defining moment for La Farge. He tapped into something that was bubbling up in American culture and stirring within him. Other folksingers began talking about his intensity as a performer at the Gaslight or other spots in and around New York. He tried to improve as a guitarist and musician, but he was limited. "He idolized Josh White," Paxton says. "He tried to base his guitar playing on Josh White's guitar playing, but he wasn't successful. I saw him perform many times. He was a fish out of water. He was not like any other performers you would see around the village." Yet John Hammond saw something in La Farge, and he decided to offer the musician a record contract. As Tom Russell later wrote: "La Farge was the first of the Greenwich Village 'new folk' circle" to sign to a major label. "He beat Bob Dylan by a few months."

Recording with Hammond and Columbia was a dream for La Farge. Over a few short sessions he completed *"Ira Hayes" and Other Ballads*. The following songs are on the album: "Ballad of Ira Hayes," "Rodeo Hand," "Easy Rider," "Sod Shanty," "John Henry," "Head Hammer Man," "I Gave My Love a Cherry," "John Brown's Body," "True Love Is a Blessing," "Alabama Bound," and "St. James Infirmary." La Farge was quite pleased because the recording felt strong and vibrant. Without a doubt, the standout track was "Ira Hayes." Columbia hoped that the growing folk audience would connect with it and maybe make the tune a hit.

When La Farge recorded it on August 25, 1960, at Columbia's Thirtieth Street studios in Manhattan, all those in the recording session must have been moved. The song held nothing back:

Gather round me people there's a story I would tell
About a brave young Indian you should remember well.
From the land of the Pima Indian
A proud and noble band
Who farmed the Phoenix valley in Arizona land.

Down the ditches for a thousand years,
The water grew Ira's peoples' crops.
'Till the white man stole the water rights
And the sparklin' water stopped.

Now Ira's folks were hungry
And their land grew crops of weeds.

When war came, Ira volunteered
And forgot the white man's greed.

Chorus: *Call him drunken Ira Hayes,*
He won't answer anymore.
Not the whiskey drinkin' Indian
Nor the Marine that went to war.

There they battled up Iwo Jima's hill,
Two hundred and fifty men,
But only twenty-seven lived
to walk back down again.

And when the fight was over
And when Old Glory raised,
Among the men who held it high
Was the Indian, Ira Hayes.

Ira returned a hero
Celebrated through the land
He was wined and speeched and honored
Everybody shook his hand.

But he was just a Pima Indian
No water, no crops, no chance
At home nobody cared what Ira'd done
And when did the Indians dance?

Repeat chorus

Then Ira started drinkin' hard
Jail was often his home.
They'd let him raise the flag and lower it
like you'd throw a dog a bone.

He died drunk one mornin'
Alone in the land he fought to save.
Two inches of water in a lonely ditch
Was a grave for Ira Hayes.

Repeat chorus

Yeah, call him drunken Ira Hayes
But his land is just as dry
And his ghost is lyin' thirsty
In the ditch where Ira died.

On that day, La Farge also recorded "Gather 'Round" and "Please Come Back, Abe." And over the next year, at Columbia's Studio D at 799 Seventh Avenue, he recorded twenty or so tracks, with Hammond producing all the way through. *"Ira Hayes" and Other Ballads* was released in the spring of 1962. "It came out just when hard-hitting songs were emerging everywhere," The New Lost City Rambler's John Cohen says. John Trudell explains that La Farge's significance as a songwriter, in particular his song "Ira Hayes," encapsulated Native resistance:

In my own personal opinion, for the 1900s—let's call it that [twentieth] century—I think that the resistance in that century continued differently from the previous century. In the 1800s we could go out and fight. Then in the 1900s we resisted through a more traditionalist movement, which meant that we kept our traditions the best that we could, like our language, ceremonies, our way of life. Meanwhile, the colonizing process was trying to brainwash, colonize Native people through the education and religious system in an effort to make them white. I think it reached the point that the first resistance fighter, what I'm going to call a fighter in the 1900s, is the one that became the drunken Indian like Ira Hayes. What is stereotyped as the drunken Indian, are Native people that the government decided they wouldn't allow to be Native.

But the Native people didn't want to be white, so they became the drunken Indians. They kept us alive. It was the only form they could take without being formally exterminated. They wouldn't submit but became drunk instead.

When he wrote the album's liner notes, Oliver La Farge Sr. put aside for a moment the tension that so long defined his relationship with his son, offering instead pride and understanding: "Listening to his albums of ballads, the father of Peter La Farge finds admiration and delight mixed with a sense of astonishment that this young man could descend from him, a prose writer. Peter has crowded into the still short span of his life a variety of experiences that ought to be indigestible. When you hear him sing, you know that these experiences have given him a reality as a folksinger, for they have made him brother to many of the kinds of people from whom folk-stuff springs. . . . It comes out of profound feeling and it has a bitter humor that beats common anger all hollow. I defy anyone with normal feelings to listen to 'Ira Hayes' without getting goose pimples."

Soon after bringing La Farge to Columbia, Hammond turned his star-making attention to his newly signed folksinger, Bob Dylan. La Farge and Dylan were both on their way. At least that's what La Farge hoped, especially after a profile of him appeared in the September 1962 issue of *High Fidelity* magazine. Under a picture of La Farge seated with his guitar and singing, the magazine wrote in bold letters, "The Strongest Medicine Offered to American Audiences Since the Heyday of Woody Guthrie." The article itself is full of praise: "Another talented newcomer—but one solidly rooted in the present—is Peter La Farge . . . a new and impelling voice . . . influenced by Josh White, Cisco Houston, and Woody Guthrie." La Farge couldn't ask for anything more. To be listed in the same breath as three of the best folk musicians of the past thirty years was a true honor.

Turning to the Columbia album, *High Fidelity* wrote, "In his first album, La Farge runs the gamut from exuberance ('Rodeo Hand') through lyricism ('I Gave My Love a Cherry') to earthiness ('Sod

Shanty')," singling out "Ira Hayes" as "the pinnacle of his art," a "searing composition" that "reveals La Farge as a master of understated bitterness." The article concludes: "No one will listen to it without wincing." At the end of that month, La Farge performed at Town Hall. Conrad Osborne of the *New York Herald Tribune* wrote on October 1: "In two deeply-felt pieces of Indian reference (one concerned with the breaking of the government treaty of the Seneca Indians, the other—a moving number which concluded the evening—with the death of Ira Hayes), Mr. La Farge demonstrated that he can create moods of bitterness and mournfulness. He was well received."

ON THE same day that La Farge was waking up to positive notices, James Meredith was attempting to become the first black student to enroll at the University of Mississippi. A race riot broke out, leading to the deaths of two people and the injury of seventy-five. The story made international headlines. "All the old hates of the civil war 100 years ago are boiling over," the *London Daily Express* wrote. In Berlin, the East German news service ADN proclaimed that the U.S. government "bowed to fanatical racists." Stockholm's *Expressen* reported, "The spokesmen for segregation were not waging more than a delaying fight against development." The BBC believed that the Mississippi governor had enflamed the situation: "Despite Governor Barnett's assurances that his police would carry out their duties, there have been reports that they neglected to provide adequate security, and additional troops and marshals were called in." This was a direct violation of an executive order President Kennedy issued only a few days before, on September 30. Meredith told the gathered news media, "This is not a happy occasion."

On December 6, 1962, in Columbia Records Studio A, Bob Dylan recorded "Oxford Town," which is about the Meredith incident and includes the lyrics, "He went down to Oxford Town / Guns and clubs followed him down / All because his face was brown / Better get away from Oxford Town." As Josh Dunson says, Dylan and "La Farge were just aghast at what was taking place." This outrage was finding its way into their music. The *New York Times*' Robert Shelton had just written that folk music was playing a key role in the civil rights movement and its success in certain parts of the country. Shelton highlighted Alan Lomax and Guy Carawan's album *Freedom in the Air*, a documentary about Albany, Georgia, in 1961–1962 that "captures the spirit of the nonviolent resistance to segregation" and "is the most effective documentary recording to grow out of the integration movement." The album was based on an original idea and fieldwork by Guy Carawan. "The freedom songs are playing a strong and vital role in our struggle," declared Martin Luther King Jr. during an Albany Movement event. "They give the people new courage and a sense of unity. I think they keep alive a faith, a radiant hope, in the future, particularly in our most trying hours."

SMOKING FOR a minute, the two men stood quietly on the Manhattan sidewalk near the corner of Carnegie Hall, where Andrew Carnegie had addressed a throng of people and reporters more than seventy years before. "It is probable that this hall will intertwine itself with the history of the country," Carnegie had told the enthusiastic crowd. "All good causes may here find a place." As Ed McCurdy and Johnny Cash stood on the street, breathing in the cool spring air, McCurdy suggested that they go down to the Gaslight in Greenwich Village to check out some music. Cash agreed to go.

The club was crowded with couples out for the night, mixed in here and there with folksingers, poets, writers, and a tourist or two. As waitresses bustled around the place serving drinks, the musicians settled in at a table in the back corner. They talked, sharing a drink or two and checking out the performance every once in a while. Soon, Peter La Farge was on the stage singing some Indian protest ballads, including "Ira Hayes." Ed got up there, too, singing the Irish ballad "Molly Malone." Afterward, McCurdy introduced La Farge to Cash.

"Johnny Cash appeared on the folk scene, trailing his majesty down the steps of the Gaslight coffeehouse of MacDougal Street, beside Ed McCurdy," La Farge wrote in *Broadside* about meeting Cash.

"The hillbilly minstrel who'd walked too many lines next to the man who wrote 'Strangest Dream.' It was a valid passport. 'That's Johnny Cash' . . . 'What's he doing here?' . . . 'What does he want?' the murmur went. He wasn't looking for much, just himself." Cash later recalled the time in New York with McCurdy and La Farge: "I was off for a while after Carnegie Hall, so I started hanging out with Ed, and for a few days I didn't do any amphetamines. One afternoon, though, Ed came by with a friend of his, Peter La Farge." The three musicians spent time hanging around the Village, checking out the new folksong scene. At one point, Cash refused to go out until he took some Dexedrine. McCurdy protested and then relented. La Farge happily joined Cash in popping some pills.

La Farge and Cash seemed to be kindred spirits, having similar, often provocative, sometimes troubled, even outsider sensibilities. "La Farge was more the kind of guy that would have said, 'You need to hear this whether you like it or not,'" Dick Weissman says. Cash was like that too. Both also treated their troubles with pills. At one point in their time together, Cash gave La Farge Dexedrine and Thorazine, the latter to help with coming down from the former. The next day McCurdy called Cash to tell him that La Farge was not waking up. He had taken all the Thorazine. Cash later said: "We were really worried, but while Peter slept for three or four days, he didn't die." They were all lucky.

Oscar Brand knew this side of Peter La Farge very well. "He could zonk out faster and harder than anyone I ever met and wake up three days later." Like McCurdy, Brand was a true one-of-kind character in American popular culture. Brand seemed to do it all, from being a musician to scoring ballets to serving as the host of New York Public Radio's *Folksong Festival*, which somehow managed to survive the McCarthy blacklist even though targets of the anticommunist group such as Pete Seeger were frequent guests. He performed with Woody Guthrie, Josh White, Leadbelly, and scores of other heralded musicians. On October 29, 1961, Brand invited Bob Dylan on his radio program to promote the young musician's upcoming Carnegie Chapter Hall show. ("Chapter" is what it was called then.) Brand also had befriended La Farge, and they often performed together on the *People's Song* program. "Pete was like Woody, a will-o'-the-wisp," Brand recalls. "He just disappeared for extended periods of time. He did more of the slipping away, of not being where they wanted him to be, than anyone I know. Just like Woody." At a party not long after Dylan's appearance on Brand's radio show, La Farge showed up "a little shaky," Brand remembers. "So rather than let him roam around and fall out of the window—we were on the sixth floor—I led him over to one of these majestic chairs with big plush padded backs and great arm rests. The first thing people saw when they came in was Peter. One beautiful young woman asked me, 'He's royalty, isn't he?' I said, 'Oh, yes!' Peter always said he had come from a family of chiefs anyway."

After his time with McCurdy and La Farge, Cash headed back to the Barbizon Plaza Hotel on Central Park South. It was time to check out and travel to the next stop on the tour. Cash's manager Saul Holiff wanted only the best for his client, and the Barbizon Plaza Hotel, an audacious building perhaps rivaled only by the Chrysler Building, was one of New York's premiere hotels. As Johnny Western explains, Holiff felt it reflected Cash's star status perfectly. Upon arriving, Cash went straight for Western and Terry's room. "We hadn't seen John since he left the stage," Western says. "After the show we just went back to our room and commiserated." Western's younger brother, who was stationed at the nearby Naval Air Station in Lakehurst, New Jersey, was coming over to join them before they left. The musicians were busy packing, and still trying to shake off the disappointment from the night before, when Cash suddenly appeared at their hotel room door.

Western let him in. The musicians were all uncomfortably quiet for a moment. Then Cash started to speak: "I'm sorry for getting on you guys last night. It wasn't your fault. It was my fault." The previous night, say both Western and Grant, Cash had tried to find fault with everyone except himself. His excursions with McCurdy and La Farge, in some strange way, had righted him a bit. He knew what he'd done the night before. "He realized that the show was in the toilet," Western says, "that he was totally responsible because of the amphetamines and so forth. He apologized. We accepted. We always accepted." Cash made his rounds and made amends with everyone he could. Now was the time to gather together and get straight for the next set of performances, including a stop at the Hollywood Bowl.

As the performers met out in front, on the corner next to the hotel, Western introduced Cash to his brother and the men spoke briefly. It was time to put the Carnegie Hall catastrophe behind them. That morning's *New York Times* contained a review of the show. Robert Shelton could have cut Cash down in the review, but instead he gave Cash a pass by focusing the article away from the troubled music star and training it on the appearance of Mother Maybelle Carter: "Although the star, Johnny Cash, was suffering from a throat ailment, which made it difficult to judge his performance, the evening afforded several diverting moments. Chief among these was the appearance of Mother Maybelle." "It could have been a devastating review," Western says. Grant agrees, saying, "Shelton, who was a fan of Cash, looked out for him." The review ended with Shelton asking audiences to give Cash another listen despite the "incohesiveness of his performance."

The band members thought it was best not to show Cash the review. Grant says, "We were just happy to get out of New York City and get to the next place and put this behind us. But with John, you just never knew what was ahead. You never knew."

PART TWO
A Guitar

Johnny Cash warms up backstage at Carnegie Hall as part of the New York Folk Festival in July 1965. *Photo by Michael Ochs Archives / Getty Images.*

The Whippoorwill Cries,
the Fox Whimpers

JOHNNY CASH FELT lucky. The Carter Family, faithful and true, were standing by his side and had been a major part of his show for several years. For many years before that, the group's music had been a defining part of Cash's life. Although he was still married to Vivian with four young children, his relationship with June Carter had been moving for some time into something more than a passing affair. On the night of the Carnegie Hall debacle, June was the first person who tried to cut through Cash's haze and console him. "I thought you were very good but your voice just wasn't there," Cash later recalled June saying. "I feel really sorry for you about that." But Cash was too muddled and defeated at the time to hear her. He responded angrily, "Well, *I* don't feel sorry for me," forcing June into silence. Yet Cash, regardless of the momentary misfortune, was uncannily tenacious. He could turn misfortune to his creative advantage and spark his own artistic rebirth. This was proven a month later when, performing essentially the same show, he played to a packed house at the Hollywood Bowl. Cash's manager Saul Holiff, four years earlier in 1958, had convinced Cash that he had the potential to become a true music star. Now Cash could boast that he had performed at both Carnegie Hall and the Hollywood Bowl within one month's time. "The show was a rousing success in every way that

Figure 2.1. Publicity photo of The Carter Family at the time of Johnny Cash's Carnegie Hall debut, circa 1962. From left: Mother Maybelle Carter, Anita Carter, June Carter (seated), and Helen Carter. *Courtesy of Carnegie Hall archives.*

Carnegie Hall was a disaster," Johnny Western says. "Everyone was great that night but John was amazing."

As Cash finished out the year, alternating between being awful and dazzling on stage, his determination to record another Americana album was growing stronger. At the start of 1963, the folk revival had become a full-fledged pop culture sensation. Robert Shelton, the *New York Times* music critic, seemed to write articles almost daily about the new music scene. "In recent months there has been a scramble among several labels to increase their stables of city folksingers," Shelton wrote.

Never losing sight of his struggles growing up in poverty, Cash decided to record an album dedicated to the American workingman.

Once again producer Don Law was at the boards, this time aided by Frank Jones. Released in February 1963, *Blood, Sweat and Tears* included Cash performing music by Alan Lomax and Vera Hall ("Another Man Done Gone"), Merle Travis's classic workingman's tale ("Nine Pound Hammer"), his hero Jimmie Rodgers's railroad masterpiece ("Waiting on a Train"), character actor Sheb Wooley's satirical story ("Roughneck"), and two songs by country songwriting great Harlan Howard ("Chain Gang" and "Busted"). Electrified by the ascendant folk scene, Cash displayed a fresh songwriting approach by taking traditional tunes and putting his own stamp on them. He did this best with "The Legend of John Henry's Hammer" (written with June Carter), "Tell Him I'm Gone," and "Casey Jones."

While Cash and Law were happy with the record, Columbia's response was lukewarm at best. What they wanted from Cash was more country hits and as many crossover hits as he could muster. They didn't see any really big hits among the ballads on *Blood, Sweat and Tears*. The record undeniably fared better than Cash's previous Americana recordings, which had been derided by the music press for being "overly sentimental" and "corny." The album's archetypal folk ballad feel produced two standout songs: "Casey Jones" and "The Legend of John Henry's Hammer." The album is classic Cash: the music is bound together with equal measures of subtlety, emotion, and sparse artistry. Record sales, however, were sparse too. In the eyes of some executives at Columbia, Cash's decision to record such personal music was beginning to chip away at his market value. Cash said, "I got a lot of credit for it among other artists. A lot of other people openly admired them but some people didn't want to accept the fact that a country artist was doing things like [*Blood, Sweat and Tears* and *Ride This Train*]. I had a few people tell me that it wasn't country and that wasn't right for me to do it. They said it wasn't commercial, and all that jazz."

INSTEAD, THESE concept albums captured Johnny Cash as both an artist and a person curious about and engaged in the world around him. He wanted to challenge his audience rather than do what was easy or expected of him. "He could have done songs like 'I Walk the Line' forever and a day," Bob Johnston says. "But he always wanted to do something more." Not surprisingly, the shifting American political and cultural landscape began to affect Cash as he became more and more interested in what was unfolding outside the concert hall and studio walls. President Kennedy's betrayal of the Seneca with the Kinzua Dam project outraged Cash, who often claimed to be part Indian with Cherokee blood running through his veins. "Cash was sincerely affected by what was happening to the Seneca as a result of the Kinzua Dam," activist and scholar Laurence Hauptman explains. "He just immersed himself in learning all he could," Cash discographer John L. Smith says. "It was something he believed in sincerely and deeply," Marshall Grant confirms.

The Kinzua Dam project was seen by Native people across the country as a continuation of what the first Europeans had started when they came to the Americas five centuries earlier: the systematic and frequently coldhearted seizure of Native land that led to the elimination of many eastern tribes or forced them to relocate to cities and towns.

Realizing that establishing peace between various tribes could protect Native people from further harm, the Seneca had decided to come together some time between 1570 and 1600. They developed the League of the Iroquois, a remarkable confederation comprising the Cayugas, Oneidas, Mohawks, Onondagas, and the Seneca. Later, after the Tuscaroras joined, the League of Five Nations became "Six Nations."

When the Pickering Treaty of 1794 was signed between Washington and the Seneca, the Seneca were led by Kaintwakon (*By What One Plants*), who steered his people away from war, seeking a new direction in cultivating land in order to create a sustainable and independent life for his people. As a result of Kaintwakon's work, he was called Chief Cornplanter. The Kennedy administration's decision to take the Seneca's land was all the more tragic. Kennedy, who had been elected based on promises to make the country more prosperous, knew that turning away from public works projects like the Kinzua Dam could hurt his chances for reelection in 1964. The project meant jobs and hundreds of millions of dollars in money spread around an area desperately in need of financial help. Weighing this political reality against breaking a treaty, the decision was easy: the treaty with the Seneca was blocking progress. Maurice K. Goddard, Pennsylvania's secretary of the Department of Water, wrote a letter to the editors of the *New York Times,* asserting that the needs of millions of people in Ohio and Pennsylvania outweighed the needs of a few hundred Seneca. He further argued that there was simply no alternative to flooding them out of their land to make way for the public works project, dismissing a plan that had been put forward by Dr. Arthur E. Morgan, the former chairman of the Tennessee Valley Authority.

Morgan had studied the Kinzua project closely. No one could dispute that flood protection was needed. In fact, the Seneca were the first to admit that something needed to be done but they believed there was a better way, one that would not lead to their displacement. When Morgan met with the House Appropriations Committee in 1960, he explained that the "best way to control the Allegany floods" was the Conewango-Cattaraugus project, which would "store three times as much flood water" as Kinzua proposed and "save $100,000,000.00." Morgan evaluated the alternative plan in the *Pittsburgh-Sun Telegraph:* "There is every indication that permanent and complete control of the flood waters originating in the Upper Allegheny River should be accomplished by diversion. The proposed diversion to carry the flood waters into Lake Erie would be approximately 41 miles long. It would be capable of safely handling a flood of 200,000 cubic feet per second." In an effort to prevent the Seneca from losing their land, Morgan came up with five alternatives, all of them more efficient, inexpensive, and environmentally sound than the government's proposed plan to flood the land and erect the massive dam. One lawyer working on the dam project joked that Morgan's proposal of "flooding the Conewango valley would provide more water for Pittsburgh. But it would flood out white folks! They vote." Morgan's proposals were repeatedly dismissed and rebuffed, prompting him to take his case to the public. In a 1961 letter to the *New York Times,* Morgan explained, "When, however, America's oldest treaty is at stake, the dishonoring of which would quickly become known throughout the world, then the whole country has a vital interest in seeing the Conewango alternative honestly and fully studied."

Even though Morgan backed up his study with copious economic and land-survey analyses, he was derided by political and business leaders who had a lucrative stake in Kinzua. "The Army Corps of Engineers had many viable alternatives but never gave them any airing," author Charles Wilkerson wrote. Asked to submit additional materials to support his findings, Morgan knew exactly what was going on. Since the end of World War II, the United States' domestic priorities had centered on economic development that depended on private initiatives (industrial factories, new consumer products, and residential subdivisions) and public works projects (dams, power plants, and highways). Native lands offered prime locations for building many of these projects and the tribes had little or no political power to resist the encroachment. So the government seized the opportunity to claim these lands, starting with policies like termination. When termination was not as effective as the government would have liked because forced assimilation proved harmful to the terminated tribes, they resorted to breaking treaties.

According to Native activist and musician John Trudell, it was the legal aspect of the Native struggle that distinguished it from the black civil rights movement. "In my mind," he says, "the Indians could never have a civil rights movement. The civil rights issue was between the Blacks and the whites, our issue was around law. It was legal." Trudell continues: "There's five kinds of law in America: common law; criminal law; constitutional law; statute law; and treaty law. That's important to note—treaty law is one of the five principal laws in America. The agreements that the United States made with the tribes were legal agreements. So our movement was based around treaty law and making sure these were upheld and not broken. This isn't about morals and ethics—I mean, of course it is to a degree—but the United States has a legal responsibility to us. So in the end this is about the law." Trudell concludes: "If you're a nation of laws, then you have to respect this, and if you don't respect these treaties then we get that you're not really a nation of laws. It's all about the rule and if you don't adhere to that then it's all bullshit."

In a series of powerful articles for the *New York Times* that followed the Kinzua Dam story, Brooks Atkinson (the leading theater critic in the country at the time) concurred with Trudell. If a country that preaches to the world about morals and rights breaks its own laws, what do you have left? In his "Critics-at-Large" column, he wrote directly and passionately about the injustice being waged against the Seneca. Atkinson's outrage grew with each column as he tried to use his writing as a platform to rally non-Native support for the Seneca cause. Writing just after Kennedy had broken his promise not to "dishonor" George Washington's pledge that "the United States will never claim the same, nor disturb the Seneca nation. Never," Atkinson offered this searing indictment: "For the moral question is one no one dares face: Is the Kinzua Dam right or wrong? It is wrong." Atkinson wrote that the "Seneca have all the decency and goodwill on their side" because they understood the need for flood protection and were willing to find a solution (which they had done with Dr. Morgan's assistance) that would benefit—not harm—any of the parties involved.

Atkinson's column became one of the strongest voices for the Seneca cause, pressing the issue almost daily to stir public support. He rallied against the unilateral abrogation "without negotiation" of the treaty and judged the government's efforts to compensate the Seneca people as "the legal power to pay for bad faith with money." Atkinson took every opportunity to remind his readers that the Seneca were facing such an unfortunate situation because Kennedy had gone back on his word and broken the law.

Despite the legal and political challenges the Seneca tried to mount against the dam project, it moved forward on track to reach the 1965 completion date. The Seneca possessed few resources but managed to organize a public relations campaign that included television and radio appearances. As the situation grew desperate, Senator Joseph S. Clark brushed aside claims that the government was acting illegally or immorally: "The people and communities who need the protection and clean water that Kinzua will give also have moral rights." Besides, Senator Clark added, the Seneca would be better off once they were resettled. To which Atkinson responded: "Souvenir stands and hot dog stands will be small compensation for the loss of the site of Seneca's Longhouse religion," referring to the sacred site that would be flooded by the dam.

When Native people from around the country gathered in Chicago for a conference in June 1961 to address issues critical to Native people including self-determination and treaty violations, the Tuscarora and Seneca were the focus of much attention. The budding Native movement, including the National Indian Youth Conference, refused to be discouraged by these events. Instead, they used the Tuscarora and Seneca as symbols to mobilize Native people across the country, transforming the movement into one that was more vocal and active. One of the key Native activists, Vine Deloria Jr., later wrote: "We never forgot that the Tuscarora had stood up for Indian treaty rights and the international status of tribes at a time when few men were willing to stand up for any principles at all."

The United States government thought that Native people, like everyone else, had their price. Paying the Seneca and Tuscarora a few million dollars seemed like the best way to redress the loss of tribal land. "They've been doing this kind of stuff since they got here," according to artist and activist John Trudell. "They cut down the forest to build their settlements, to graze their herds. It's nothing new happening here."

Less than ten years earlier, 533 acres of Tuscarora tribal land had been turned into a reservoir. The tribe was paid $850,000 while Niagara University was given $5,000,000 for two hundred acres that the government used for part of the proposed power plant. For thousands of acres of tribal land that was worth much, much more, the Seneca were paid $3,000,000 in 1965. However, the Seneca's land could not be valued in terms of capital but as a spiritual center and a source of identity. "The reality of it is for us to remember and understand as Native people that our tradition is based upon respect," Trudell explains. "This includes respecting our lands protected by treaty, by law. To protect and preserve our identity, we need to remember that spirituality and our way of life is based upon respect."

With this in mind, the National Indian Youth Conference built into its platform the "importance of educating new generations of Native environmentalists invested in improving both tribal and national land by creating hybrid scientific and social frameworks of ecological understanding." With Morgan's help, the Seneca had done exactly that by presenting an alternative to flooding the land with a forward thinking and environmentally sound approach. The government, by contrast, merely proposed to flood 10,000 acres—roughly one-third of the Seneca's tribal land. Even more troubling, the land at issue was the tribe's most fertile and lush. As Charles Wilkerson later explained, "The rich bottomland and low-lying forests down by the river, the prime berry and fruit gathering places, the finest deer and bear habitat, the best farmland, none of it would ever be seen again." In the more evocative, pained words of the Seneca: "When the Whippoorwill cries in the east, close by the house, some evil will befall the family; when a fox is heard whimpering in the woods, a death will follow."

When Arnold H. Lubasch wrote a special report for the *New York Times* in 1962, he called the situation an "engineering triumph that is causing human tragedy." He described the solemn ceremony conducted by Seneca Melvin Patterson at the site of Chief Cornplanter's simple stone monument. "From this day forward," Patterson said, "we of Indian blood will call the waters that will flood this reservation practically out of existence the Lake of Perfidy." Lubasch's article was followed by an op-ed in the *Times* that declared: "It is too late to stop Kinzua Dam. The cranes are working at the site and soon the water will begin to back up to form what the Senecas will henceforth call 'The Lake of Perfidy.'" In addition to the massive displacement they would face, the Seneca would also be denied access to the river that was central to their way of life. Even more, their burial sites would be desecrated while tribal elders feared that their Longhouse faith, founded by Cornplanter's half brother, Handsome Lake, would ultimately be destroyed. "About 400 of the 800 Senecas who will be displaced maintain their tribal faith by marrying, naming their children, and burying their relatives according to Longhouse belief and ritual," Atkinson wrote. "It is the foundation of their social and spiritual life." For many political leaders, the number of individuals affected was too insignificant to matter, but as the *New York Times* op-ed pointedly suggests, "Injustice cannot weighed by numbers. If the agents of 186,000,000 people do wrong to a few . . . it is nevertheless wrong . . . this is not the first time such a wrong has been done to the Indians. Is it unreasonable to hope it will be the last?"

As THE Seneca story continued to unfold, the fortunes of Peter La Farge were at once rising and sinking. Columbia decided to drop him after poor sales and an even poorer attitude. "It was probably the drinking, and also no one bought the record," insists writer and musician Tom Russell. "He didn't really have much melody in his singing. It was more like spoken word. He was a very great lyricist and poet, but the music was basic." "John Hammond almost wouldn't release that first record because of its raggedness and unprofessionalism," Seymour Krim later explained. "He came to sessions unprepared, drunk [and] drugged." La Farge admitted, "I thought the best way to make a record was with a bottle of brandy." Regardless of La Farge's lack of success at Columbia, he held a central place in the folk scene that was emerging around New York City and on the festival circuit. La Farge's regular shows at the Town Hall's 99 Cent Hootenannies were perhaps his best moments as a musician. "His performances at Town Hall were intense even though he was not very good on guitar," Josh Dunson recalls. "His voice carried him very, very well. He was charismatic and had a presence that matched well with the beautiful setting of Town Hall. He wrote just beautiful

Figure 2.2. Peter La Farge performing at Town Hall, circa 1963. *Jim Marshall.*

songs that moved people. It was a good place for him as the audience
was very open to different styles of singing."

LA FARGE seemed to move in the world in a way that found him taking one step forward and two steps back as he increasingly shifted between moments of calm and bouts of erratic behavior (he was even
known to brandish a bullwhip and carry around Colt single repeater
pistols that he later gave to Bob Dylan). He was a walking contradiction to his fellow musicians and artists, appearing haunted and troubled to some, sweet and subdued to others. "He was quiet and laid
back," says his friend, photographer Jim Marshall. "He wasn't a dynamic performer but his music was sheer poetry." According to Tom
Paxton, "He had a lot of bitterness about what had been done to Indians in this country and of course this came out in a lot of his songs.
He carried that weight heavily." To others, it was clear that La Farge
lacked discipline, and his escalating drinking and drug problems only

Figure 2.3. Bernice Johnson Reagon and Julius Lester performing at a *Broadside* magazine concert in September 1964. *Photo by Diana Davies, courtesy of the Ralph Rinzler Folklife Archives and Collections, Smithsonian Institution.*

served to undermine his work further. His reputation as a musician was becoming overshadowed by his troubled emotional state and reckless behavior. "I think that his personal problems made it very difficult for him to concentrate on getting the very best out of a song that he could," Paxton explains. "The folk community had ambivalent feelings about Peter," writer and musician Julius Lester says. "He did not have the greatest voice, nor did he have a lot of showmanship on stage. He wasn't polished. What he did have was a 'sincerity.' He was real. I think we both felt kind of like outsiders in the folk music world because we may have been more serious, a little more sincere about the things we were singing about. Protest music was not a 'career' move for Peter; it was what he believed in."

After Columbia cut him loose, La Farge was signed by Moe Asch of Folkways Records. "It's interesting how much Moe Asch recorded

Figure 2.4. Radio host and folksinger Oscar Brand (right) with musician Erik Darling (left) in 1957. *Courtesy of Doug Yeager.*

La Farge after what happened with Columbia," folk musician Dick Weissman told me. "I also suspect there's stuff beyond what got released because Asch really believed in La Farge despite a track record that suggested maybe he couldn't deliver." La Farge was trying to steady himself in a world that felt like it was spinning around him in a frenzy. Consequently, La Farge's relationship with Asch, while productive, was frequently contentious as a result of the musician's extreme mood swings and troubled mental state. And since La Farge was not one to do things halfway, when he drank, he drank everything around him and when he popped pills, he did the same. He also thought nothing of mixing drugs and alcohol with the medication he took for his mental illness. "His was a voice crying in the wilderness," Johnny Cash said. "I felt lucky to be hearing it. Peter was great. He wasn't careful with the Thorazine though." His reckless behavior made him appear sinister at times and docile and completely detached from reality at others. "There was more than one time when I performed with Peter that he was long ago and far away," Oscar Brand remembers. "One time at Town Hall, he was backstage standing completely still not saying anything. When I came over to him he said, 'Oscar, what's going on here, where are we?' But all I needed to do is get him in front of the microphone and he seemed to be all right."

Figure 2.5. Folkways Records founder Moses Asch in his New York office, circa 1964. Asch gave Peter La Farge the opportunity to continue recording his music. *Photo by Diana Davies, courtesy of the Ralph Rinzler Folklife Archives and Collections, Smithsonian Institution.*

Moe Asch, a deeply respected figure in the folk community, started Folkways in 1948, putting out records that included Woody Guthrie's children's music. (Interestingly, Asch convinced Seeger to sign with Columbia, thereby having a hand in losing his best-selling artist because he knew Seeger would reach many, many more people through his music with backing from Columbia, which had considerably more resources than Folkways.) Working out of an office on Seventh Avenue in New York, Asch was not motivated by record sales or commercial success, goals that were too restrictive for a music lover who found joy in all musical genres and sought to provide a range of musicians with an outlet. In his eclectic career, Asch recorded jazz, audio drama, and classical music from the Renaissance to the twentieth century. He was particularly interested in promoting artists that were, as Julius Lester says of La Farge, "real" and "sincere." More often than not, these musicians didn't fit neatly into the limited confines of the pop music world. "Asch's label was shaped by the ideas of the American Left between the world wars, which hoped to find the voices of 'the people,'" music writer Jon Pareles explained. "It tracked down unknown singers and storytellers. It wasn't the first company to record grassroots musicians, but it revived that tradition while other labels concentrated on reaching large mainstream audiences."

As La Farge started recording for Folkways, his music moved between cowboy ballads and topical songwriting. At the time, a correspondence grew between Oliver La Farge and Asch, who sought the writer's counsel on what would be appropriate album art for his son's records. "Most Indian material would support another collection of tom-toms and the land of Sky-Blue Water," Oliver wrote on October 16, 1962. "I suggest that you get hold of the Golden Books edition of my book *The American Indian* . . . and look at the Iroquois masks."

Peter La Farge found plenty to write about in the midst of the Kinzua Dam controversy. When he read Atkinson's article detailing the devastating effects the dam would have, it must have enflamed La Farge's already white-hot anger. He saved various press clippings, using them as inspiration and as a framework for shaping the song he was working on. La Farge learned that the United States based its constitution on that of Six Nations, namely that of the Iroquois. At the Broadside gatherings at Sis Cunningham and Gordon Friesen's Manhattan apartment, he started to craft the song. While studying the history of broken treaties between the United States and the Native peoples, certain phrases from the promise the government made to the Natives leapt out: "as long as the grass shall grow and the waters flow"; "as long as the sun rises and sets." With the simple words "*as long as*," the song poured out of La Farge.

IT WAS equally hard for Cash not to be stirred by the events of the civil rights movement. The movement had become a fixture in the United States, and the media reported daily on the swelling confrontation. Pushed along by a rising counterculture tide, the defiant movement touched the entire country, and no one could ignore the signs that the United States was changing and coming apart at the seams. Political divisions were growing more extreme as the stakes rose higher and higher. When George C. Wallace was elected governor of Alabama in January 1963, he defied the Kennedy administration's call to ease the hostilities surrounding desegregation. He declared: "Segregation today, segregation tomorrow, segregation forever."

Kennedy was losing his grip on the country as violent clashes between southern segregationists and civil rights activists escalated, and he received little sympathy from civil rights leaders, who were ratcheting up their efforts due to a lack of trust that the government would do anything to help or protect them. The Southern Christian Leadership Conference, under the leadership of Martin Luther King Jr., Ralph Abernathy, and Fred Shuttlesworth, targeted Birmingham, Alabama, where Sheriff Eugene "Bull" Connor was well known for violently suppressing—without hesitation or remorse—any civil rights protests. Calling the plan "Project C," the SCLC's strategy was to "confront segregation through peaceful demonstrations, rallies, boycotts, and appeals to justice."

They organized a sit-in on April 3, followed by a march through Birmingham on April 12. King, Abernathy, and Shuttlesworth, along with hundreds of others, were arrested for "parading without a permit." While in jail, King set about writing an impassioned defense of the civil rights movement, declaring, "We will have to repent in this generation not merely for the hateful words and actions of the bad people but for the appalling silence of the good people . . . Injustice anywhere is a threat to justice everywhere." Folksinger Tom Paxton says of the moment: "It was a really fiery time. The war hadn't started yet. The civil rights movement was in full force. It was being resisted violently in some parts of the country, of course in the South, but places like Boston and Detroit too."

The decision by Martin Luther King and the SCLC to challenge Sheriff Connor garnered national attention and public sympathy. On May 2, thousands of blacks, many of them children, were arrested while photographers snapped pictures and network television crews filmed Sheriff Connor's police force spraying protestors with fire hoses and attacking demonstrators with police dogs. As Cash watched the terrible scene on television, a sense of anger welled inside him that would take root and find expression on his next record.

WITH SO much happening around him, Cash was bursting with song ideas and was eager to move his songwriting into areas he felt were receiving little attention in the press or on the floor of Congress. He was quick to point out—as he did in a widely read profile that appeared in *Time* magazine in 1959 following his move to Columbia—that what he really had set out to do was to make "authentic folk music." He wanted to explore this creative side of himself but felt constricted by the demands of Columbia. Even though *Blood, Sweat and Tears* produced a minor hit with "Busted" when it reached number 13 on the *Billboard* country charts, it barely registered on the *Billboard* pop charts, peaking at number 80. Columbia wanted more crossover hits like "Folsom Prison Blues" and fewer commercial forays into conceptual Americana records like *Ride This Train* or *Lure of the Grand Canyon*. "The suits never understood John," record producer Bob Johnston said. "He always had to go his own way on his own terms. But it worked. It had to or you really wouldn't have Johnny Cash."

Johnston was right: Cash hadn't gotten to where he was without a keen sense of what worked best for him both as a musician and as a person. After all, Columbia did move into the folk revival scene by recording Seeger, and signing La Farge as the first of the "new breed" and then Dylan. Cash had stopped in a few times to see Hammond while Dylan was recording his first record, *Bob Dylan*, with the Columbia producer. As the studio heads became increasingly concerned that Hammond had lost the Midas touch when it came to discovering musicians, worried whispers turned to direct indictments that Hammond was wasting the label's time and money. Some Columbia executives mocked Dylan as "Hammond's folly," and when *Bob Dylan* was released, its slow record sales did little to ease the studio's concerns.

None of this bothered Hammond, perhaps because he knew he was basically untouchable. Almost two decades prior, he had saved the fledgling label and had given it the most impressive jazz catalogue in music. And the man at the top, Goddard Lieberson, owed Hammond his job. There was another powerful ally supporting Hammond: Johnny Cash. He later explained that Cash played an important role in Columbia's patience with Dylan: "Johnny Cash was one of Dylan's big boosters at Columbia." Hammond told writer Anthony Scaduto: "Way back there in '62, whenever Dylan was in the studio or playing in town, Cash would come around. They hung out together back then. Johnny dug me because I brought Seeger to the company and I brought Dylan to the company and he was behind me all the way. Cash was behind Dylan every which way and everybody in the company knew it. Cash made it known he thought Dylan was a giant. There's no higher recommendation." In May 1963, Cash and Hammond were vindicated when Dylan released *The Freewheelin' Bob Dylan*. Recording mostly his own material, Dylan broke free, showcasing a rare, exceptional songwriting talent beyond anything in pop music at the moment. The track that opens the record is the meditative protest song "Blowin' in the Wind." One month after the record's release, the song became an international hit for folk trio Peter, Paul & Mary, who were managed by Albert Grossman.

Cash faced a similar situation to Dylan's because he needed to silence his doubters inside Columbia. A hit song would surely stifle the executives, but would it provide him with the crucial cover to record some of the more personal records he had in mind? Once again, Cash turned to the creative and familial support of his other family: the Carters. While spending time with Pop Carter, Cash was impressed by the man's daily routine of hard work, which included breaking rocks. "He'd be out there with a nine-pound sledgehammer, bustin' rocks in the heat of the summer," Cash said. "I just couldn't understand a man lovin' that kind of torture. I mean he did it all day long, like a convict. Then he'd come in and cook supper." Seeing the dignity with which Pop carried himself even in the most laborious, unglamorous activity reminded Cash of the value of hard work and the commitment he had made to himself when he first picked up a guitar—to bring humility and integrity to bear on anything that he did. As Cash watched Pop, the sound of the hammer ringing off the rocks stuck in his head. He decided to take the traditional

Figure 2.6. Photo of Bob
Dylan taken by Jim
Marshall at the Newport
Folk Festival, circa 1963.
Dylan was participating in a
topical folksong workshop,
where Peter La Farge also
performed. *Jim Marshall.*

ballad "John Henry," and create his own version: a nine-minute tribute
to hard work called "The Legend of John Henry's Hammer." Naturally,
the Carter sisters provided background vocals.

It's impossible to measure The Carter Family's impact on American popular music. They were the first family of country, and their
fingerprints are everywhere a musician picks up an instrument to play.
New folksingers may look to Woody Guthrie as their playful patri-
arch, but Guthrie himself worshipped The Carter Family as folk gods.
He "borrowed" music from them freely, laying his own socially conscious lyrics over their classic melodies. One of Guthrie's best-known
songs, "This Land Is Your Land," borrows the melody virtually note
for note from "Little Darlin' Pal of Mine," which had been inspired by
a southern gospel hymn, "Oh, My Loving Brother." "My father
revered The Carter Family," Arlo Guthrie said. "Even though they
were in the old tradition, they were not purists in their attitude. They
were capable of writing their own songs and playing in a style that

was part serious and part fun. And because of this and the fact that they were a 'family,' my dad was influenced and inspired by them. For him, they were down to earth, unpretentious, possessed a uniquely American style that was entirely theirs."

Much of these qualities easily fit Cash. His connection to The Carter Family ran deep because, after all, he grew up listening to Carter Family 78s. "I think The Carter Family were really key to John," Arlo Guthrie says, "because they also helped him battle his demons head-on." According to folklorist Archie Green, "When Cash was young, coming out of a rural Arkansas culture, The Carter Family served as a model for sure. One time when he came to perform at a fair outside of Chicago, I invited him back to our house. I asked him if he'd put his guitar aside and asked him to sing some of his father's songs the way he remembered them as a boy. He just launched right out into a railroad ballad 'Wreck of the '97' unaccompanied and giving it all the vocalizations of a traditional singer. He never forgot it. This was a direct influence from The Carter Family."

When Anita Carter, June's sister, recorded "Ring of Fire" for her Mercury release *Folk Songs Old and New,* Cash heard the song differently in his head. There was something about the song that struck him, and given the chance, he felt he could score a hit with it. "I'll give you about five or six more months," Cash told Anita. "If you don't hit with it, I'm gonna record it the way I feel it." Johnny Cash recorded his own version of "Ring of Fire" in May 1963 and Columbia released it as a single the next month. Mother Maybelle and the Carter sisters sang harmony on the recording, and Cash and producer Don Law decided to add mariachi-style horns. The song hit the top of the *Billboard* country charts in June and climbed to number 17 on the pop charts. Cash had his hit and with it much-needed leverage with Columbia. He would need every bit of it.

"IF TAPE recorders at Pete Seeger's Carnegie Hall concert Saturday night caught even a modicum of the folksinger's masterful performance, they should provide material for a great recording," wrote Robert

Figure 2.7. Pete Seeger backstage at Town Hall in New York City, circa 1962–1963. Seeger took an interest in helping La Farge as a performer and a musician. Seeger also included La Farge's "Coyote, My Little Brother" in his own repertoire. *Jim Marshall.*

Shelton in the *New York Times* on June 10, 1963. John Hammond, who recorded the entire show, was in full agreement with Shelton. "The freshest part of the evening was devoted to the new song writers who are keeping the leaves of the folk tree green," Shelton remarked. "With a raucous performance that brought the capacity crowd to its feet for most of the night to sing along, Seeger performed songs from Tom Paxton, Bob Dylan, and Malvina Reynolds." He opened the show by playing his homemade mountain banjo and then performed folk music from around the world, including West Indian sailor rants, magisterial gospel songs, and Rhodesian and Brazilian music.

Three days after Seeger's concert, President Kennedy offered the country his strongest remarks in support of civil rights, promising legislation that afforded "the kind of equality of treatment that we would want for ourselves." The announcement was met with violence throughout the South, setting the stage for even greater confrontations in the days and weeks ahead. While Kennedy was delivering his speech, Byron De La Beckwith was lurking in the bushes outside the home of the Mississippi NAACP field secretary, thirty-seven-year-old Medgar Evers. De La Beckwith aimed his rifle and shot Evers, murdering the civil rights leader as he walked from his car to the front door of his home. John Hammond, who at one time had served on the NAACP board, knew Evers. He decided to attend the funeral of the slain civil rights leader, which took place at the Masonic Temple Hall on Lynch Street in Jackson's black section. The NAACP's executive secretary, Roy Wilkins, delivered the eulogy before a crowd of thousands who had gathered to mourn Evers: "There have been martyrs throughout history, in every land and people, in many high causes. We are here today in tribute to a martyr in the crusade for human liberty, a man struck down in the mean cowardly fashion by a bullet in the back." Wilkins stirred the bitter anger of the mourners by condemning a society that "imprisoned the negro." The memorial service concluded with an emotional rendition of "We Shall Overcome." When the mourners left the church chanting, "After Medgar, no more fear," Hammond feared a riot would ensue and trigger a violent clash between the mourners and the police. Not long after, Columbia released a live album of Seeger's June 8 Carnegie Hall performance. With an estimated 500,000 copies sold, the album, called We Shall Overcome, was a huge success. The civil rights anthem that closed the show and gave the album its name, "We Shall Overcome," had become a pop hit.

The murder of Medgar Evers was a catalyst for many musicians in the folk revival. On July 6, 1963, Bob Dylan, Josh White, Theodore Bikel, and Pete Seeger performed at a voter registration drive in Greensboro, Mississippi. "The racial crisis in the South has become a theme of major importance for folk singers of the North," observed the New York Times. "New songs on this theme are not only weapons of the civil-rights arsenal, but are also developing into valuable commodities in the music industry." Evidence supporting this claim was everywhere. Dylan wrote "Only a Pawn in Their Game," a stirring tribute to Evers. Tom Paxton composed "The Dogs of Alabama," a scorching condemnation of southern justice. Peter Seeger and Lee Hay's "The Hammer," an antidiscrimination song, sold 788,000 copies, becoming a key "freedom song" in the movement.

FOR LA FARGE, working closely with many of these musicians in the New York folk revival music scene inspired him to work vigorously on his songwriting efforts on behalf of Native people. Following the Kennedy administration's betrayal of the Seneca, there was a series of standoffs between the government and Native people. In Washington State, a long simmering battle over fishing rights, guaranteed by long-standing treaties that the state government saw fit to break, erupted into an uprising. When Washington had first sought to control Indian fishing in 1957 in *State v. Satiacum*, they pressed the case all the way to the Supreme Court. In 1958, the Court ruled in *Tulee v. Washington* that the treaties signed by Governor Isaac Stevens in 1854 were legally binding and took precedence over state laws. The state dug in its heels, refusing to ease up on efforts to regulate Native fishing in the interest of protecting game fishing.

In the June 11, 1961, issue of *Time* magazine, Oliver La Farge Sr. warned that the temper of the Indians had reached a "boiling point" and urged that a "new frontier" was needed. La Farge's forecast became a reality on March 18, 1962, when Nisqually, Puyallup, Squakine, and other Washington State Indian tribes rose up in what officials deemed the "biggest rebellion against the white man since Chief Joseph's 1877 uprising in Nez Perce." Then, in 1963, the state scored a crucial legal victory when the requirement to obtain consent to external jurisdiction onto Indian reservations was ruled "no longer necessary, paving the way for the State to control Indian fishing." The state's supreme court further undermined the treaty signed by Governor Stevens in 1854 when it ruled in favor of restricting Indian fishing, defending the decision by explaining that fish conservation must be maintained. A former marine, Billy Frank Jr. could no longer sit by and watch the continued denigration of his people's way of life. The Nisqually had a saying, "When the tide is high, the table is set." Leaders of the National Indian Youth

Council, including Hank Adams, were slowly making their way to the Nisqually River to join Frank in the showdown with state authorities.

Coming on the heels of all of this, La Farge produced his next great song, "As Long as the Grass Shall Grow." Based on the recording session notes from Cue Studios in New York City, La Farge was producing songs at an extraordinary pace, and his output at this time represents some of his most ambitious and socially conscious music. In the opinion of Jim Marshall, "'As Long as the Grass Shall Grow' is one of the very best songs to come out of the folk revival. Actually, with 'Ira Hayes,' I think it's the best music. I photographed [La Farge] a ton around this time, including his performance at Newport in '63."

In July 1963, La Farge had been invited to perform at various workshops during the Newport Folk Festival, where he was joined by Paxton, Seeger, Dylan, Jim Nettle, the Freedom Singers, and Phil Ochs. La Farge felt a particular kinship with Ochs, who was part of a loose-knit group of topical folksingers that included Mark Spoelstra, Dylan, Happy Traum, Patrick Sky, and others. A former journalism student who proudly embraced the label "topical singer" rather than "folksinger," Ochs was described by the New York Times as a "musical editorial writer . . . his satire is trenchant and opinions controversial." In Sing Out! Gordon Friesen singled out Ochs and La Farge as the best of the "new breed . . . Ochs researches his material widely before writing a song on any subject. His lyrics are blunt and his wit razor sharp." Similar to La Farge, Ochs first signed with a major record label, but unlike La Farge, the company decided not to release the album, claiming the material was too controversial.

"La Farge really did well in the workshop setting," Dunson recalls. "His laid-back performance style really suited that environment," Marshall adds. When they gathered at Newport, La Farge performed "As Long as the Grass Shall Grow." The song is a beautifully composed ballad about the Seneca's loss:

As long as the moon shall rise, as long as the rivers flow;
As long as the sun will shine, as long as the grass shall grow.

The Senecas are an Indian tribe of the Iroquois nation
Down on the New York-Pennsylvania line, you'll find their
  reservation.
After the U.S. revolution, Cornplanter was a chief;
He told the tribe these men they could trust, that was his true
  belief.
He went down to Independence Hall and there was a treaty
  signed;
That promised peace with the USA and Indian rights
  combined.
George Washington gave his signature, the government gave its
  hand;
They said that now and forever more that this was Indian land.

La Farge then adds the chorus that paints, in vivid detail, the tragic
story shared by so many tribes throughout the country:

As long as the moon shall rise . . .
On the Seneca reservation there is much sadness now.
Washington's treaty has been broken and there is no hope no
  how.
Across the Allegheny River they're throwing up a dam.
It will flood the Indian country, a proud day for Uncle Sam.
It has broke the ancient treaty with a politician's grin.
It will drown the Indians graveyards; Cornplanter can you
  swim?
The earth is mother to the Senecas; they're trampling sacred
  ground.
Change the mint green earth to black mud flats as honor
  hobbles down.

The Iroquois Indians used to rule from Canada way south,
But no one fears the Indians now and smiles the liar's mouth.
The Senecas hired an expert to figure another site,

But the great good army engineers said that he had no right.
Although he showed them another plan and showed them
   another way,
They laughed in his face and said, 'No deal, Kinzua Dam is
   here to stay.'
Congress turned the Indians down, brushed off the Indians'
   plea.
So the Senecas have renamed the dam; they call it Lake Perfidy.

Washington, Adams, and Kennedy now hear their pledges ring.
The treaties are safe, we'll keep our word, but what is that
   gurgling?
It's the back water from Perfidy Lake; it's rising all the time
Over the homes and over the fields and over the promises fine.
No boats will sail on Lake Perfidy; in winter it will fill.
In summer it will be a swamp and all the fish will kill.
But the government of the USA has corrected George's vow.
The father of our country must be wrong; what's an Indian
   anyhow?

On August 2, 1963, Oliver La Farge died at the age of sixty-one due to complications following surgery for a heart ailment. The *New York Times* noted that La Farge's "tireless efforts spurred public and private projects to improve the Indian's welfare and assure his social, civil and constitutional rights." Responding to La Farge's obituary that appeared in the *Times*, a reader described him as throwing "his arm in kindness and affection around the shoulder of a forgotten man. No racial minority ever had a more resolute friend." Yet not everyone agreed that La Farge was a "resolute friend." In fact, throughout his long career as an advocate for Native people, La Farge faced sharp criticism and occasionally received the harshest treatment from those he had dedicated his life to helping. Navajo tribal chairman Paul Jones, leader of the largest Native tribe, believed that it was "Indians and Indians alone" who should decide their future and that "spokesmen like Oliver La Farge" merely served to weaken the cause. According to Seymour Krim and writer Jim Nash, after Pete learned of his father's death, he "disappeared into the Canadian Alps." "After a couple of weeks Pete came back illusorily cleansed and sobered and started something called the Federation of Indian Rights," Krim explained. La Farge hoped the group would raise money to help fight legal battles like those involving treaty rights. La Farge received little support from those within and outside of the folk community. "It was probably a combination of things," Krim wrote. "But for whatever reasons, Pete's possibly noble gesture died a slow death from disinterest and cynicism."

THREE DAYS after La Farge's death, the United States, United Kingdom, and Soviet Union signed a nuclear test ban treaty. A few days later, comedian and activist Dick Gregory was arrested for "causing a racial disturbance" in Chicago and was released on August 23 after spending twelve days in jail for refusing to sign a recognizance bond on a disorderly conduct charge. That same day, actors Marlon Brando, Paul Newman, Anthony Franciosa, and Virgil Frye faced accusations of "rabble rousing" from Mayor Lesley Gilliland in response to their efforts to promote racial equality in Gadson, Alabama. The four men had come to the small town to speak to political officials about racial problems but were turned away. They then met with leading businesses including the Republic Steel Corporation and the Goodyear Rubber Company. Brando served as the group's spokesman. "We are here as devoted and peaceful representatives of good will," Brando explained. "We are not here as agitators, interlopers or interferers."

The group tried to introduce a more reasoned and nuanced discussion by explaining that they were not singling out southerners as the primary perpetrators of racial inequality. "We have trouble in New York, in the West, the East and the South," Brando told the press. "Southerners can point to the North and accuse them of hypocrisy, insulated, and restricted thinking, just as easily as the finger can be pointed the other way." Brando added that for too long, the South has "been accused as the sole source of friction and trouble between the races." Paul Newman defended the group's right to speak out on behalf of racial equality, explaining that the State Department had asked the actors to be ambassadors of good will abroad. "We would like to hope that we can be considered the same kind of ambassadors in the South," Newman said. "It's all right when we come down South to raise money for a hospital. And it's perfectly all right when we are asked to donate our services for other humanitarian causes. They don't call us rabble rousers then."

Dick Gregory and Brando's group were moving the discussion from civil rights to human rights. "The only people in the world who have been treated worse by this white racist system than we Blacks have been treated are the Indians," Gregory said. "After I saw what was happening to them in regards to treaties, fishing rights, and their land, I began to work harder for human rights, not civil rights." Following his time in the South, Brando became active in the Native cause. "I always figured that the civil rights movement had hundreds of artists and celebrities helping," says musician Buffy Sainte-Marie. "Nobody else was covering this base, so I did what I could at the grassroots level. Marlon Brando and others tried to help too."

Brando offered financial support and advice—sometimes unwelcome—encouraging the National Indian Youth Council to "adopt elements of the civil rights campaign" to engender public sympathy and mass media attention. But Vine Deloria reiterated that the Native issue was one of self-determination; Native people must seize their responsibility to work for that right and not choose to remain "invisible" or "opt out" by participating in civil rights, which was a movement based on "race equality." The Native movement was one of defending against the removal of a people's culture as well as protecting the legal status guaranteed by federal treaties. In line with Deloria's belief, many young activists in the Native movement decided not to participate in the upcoming civil rights gathering known as the "March on Washington for Jobs and Freedom."

"There was Bob Dylan on one corner and Odetta on another corner," former Franciscan priest and civil rights activist Jack Healey recalls. "The music just caught you and brought you forward." Healey helped organize the march and was standing only a few feet from King when he arrived at the steps of the Lincoln Memorial in Washington on August 28, 1963, to deliver his speech, "I have a dream." The March on Washington, envisioned by labor leader and founder of the Brotherhood of Sleeping Car Porters, A. Philip Randolph, brought out over two hundred thousand people in support of civil rights. "Music was the element that bound people together," Julius Lester says. "Music sung together creates community." Musicians came out to lend their voice in the effort, including Marianne Anderson, Josh White, Peter, Paul & Mary, Joan Baez, and Mahalia Jackson in addition to Dylan and Odetta. "Listening to all those musicians gave me that sense of movement in music and the power of music," Healey says. "So, I thought when you deal with human rights, you either deal with the aspiration of human rights, which is very idealistic, or you deal with the degradation of human rights—the oftentimes violent mistreatment of people by governments. Music can give voice to the degradation and that will provide the force to go forward." Also in attendance were Harry Belafonte, Marlon Brando, Diahann Carroll, Ossie Davis, Sammy Davis Jr., Lena Horne, and Paul Newman. Burt Lancaster read a speech by James Baldwin, who is credited with helping to galvanize the civil rights movement with his 1963 book, *The Fire Next Time*. Still, Baldwin and others in the movement, including Malcolm X, were highly critical of the March on Washington, calling it a "sellout" by civil rights leaders like King and a "takeover" by the Kennedy administration. Malcolm X said afterwards: "They wouldn't let [Baldwin] talk because they couldn't make him go by the script." Baldwin later said, "What struck me most horribly was that no one in power (including some blacks or Negroes who were somewhere next to power) was able to remotely, to accept the depth, the dimension, of the passion and faith of the people."

IN A matter of months, much had changed for both La Farge and the country. Still reeling from the death of his father a month earlier, La

Farge poured all his energies into his music. He eagerly agreed to serve as host of the "99 Cent Hootenanny" at Town Hall on September 13, 1963. Town Hall was his performance venue, a place where he felt comfortable and safe. On this evening, La Farge invited Guy Carawan, Phil Ochs, and Buffy Sainte-Marie to perform with him. Carawan had met La Farge at the Lomax gatherings and was now a highly respected and well-known musician, thanks in large part to his work with Highlander and their prominent role in the civil rights movement. Carawan recalls: "La Farge was a very intense but quiet person. He addressed a very unpopular social justice issue with the Native American cause. I found him to be courageous in his efforts."

Filled with a soaring spirit and a gifted songwriting and guitar playing talent, Buffy Sainte-Marie was the new voice on the scene. Sainte-Marie admired La Farge for his principled stance on behalf of Native people and for being the only folksinger to tackle the challenges facing them. Unlike La Farge, who promoted the fiction that he was a "full blood Indian," Sainte-Marie was genuinely Native from the Piapot Cree Indian Reserve in the Qu'Appelle Valley, Saskatchewan, Canada. In her first ever performance in Greenwich Village at the Gaslight, she impressed music critic Robert Shelton, who described her voice as "echoes of Edith Piaf and Anne Sylvestre." Sainte-Marie showcased a songwriting ability that was sophisticated and intelligent beyond her twenty-one years. Two songs quickly became standouts: "The Universal Soldier" and "Cod'ine." The latter is about the terrors of drug addiction. The former, written in Toronto, addressed the debate in Canada over accepting U.S. nuclear warheads.

La Farge was so impressed by Sainte-Marie that he wrote a *Sing Out!* profile that was part love letter and part music tutorial. "If this article is somewhat short of a love letter, it's because I care so damn much," La Farge wrote. He filled the article with prose that provides deep insight into Sainte-Marie's potential greatness, proclaiming, "This powerful, fragile, pretty and magnificent folk queen has more going for her, and more going without her, than anyone else in the art." La Farge quoted Sainte-Marie as she explained why her work

Figure 2.8. Buffy Sainte-Marie performing at the Broadside Hootenanny for Miners, May 1965. Sainte-Marie became an indefatiguable voice for Native and human rights. *Photo by Diana Davies, courtesy of the Ralph Rinzler Folklife Archives and Collections, Smithsonian Institution.*

takes such an insightful, progressive posture: "If you want someone to hear you, you must talk softly so they'll want to hear more." La Farge appeared mesmerized by Sainte-Marie, declaring her "an artist . . . she is a folk poet with the ability to instill truth into simplicity," and adding, "Her message would not be heard in this country, where people don't believe in Indians."

La Farge was also moved by Sainte-Marie's courage, which she carried with "pride and strength . . . in an overcrowded heart." Sainte-Marie's intrinsic sincerity, tempered by a commitment and a compassion for the world and its people, led her to write great songs. In the article, La Farge singles out one in particular, "Now That the Buffalo's Gone," written in support of the Allegany Seneca. In the song, Sainte-Marie asks, "But even when Germany fell to your hands / consider, dear lady, consider, dear man / you left them their pride and you left them their land / and what have you done to these ones?" Her response captures the bitterness many Native tribes felt as their treaties were tossed aside: "Has a change come about, Uncle Sam? / Or are you still taking our lands? / A treaty forever George Washington signed / He did, dear lady, he did, dear man / And the treaty's been broken by Kinzua Dam."

"This song was on my first album and I'd have thought it would be obsolete by now," Sainte-Marie explains. "But governments are still breaking promises and stealing indigenous lands, and I still believe that informed people can help make things better."

The success of the Town Hall show allowed La Farge to return as host for another 99 Cent Hootenanny, this time on October 5. The performers included Malvina Reynolds, well known for her whimsically mocking song about suburban living, "Little Boxes." La Farge's friend Len Chandler also performed. Chandler was a forceful and dynamic musician specializing in "freedom songs." According to a review that ran in the *New York Times,* Chandler's performances of "'To Be a Man' and 'Turn Around Miss Liberty' commanded attention." La Farge ended the show with a new song, "Father, Oh My Father," which he dedicated to Oliver La Farge and included on his Folkways record *On the Warpath*. It is a song of praise for his father's legacy: "Father, oh my father / The torch you lit burns high / and the trumpet beacons of freedom char the sky."

The months following the show would forever alter the course of U.S. and world history. On October 8, Sam Cooke and his band were arrested after trying to register at a "whites only" motel in Louisiana. On November 2, South Vietnamese President Ngo Dinh Diem was assassinated in the wake of a military coup. Four days later, General Duong Van Minh, leader of the coup, became leader of South Vietnam. The escalation of war in Vietnam was moving at a ferocious pace. Then, on November 22, 1963, riding in an open car through Dallas, accompanied by his wife and John Connally, the governor of Texas, President Kennedy was assassinated. The bullet that took his life seemed to take something more: hope. The nation's mourning was intense and profound. With his death came uncertainty and confusion, as the civil rights movement seemed to have become paralyzed.

Figure 2.9. Len Chandler performing at a *Sing Out!* Leadbelly concert at New York's Town Hall, date unknown. *Photo by Diana Davies, courtesy of the Ralph Rinzler Folklife Archives and Collections, Smithsonian Institution.*

"The movement came to a temporary standstill, and many civil rights leaders were even more afraid for their lives," Dick Gregory later said. "If the president could be murdered in cold blood in front of millions of people in the middle of the day, surely Black leaders" and anyone speaking out against war or on behalf of Native people "were sitting ducks. I had begun to realize we were dealing with a conspiracy against anyone trying to help."

As the year came to a close, the Senate continued to pursue Native land removal. Senator Henry Jackson from Washington, chairman of the Senate Interior Committee and a strong proponent of termination, introduced a bill calling for the termination of the Seneca. The bill died in committee but it was clear to young Native activists like Hank Adams, Clyde Warrior, and his wife, Della, that the government was not going to change its approach toward Native people, who were being pushed toward the bottom rungs of society. The Cheyenne River Sioux in Eagle Butte, South Dakota, for example, reported, "97 percent of the occupied housing structures were deficient, dilapidated, or un-safe" and "unemployment exceeded 75 percent."

With the country still in shock and mourning the death of the president, the self-determination sought by Native people seemed beyond their reach. Peter La Farge felt it all slipping away, and the frustration unmoored him. He sought solace in pills and alcohol but instead found it only intensified his sense of alienation. "He was calling me a lot during this time," Povy La Farge says. "I think he had enough of being out there and really wanted and needed to come back to New Mexico." Soon he must have felt out of place in the folk scene, where the issues that concerned him were mostly ignored. He was joined by fellow folksingers Buffy Sainte-Marie and Patrick Sky in spreading the word about Native rights, but the overall folk movement expressed little interest in the cause. "The Indian issue was not of interest to the majority of folksingers," Weissman explains. "We wanted to focus on Black issues. Why wasn't there room for more than that? It wasn't like African Americans were the only group that had issues that needed to be addressed."

In reality, what La Farge, along with Buffy Sainte-Marie and Patrick Sky, were doing to support Native issues in folksong was not filtering into the American mainstream in the way that Dylan's topical folksongs had. "There were other songwriters around—like Phil Ochs ('I Ain't Marching Any More') and Bob Dylan ('Masters of War')—who were making heavy-hitting topical songs that were irresistible to anybody who heard them, really works of genius," Sainte-Marie says. "It was like Peter and I both were outsiders from the weeds, a little fragile, no professional or business connections, and expected not to last; so just get it down on tape and put it out. Folklore, Vanguard, Smithsonian recording people had a high tolerance for amateur genius, and in Peter's case I guessed that a real producer might have improved his performances of his songs."

Then again, La Farge had other problems to contend with as his psychiatric hospital stays became more and more frequent. And even though his relationship with Moe Asch was often combative, the troubled troubadour felt fortunate that Asch stuck by him, providing the only viable outlet for his music. La Farge also knew he was lucky to retain the best folk manager in the business, Harold Leventhal. With Leventhal on his side, La Farge felt a sense of safety and certain success as the veteran manager did his best to support the impulsive musician as he cycled in and out of the hospital. In a letter dated December 31, 1963, La Farge wrote to Leventhal: "When I get well enough, which the doctors indicate is in the foreseeable future, I will want to sing from now on, on a reasonably profit-making basis." On the eve of a new year, La Farge was raising himself up, hopeful that what lay ahead for him was peace of mind.

Broken Hearts,
Bent Journeys

IN SEPTEMBER 1963, a quiet, thoughtful musician from Chattanooga, Tennessee, already considered the best Dobro (resonator guitar) player around, had come to the end of his stint in the U.S. Army. Before entering the army in 1961, Norman Blake had established himself as a musician's musician, someone with the ability to play anything in any situation. Mother Maybelle of The Carter Family first noticed Blake in the 1950s when they appeared on stage together at an amusement park in Tennessee. The music legend was impressed. "Around 19 and 60, in Chattanooga where I'm originally from, there was an agent Gene Goldfort," Blake says. "He was booking people out of Nashville for various and sundry things. There was an amusement park in Chattanooga and I had performed there. That's when I got to know Mother Maybelle and the Carter sisters. Then about 19 and 60, June Carter came down for the TVA co-op shows close to Chattanooga and I was in sort of a pickup group that played with June."

When Blake was drafted his music career came to a standstill, but June Carter never forgot him. Blake says, "I went off to the army in 19 and 61 'cause I was drafted. When I came out of the army in 19 and 63, a fellow by the name of Bob Johnson—no connection to the Bob Johnston the producer at Columbia—a banjo player and a various instrument musician down here that I had worked with ended up connecting with John." Johnson played on sessions with Cash over in Nashville while Blake was in the army. "Okay, when I came in from the army he came over and said to me, 'Well, I'm going over to Nashville to do this session with Johnny Cash,' and he says, 'Do you want a ride over there' so I said 'Yes, I'll go over' and went over," Blake recalls. "We walked into the studio and June says to John, 'This is Norman Blake, I told you about him and he plays guitar and he plays Dobro.' John turns to me, he'd never heard me play a note at all, on the strength of what June told him about me, he says, 'Well, I've been wanting to use a Dobro with mariachi trumpets'—like they did on 'Ring of Fire'—'if you can get a Dobro by tomorrow, come over and I will use it on the session.' It was just like that . . . he'd never heard me play."

Blake borrowed a Dobro from Josh "Uncle Josh" Graves, who is credited with making the instrument an integral part of bluegrass music, particularly through his longtime association with the Foggy Mountain Boys' Lester Flatt and Earl Scruggs, both musicians formerly of Bill Monroe's Blue Grass Band. With Dobro in hand, the first tune Blake recorded with Cash was the rebel-without-a-cause anthem "Bad News," a song that could easily have been the theme song for James Dean's Rebel Without a Cause or Brando's The Wild One. It would not be the last collaboration between the two musicians. Johnny Cash instantly loved Norman Blake—in part because they shared similar philosophies about life and music. "Certainly Woody Guthrie and the Carter Family were influences on me, especially the Carter's guitar playing," Blake says. "From the early original recordings of the Carter family to Woody Guthrie—just like for John—I've always had a high regard for Woody's work, his approach and his philosophies certainly." Cash realized that both June and Mother Maybelle were right: Blake could play anything. As Cash prepared himself for the new year and the new work he intended to record, having a go-to musician like Norman Blake—already one of the best, old-time guitar, bluegrass, and mandolin players around—would prove essential. The music star needed Norman Blake more than he realized.

To KICK off the new year, *Time* magazine named Martin Luther King "Man of the Year." But 1964 began under a cloud of growing insecurity and fear, with an unsteady and uncertain country just two months past President Kennedy's assassination. When brusque Arizona senator Barry Goldwater announced his intention to run for president, he did so by declaring he was for "extremism in the defense of liberty" and against "moderation in the pursuit of justice." As the leader of a new conservative movement, Goldwater had a reputation for saying whatever was on his mind regardless of the consequences. In December 1961, he told a news conference, "Sometimes I think this country would be better off if we could just saw off the eastern seaboard and let it float out to sea." Such comments led former President Eisenhower to tell the senator, "Barry, you speak too quick and too loud." As he broadcast his intentions that he would seek the presidency, Goldwater told journalist Stewart Alsop in 1963 that the idea of waking up one day and being president, "Frankly, . . . scares the hell out of me."

Having worked alongside Goldwater for so long in the Senate, President Johnson knew that the Arizona senator deeply opposed the New Deal, making his potential opponent vulnerable at a time that so many were looking for a protective hand from the government. Goldwater repeatedly attacked the policy, describing it as "political Daddyism . . . it's as old as demagogues and despotism." Goldwater's hard line did not fit with a new American cultural line, which was being blurred daily as the counterculture pushed harder and harder for change. For that reason, Johnson decided to present himself in stark contrast to Goldwater, unveiling his plan for a "war on poverty" as the cornerstone of his Great Society social policy program. Modeled after the New Deal, Johnson's program was bold, and carried with it the added ambitious goal to bring about racial justice.

A key element of the Johnson's Great Society program was a "war on poverty," which included assistance for the Appalachians. Integrated in the swath of Appalachia that runs from southern New York to northern Alabama, Mississippi, and Georgia are five counties of southwestern

New York where the Allegany Seneca live. With one hand, the government had taken away their land, forcing them deeper into poverty, and with the other, they appeared to be offering a helping hand. This contradiction made the Seneca—and Native activists—angrier. "That area is very depressed for the whites and Indians and the few African American people that live there," scholar Larry Hauptman says. "You wouldn't believe the conditions that I saw as the government flooded the Seneca land. They were forced into shabby hut houses and they had essentially no health services. It was just extreme poverty."

Peter La Farge and Buffy Sainte-Marie refused to accept the further humiliation and denigration of Native people. "Non-Indian people as well as most Native Americans were largely uninformed about local issues concerning Indians, and folk music audiences were receiving their first dose of Indian 101 via us two songwriters," Sainte-Marie says. "People tell me that Peter and I were their first eye-openers into Indian issues. As for me, just out of teachers college, I was always urging people to learn more and pointing out two historical quotes:

"Your great object seems to be the security of your remaining lands, and I have therefore, upon this point, meant to be sufficiently strong and clear. That in the future you cannot be defrauded of your lands; that you possess the right to sell and the right of refusing to sell your lands."—President George Washington, Proclamation to Chief Cornplanter of the Senecas, December 29, 1790

"This [Treaty of 11 November 1794] is a new and important security against your being cheated; and shows the faithful care which the United States now means to take for the protection of your lands."—Timothy Pickering, personal envoy of President Washington, to the Senecas, 1794

Using her considerable talent to draw attention to these largely disregarded issues, Sainte-Marie started "spending as much time in Indian country" as she could. Not soon after making her way to Green-wich Village in 1962, Sainte-Marie began working closely with the National Indian Youth Council and the Native American Committee in Chicago. "All during the social activism of the civil rights move-ment there were huge crowds of artists on every stage," Sainte-Marie says. "I was off doing the same in Indian country, with people like Floyd Westerman, Charlie Hill, and Paul Ortega, trying to shine a spotlight on Indian issues." If it wasn't enough to contend with polit-ical indifference, another serious obstacle for Native people was the Black civil rights movement, which was swallowing all the public and political attention. Native people were growing increasingly frustrated and concerned. "In my mind, Native people could not have a civil rights movement," John Trudell explains. "The civil rights issue was between the Blacks and the whites but I never viewed our cause as a civil rights issue for us. They've been trying to trick us into accepting civil rights but America has a legal responsibility to fulfill those treaty law agreements. If you're looking at civil rights, you're basically say-ing, 'Alright, treat us like the way you treat the rest of your citizens'— I don't look at that as a climb up [in U.S. society]."

Just a couple of years removed from the conference in Chicago in 1961, young Native people were defiantly rejecting the old approach for dealing with the United States government when it came to seeking redress. The idea that they should join along with the civil rights movement or remain patient and content to take what the government was willing to give them was simply no longer tolerable, if it ever had been. While they understood that the various movements—antiwar, free speech, civil rights—were providing space for them to advance their own issues, they also saw the danger of being swept into those movements where they would remain hidden. This is one of the main reasons that Native people refused to participate in 1963's March on Washington.

Clyde Warrior, Hank Adams, Walter Funmaker, and Thelma Stif-farm and the growing NIYC just kept pushing and pushing. Sainte-Marie was working with them all, as their fresh, hands-on style was something that the movement desperately needed. "This was one very powerful group of young people, and very early made significant changes. I remember riding around with Clyde Warrior and Mel Thom in some beat-up car in Ponca City, Oklahoma, and there were still signs in store windows: *Help Wanted. Indians Need Not Apply*," Sainte-Marie says. "There was really no American consciousness about Indians. Everybody was mis-educated. Most Americans have never had the chance to learn our realities. It's like being invisible. We are a tiny population compared with African Americans, let alone white people." These young Native activists were following a different path, one that they believed was appropriate and connected to their specific needs. Confidently and brilliantly, Clyde Warrior stepped forward with proposals and ideas that alarmed the Native old-guard but excited the young with bold, new ideas and visionary leadership.

CLYDE WARRIOR was born on August 31, 1939, in Ponca City, Oklahoma, and from early on displayed an activist's commitment to justice for Native people. As a student at Cameron Junior College in Lawton, Oklahoma, Warrior was elected president of the Southwest Regional Indian Youth Council. While working on the Youth Council, he developed the idea that a national youth council was needed. By 1961, Warrior was instrumental in the Native youth movement. For his efforts, he was invited to the American Indian Chicago Conference. As part of a new group of young activists, Warrior openly expressed his frustration with what he perceived as the older generation's harmful acceptance of BIA policies, calling them "Uncle Tomahawks." Deloria singled out Oliver La Farge Sr.: "Perhaps the best known and most skillful manipulator of Indian people" who "dealt primarily with uncle tomahawks, who would say anything to stay on the good side of him."

"It was sickening to see American Indians get up and just tell obvious lies about how well the federal government was treating them, what fantastic and magnificent things the federal government was doing for us," Warrior said. An impasse between the two generations was spilling over into open hostility, reaching a boiling point when the Native youth began to vocally dissent during the '61 conference. Indian elders would have none of it and decided to shut down what they perceived as a "dangerous" and "radical" element. The resistance only emboldened the youth, who later met in Gallup, New Mexico, to found the National Indian Youth Council. Warrior and the other youth leaders saw no future in the old way of doing things—compromise and conciliation had led Native people further down a road of no return. As an alternative, the NIYC pledged to be unyielding in their aim of "attaining a greater future" for Native people, doing all they could to develop a grassroots movement to protect and promote tribal sovereignty and self-determination.

"This is all I have to offer. The Sewage of Europe does not flow through these veins." This was, more or less, typical of Warrior's fiery rhetoric, which served as notice of a new generation of Native people who were ready to forge a different path, a group that refused to bow down to the "white father" and instead called for swift action and immediate justice. According to writer Charles Wilkerson, "That kind of talk made many Indians uncomfortable. Their schooling had taught them that Anglo culture was good, that Indian ways were bad. No matter, Warrior never toned down his rhetoric. A compelling public orator and steeped in history and Indian rights, he pressed forward, relentlessly challenging assumptions, breaking the mold, making converts."

One of Warrior's brashest and most incendiary moments came as the 1964 U.S. presidential election drew closer. Various community leaders and activists began to publicly endorse Johnson. Before long, it appeared that everyone in the different social movements had lined up to support the Texas Democrat's candidacy. Warrior saw no point in supporting Johnson. After all, this was the same man who, starting in 1937, had voted against every civil rights piece of legislation that was introduced during his eleven years as a congressman. Johnson voted against the Poll Tax, desegregation in the armed forces, and ending lynching. When he ran for the Senate in 1948, he called Truman's proposed civil rights plan "an effort to step up the police state." His words were echoed in Goldwater's speeches and public comments. In his first speech as a senator, Johnson led a southern filibuster against an attempt to impose cloture on a debate of Truman's civil rights legislation. "We of the South know that 'cloture is the deadliest weapon' against the rights of a minority such as the South," Johnson said on the Senate floor. His ninety-minute defense of the South's rights helped defeat Truman's plan. After the speech, the aging southern senators lined up at his desk to congratulate him. The first person to do so was Richard Brevard Russell, the leader of the conservative coalition from Georgia. In his biography of Johnson, Robert Caro describes him as "the young hope of those aging men in their grim last-ditch fight to preserve segregation." Soon after, thanks to the Southern bloc of senators, Johnson became Senate leader.

When it became clear that Barry Goldwater was going to receive the Republican presidential nomination, Warrior threw his support behind him and encouraged other Native activists to do the same. "The majority of tribes" lined up to "support the Johnson-Humphrey ticket in the general election," Vine Deloria later wrote. But there was one prominent and vocal Native activist who supported Goldwater: Clyde Warrior. "His basic thesis in supporting Goldwater was that emotional reliance on a civil rights bill to solve the Blacks' particular cultural question was the way to inter-group disaster," Deloria explained. Some in the movement agreed with Deloria. It seemed that the focus on passing a law removing differences missed what was truly needed. According to Deloria and Warrior, what was required is "mutual respect with economic and political independence." Holding firm to this belief, Warrior believed that Goldwater's approach—maintaining the status quo—was the only one that could open the door to what he believed Native people really needed: self-rule.

ON MARCH 9, 1964, the San Francisco Chronicle headline read: "Alcatraz Invasion." The San Francisco Examiner carried a story titled "Wacky Indian Raid, Alcatraz Invaded." Allen Cottier, Walter Means,

Mark Martinez, Richard McKenzie, and Garfield Spotted Elk, all Bay Area Sioux, had taken a chartered boat to Alcatraz to lay claim to the island as "Indian land." In a prepared statement, Cottier, president of the Bay Area branch of the American Indian Council, declared: "Under the U.S. Code, we as Sioux Indians are settling on federal land no longer appropriated. Because we are civilized human beings, and we realize that these acts give us land at no cost, we are willing to pay the highest price for California land set by the government: 47 cents per acre. It is our intention to continue to allow the U.S. government to operate the lighthouse, providing it does not interfere with our settlement." The Sioux intended to use the land for a cultural center and to establish an Indian university. The occupation lasted only four hours but many current and soon-to-be Native activists were watching and learning

The Alcatraz protest notwithstanding, 1964 brought little relief for Native people from the failed policy of termination and continued disregard of legal tribal treaties. This time, tribes in the Northwest were facing the removal of their fishing rights brought on by the demands of sports fishermen. "It may well be that all Indian fishing will eventually be regulated by the states if the Northwest succeeds," Deloria wrote. "This would be quite tragic as there is a fundamental difference between Indian and sports fishing. Indian people are fishing for food for their families. Sportsmen are fishing for relaxation and recreation. Indians may have to starve so that whites can have a good time on the weekends, if the present threat continues."

While Native people were subject to state law when it came to fishing for salmon and steelhead trout off their tiny reservations, the main point of friction was the state regulations ban on the use of traditional Native fishing methods including nets and traps. Tribal members pointed out the obvious contradiction in light of the rights guaranteed by treaties signed by territorial governor Isaac Stevens in the 1800s. As Washington State attempted to break these treaties while continuing to arrest and prosecute tribal members, Hank Adams and the NIYC saw an opportunity to rally and unite Native people around the right to fish. Adams, who had refused induction into the U.S. Army as a protest until the federal government made good on all treaties with Native people, traveled to Frank's Landing in Washington State to lead the NIYC's organizing efforts.

When Billy Frank Jr. of the Nisqually tribe tried to continue fishing in Washington State, his cedar canoe was rammed and capsized by an aluminum boat operated by state officers outfitted in riot gear. "At the beginning, these guys had no idea how to run a boat on this river," Frank said. "We figured out their favorite hiding places . . . But they got real serious about this. And this was the time of Selma; there was a lot of unrest in the nation. Congress had funded some big law enforcement programs and they got all kinds of training and riot gear—shields, helmets. And they got fancy new boats. These guys had a budget. This was a war."

The National Indian Youth Council responded by adapting a tactic of the civil right's movement: the sit-in became a "fish-in," and they fished in defiance of state law to protest the denial of treaty rights. The civil disobedience tactic worked to build public support, but it was far from easy. On March 2, 1964, the NIYC gained national attention as Marlon Brando joined clergyman John Yaryan, and Puyallup leader Bob Satiacum in a fish-in. Brando was already an outspoken supporter of the civil rights movement, and his very public support and subsequent arrest for catching salmon "illegally" in Puyallup River helped bring much needed publicity to the growing Native rights movement.

Marlon Brando had reached out to D'Arcy McNickle after reading the Flathead Indian's book *The Surrounded*, a powerful novel depicting reservation life in 1936. (In his review of the book, Oliver La Farge praised it as "simple, clear, direct, devoid of affectations, and fast-moving.") McNickle encouraged Brando to meet with the National Indian Youth Council. From that moment, Brando assumed a more active, engaged role in Native issues. Soon after, Clyde Warrior and Marlon Brando became friends. The actor was pushing the activist (and the NIYC) to adopt some of the same strategies used by the civil rights movement. The fish-in, for one, was proving an effective weapon against the encroachment on Native fishing rights. Even though Warrior and Brando disagreed on utilizing strategies of the civil rights movement, they agreed that something needed to be done to generate more public support for Native issues. The day after Brando and Satiacum were arrested, Adams organized a protest march to the state capital with over two thousand supporters including Native people from thirty-seven tribes. Adams convinced Brando to march. Native representatives met with Governor Albert D. Rosellini in Olympia, Washington, to discuss the rash of Native arrests for fishing with nets and halting the violation of two Federal treaties signed in 1855. Relying on the state supreme court ruling against the tribes' fishing claims, Governor Rosellini refused to honor the treaties.

Unfortunately, Native people found another enemy lurking on Capitol Hill. Senator Henry "Scoop" Jackson from Washington State was now the most vocal and influential proponent of continuing termination. Early in 1960, Kennedy had seriously considered Jackson for the vice-presidential slot on his ticket, but Jackson was a polarizing figure and could cost the young politician the presidency. Although Jackson was a Democrat with some liberal views, he was a devout cold warrior. Even more troubling for Native people was that he took up the cause of termination dating back to his time as a congressman chairing the House Indian Committee. Once he took control of the Senate Interior Committee, Jackson's first priority was to terminate the Coleville Reservation, the largest in Washington State. The granddaughter of Chief Moses, Lucy Covington, resisted Jackson's efforts and enlisted the support of NIYC's Hank Adams and other activists. "If an Indian doesn't have land, he has nothing," Covington said.

As Charles Wilkinson later explained, Hank Adams and other NIYC leaders including "Guy McMinds of Quinault, Ramona Bennett of Puyallup, and Janet McCloud of Tulalip stepped up their efforts in reaching out to celebrities to join their cause," the most pressing of which was fishing rights. In addition to Brando, actress

Jane Fonda and comedian Dick Gregory were soon joining the protests. "Dick Gregory and later Muhammad Ali did appearances with us, and were kind. They were blown away by our lack of clout, and our poverty—Dick Gregory especially," Sainte-Marie explains.

JUST AS Columbia was getting set to release Cash's *I Walk the Line* in May 1964—the eighteenth album of his career—thousands of students in New York, San Francisco, Boston, and Seattle gathered to march against the escalating war in Vietnam. It was the first national protest of Johnson's Vietnam policy and the first sign that the president would face another angry American chorus, this time over Vietnam. On the album, Cash recorded "Wreck of the Old '97" with Bob Johnson and Norman Blake. Woody Guthrie and Hank Snow had recorded versions, and Cash was taking his turn with the Vernon Dalhart tune that is considered the first million-selling country music release in U.S. recording history. The song is about a southern train named the Fast Mail that, while traveling from Monroe, Virginia, to Spencer, North Carolina on September 27, 1903, sped off the track and is destroyed. The "Wreck of Old '97" inspired a number of aspiring troubadours and balladeers throughout the South to pick up an instrument and play. Working with Johnson and Blake on the venerable ballad may have given Cash a good idea for how to refine and build his next record of "Indian songs."

With the ferment swirling around him, Cash decided it was time to begin work on the new record taking shape in his head. He walked into Columbia studios in Nashville three days after the fish-in in Washington State. The timing was an interesting twist of fate in light of the fact that the folk album Cash was set to record would contain nothing but "Indian protest songs." Cash was filled with anger over what was happening. "John had really researched a lot of the history," Johnny Western says. "It started with Ira Hayes." Cash, who never forgot meeting Peter La Farge and listening to his "Indian songs," got together with his producers Don Law and Frank Jones to listen to La Farge's "Ballad of Ira Hayes" and "As Long as the Grass Shall Grow."

It was clear to all of them that Cash could assemble an entire album using much of La Farge's material.

Cash wanted to do this record right, not only by putting in the time to learn about the subject but by really feeling and understanding it in his bones. He wanted to absorb as much as possible; after all, he insisted he was a descendant of the Cherokee (and sometimes in a drug haze even claimed to be a "full blood"). In reality, the small amount of Native blood he may have had couldn't have helped him understand the hardships that Native people had endured for centuries. But Cash's empathy for their plight could take him quite a long way, La Farge's music could take him a bit farther, and the right mix of musicians and sincere sensibilities could bring him all the way to where he wanted to go. For a musician like Cash, making music is a journey filled with discovery of new relationships, cultures, lives, truth, and in the end, liberty.

Since La Farge's "Ballad of Ira Hayes" provided the spark for Cash's vision of the music he hoped to produce, it felt right that he should learn more about the song's subject. Cash contacted Ira Hayes's mother, asking if he could come to Arizona and visit with her and the family. She agreed. The trip changed Cash in a way that gave him a clearer sense of purpose and some much needed confidence to get the record right. He needed it badly at this point in his life as his struggles with addiction continued to wear him to the bone. Before Cash left the Pima Reservation, Hayes's mother presented him with a gift, a smooth black stone that turned translucent when it was held up to the light. The Pima call the stone an "Apache tear," and it is found only in remote parts of Arizona and New Mexico. The legend behind the opaque volcanic black glass is rooted in the last cavalry attack on Native people, which took place in Arizona. Just as the U.S. Cavalry had done at Wounded Knee, the soldiers were ordered to leave the bodies of the Native people they slaughtered on the ground. Then they rounded up the women, children, and men who couldn't fight and marched them off to a train bound for a reservation. The brutal ordeal was compounded by the soldiers' refusal to allow the Apache women to put the dead on stilts, an age-old sacred tradition of the tribe. Overcome by grief, legend has it that for the first time ever, Apache women shed tears. Leaving the men's bodies behind to rot on the ground, the women cried tears that fell to the earth and turned black. Cash, deeply moved by Hayes's mother's gesture, took the stone, polished it, and mounted it on a gold chain, and kept it around his neck from that time forward.

Wearing the Apache tear, Cash met his producers Don Law and Frank Jones in Nashville to discuss the musicians they would need to have any chance of pulling off this ambitious recording. Norman Blake was one of the first musicians Cash wanted. Law invited Blake and Bob Johnson to the recording session. "Don Law—the Englishman—and Frank Jones were there for this record," Blake says. "Law always had this woman with him. I don't know if she was his wife or who she was but she was always taking notes and doing that kind of thing for him. He was a gentleman who had those half glasses on all the time. Mr. Law, as I called him." Blake continues, "I was involved at a different level to contribute certain sounds. I think John always relied on that original sound that he had. He had that nailed down—it's what they did—the tick-tack guitar and Marshall on bass and W. S. Holland, 'Fluke,' had come in on drums. But myself and Bob Johnson—I used to refer to myself on the other sessions in Nashville as the 'token folkie'—brought something different for John." Starting at ten in the morning and working until two the following morning, Cash, after polishing La Farge's lyrics a bit, cut two songs: "Big River" and "Ballad of Ira Hayes."

"When we went back into the studio to record what became *Bitter Tears*," Marshall Grant says, "we could see that John really had a special feeling for this record and these songs." All the musicians seemed to share John's enthusiasm for the material. "We always supported John—from Don Law to all of us—we had enthusiasm for John's songs," Blake explains. "We were very supportive of *Bitter Tears*." Cash invited La Farge to come down to the sessions. "He was just thrilled," Ramblin' Jack Elliott says. "I got on a plane and went to

Figure 2.10. Folksinger Ramblin' Jack Elliott was a close friend of both Peter La Farge and Johnny Cash. Elliott traveled with La Farge to Nashville for the *Bitter Tears* recording session and for a time lived in the same building as Dylan and La Farge. *Photo circa 1962–1963, Jim Marshall.*

Nashville with him. I was a good friend of both John and Peter. There was something very special about this moment for all of us." Oscar Brand adds, "The two of them together made a remarkable pair. One of them was doing an actor's job on being an outlaw and the other doing a job of being a real Indian. To me, in some ways they were like cartoons in a book. With all their differences, there was something the same. It was a feeling that they have been hustled out of the crowd and turned out the door at the good party. They were considered not wanted—who wanted a poor guy from Arkansas, or troubled kid from the Southwest? You can throw Dylan in there, too, a guy writing new songs imitating Woody Guthrie."

Cash entered La Farge's life when it appeared that his moment had passed him by. Dylan was becoming a bigger music star by the day, and others like Paxton, Baez, Seeger, and even Elliott were secure in their careers. Cash gave La Farge one giant, extraordinary shot—maybe his last—to step up and out into a new world filled with countless possibilities. "Peter was a quiet type boy, a gentleman," Marshall Grant says. "He stayed around the whole week in Nashville, even for a little while at John's place. When we recorded he sat quietly in a corner of studio. He was extremely polite and only spoke when spoken to. It was clear he was in awe of what was happening and the whole process." It was hard not to be. Cash filled the studio with the Tennessee Three, Norman Blake, Bob Johnson, and The Carter Family, who provided background vocals that gave "Ira Hayes" a haunting quality. The sessions moved easily, except when Cash was too high to find his way back to the studio after getting lost on the highway. Once Cash was there, though, he was locked in. "John came there already with all the songs written out and what he wanted to do," Grant says. "It didn't take long for the band to work everything out and we didn't rush—we never rushed through—and more importantly we were all deeply moved and impressed with the album. We loved John and Peter's song."

A few weeks before Cash knocked out the remaining seven songs of *Bitter Tears* in a Nashville studio on June 29 and June 30, Bob Dylan sent notice that he was moving in a new musical direction. On June 9, recording in a New York studio, Dylan completed *Another Side of Dylan,* his next record for Columbia. The musician who had burst forward in the folk revival scene was starting to leave that part of him behind while Cash began to explore and bring out the topical songwriter in him. Once *Bitter Tears* was finished, Cash and La Farge parted ways so that Cash could travel and make public appearances, including a stop on *The Tonight Show* followed by a performance at the Newport Folk Festival. When Cash got to Newport with The Carter Family in tow, the other performers greeted him like music royalty.

Cash took the Newport stage on July 26. "No matter where you were or what you were doing, every musician that was there came to watch Johnny Cash perform," Tom Paxton recalls. Cash's twenty-minute set included "Don't Think Twice, It's All Right," written by Bob Dylan, and some of his hits like "I Walk the Line." He closed the set with "Ballad of Ira Hayes." As Cash passed the other performers backstage after his set, most just stared at him in awe. "Just a magnificent performance," the festival's promoter George Wein says before reading me an account of the meeting between Cash and Dylan from his personal archives: "At one party in 1964 in a room full of Joan Baez, Sandy Bull, Jack Elliott and some others, Dylan and Cash sat on the floor trading songs. Joan set up a little recording machine and that's where Bob gave Johnny 'It Ain't Me, Babe' and 'Mama, You've Been on My Mind.' Johnny was there with June Carter, so shy, sweet and gentle in a room full of freaks. Afterwards Johnny took Bob aside and gave him his guitar—an old gesture of admiration."

"Johnny Cash was more like a religious figure to me," Dylan says. "And there he was at Newport, you know, standing side-by-side. Meeting him was a high thrill of a lifetime and just the fact that he had sung one of my songs, it was just unthinkable." According to Johnny Western, "Dylan [told Cash] that he once hitchhiked from Hibbing, Minnesota, to Duluth—this was back when tickets were a buck and a half or two dollars—to see him and the Tennessee Two at the Duluth amphitheater . . . Dylan told Cash, 'Man, I didn't just dig you; I breathed you.'" As rumor spread that Dylan and Cash were huddled together backstage, people made their way to catch a glimpse of the two music stars. "Johnny Cash and June Carter came by after Bob had put a couple, three tunes on tape for him on this little portable machine," Tony Glover recalls. "Johnny called him out into the hall and Bob came back a few minutes later. He was holding this guitar and he says, 'He gave me his guitar.'" Bob Neuwirth adds, "I tell Bob, 'Wow, that's an old country tradition. If somebody gives you a guitar, that's a big honor, you know.'"

Cash's Newport appearance just added to his already growing legacy. Robert Shelton wrote in the *New York Times* following the performance: "Johnny Cash, the Nashville star, closed the gap between commercial country and folk music with a masterly set of storytelling songs . . . It was a gap that Johnny needed badly to bridge." La Farge said afterwards, "When he appeared at Newport among all those folkies, he didn't have to change a note to make it fit." Yet Cash had done more than "bridge a gap"; he had incited the ire of the old guard conservative country music set. "The same qualities that the folkies liked caused the traditional country music disc jockeys to shy away from playing [*Bitter Tears*]," DJ and writer Hugh Cherry later wrote. "This eventually reached a point where Cash decided to respond to the trend" of condemning *Bitter Tears* and his advocacy on behalf of the Native people.

All God's Children
Ain't Free

Flipping through the pages of the August 22, 1964, issue of *Billboard*, readers would have come across the standard music industry fare: the upcoming release of the Beatles' film *Hard Day's Night,* the newest singles from Jan and Dean and the Beach Boys. Crammed in between music news and record reviews were ads promoting Frank Sinatra's latest concert in Las Vegas and chart listings announcing the Supremes' "Where Did Our Love Go" as the number one single for that week. But there was one advertisement about halfway through the magazine that filled an entire page and caught the eye with a bold, simple title printed in cursive: "Johnny Cash." It had not been purchased by Cash's label, Columbia Records, to announce an upcoming album or tour. Instead it was a fiery protest written by Cash himself, calling attention to the censoring of his just released single "Ballad of Ira Hayes." Many radio stations refused to play the song, and print media chose not to review the song, making Cash a target in an industry that wanted him, according to one Columbia Records studio exec, to "entertain not educate." Native activist Dennis Banks says, "Johnny Cash just smashes out with the statement that is 'Ira Hayes.' He's telling America, 'This is what you did, America. You let him die a lonely death.' To me, Cash's album is one of the earliest and most significant statements on behalf of Native people and our issues."

One year after his first smash hit of the sixties, "Ring of Fire," Cash was fighting back. When he decided to record "Ira Hayes," he didn't expect trouble. "He was at the peak of his career at this time. So doing *Bitter Tears* was a brave and risky album," says producer Greg Gellner. "It wasn't an overly commercially minded album at all and was recorded to tell a story, not make a profit. Cash also understood that he could use his celebrity and success to make a point." He thought that in the midst of a growing civil rights movement and the popularity of the folk revival, the folk record he'd envisioned would be celebrated not vilified. Cash later said, "I got a lot of flak from the Columbia Records bosses while I was recording it—though Frank Jones, my producer, had the sense and courage to let me go ahead and do what I wanted—and when it was released, many radio stations wouldn't play it." Marshall Grant adds, "Many people just didn't get it. John always looked at the Indians as being run over, just terribly treated. John was deeply committed as we all were to the issues surrounding Indians. There was no one better at telling stories and putting the right words to tell those stories and that's what *Bitter Tears* is."

Although the album's material is something of a departure from Cash's prior records, the controversy arose because La Farge's songs didn't whitewash history. Cash wanted to tell the "Indians' side of the story" and present the "Indians' viewpoint," Hugh Cherry wrote in the album's liner notes. "Listen well to these words," Cherry continued. "They are the thoughts and feelings of a people who deem Custer's Last Stand not a massacre but an Indian victory over a foe who had broken a promise. Hear the words well and you will discern that simply because we are white, that does not make us pure." Cash was taking a stand and no record executive or radio DJ could stop him from getting the songs out there. There was no going back for Cash, especially with songs like La Farge's "Custer," in which Cash nearly spits out: "General Custer come in pumpin' when the men were out a huntin' / But the General he don't ride well anymore / With victories he was swimmin' / He killed children dogs and women," and then adds, "Twelve thousand warriors waited, they were unanticipated /

And the General he don't ride well anymore / It's not called an Indian victory but a bloody massacre / And the General he don't ride well anymore / There might have been more enthusin' if us Indians had been losin'."

With "Custer," "Ira Hayes," and "As Long as the Grass Shall Grow" anchoring the album, Cash reached across the folk music spectrum to create an album that blended past and present, humanism and history. By bringing together his various musical personas—the swaggering rock 'n' roll rebel, the unadorned country crooner, the down home traditionalist, and the soulful gospel spiritualist—Cash layered his folksongs in a way that was wholly his own. He polished La Farge's songs with inspired musical arrangements, which elevated and highlighted the folksinger's stirring lyrics. The musicians took La Farge's "Drums" and gave it a traditional Native feel but with an up-tempo twist over rich, bottomless percussion filled with the lush backing vocals of The Carter Family. The song resonates with the heartbeat and pulse of a people who remain resolute: "Well, you may teach me this land's history, but we taught it to you first / We broke your hearts and bent your journeys: broken treaties left us cursed / Even now you have to cheat us, even though you think us tame / In our losing we found proudness / In your winning you found shame."

Cash offers his own song, "The Talking Leaves," and strips it bare with Norman Blake's Dobro and The Carter Family singing softly in the background. Cash doesn't sing, but speaks purposefully as he tells the story of Sequoia, a poor, crippled, uneducated, and ridiculed half-breed Indian, who developed a new Cherokee alphabet and writing system to help his people organize against the encroaching settlers. He dusted off "Old Apache Squaw," a tune he'd written in 1959 that Columbia had refused to let him record some years before. With the Apache tear hanging around his neck, Cash sang "Old Apache squaw / How many broken hearts you saw? / You've had misty eyes for years / Could that mist be tears?" Johnny Horton's haunting "Vanishing Race," and Cash's own "Apache Tears"—inspired by Hayes's mother—and "White Girl" closed out the recording. By telling the story of a doomed love affair between a white woman with "bright blonde hair" and an "Indian man," the song is a metaphor for what La Farge often referred to as "Whites Only Democracy," or the myth of inclusion and acceptance versus the reality of the superficial fetishizing or romantic racist relationship the United States has with Native people. In the song, the "white girl" takes the "Indian man" to fancy parties, plying him with whiskey while showing him off to everyone she meets: "She took me to her parties; she carried me around / and I was a proud one, the tallest man in town . . . I learned to drink strong whiskey as she took me here and there / Until my life without my whiskey I could not bear." Once again fooled into believing that there is a place for him in this land with her on his arm, he learns the harsh truth: "And she said she loved me and would not do me harm / But she would not marry an Indian, she said / She thanked me for my offer, and I wished that I was dead . . . although I'm sad with staggers when I drink that tough whiskey / For I've been a white girl's pet, a captive Indian / Shown off and discarded, just a drunk who might have been."

The release of the first single, "Ira Hayes," went nowhere. It seemed that radio stations weren't playing the song. Cash, his producer, and his fellow musicians were left scratching their heads. Could the song's length be the problem? Radio stations liked to play songs less than three minutes long to squeeze as much music into an hour set. Still, the song was a strong showcase for Cash as a musician who'd grown immeasurably since he recorded the early pop-style ballad "Ballad of a Teenage Queen." "I was very surprised that Cash would record 'Ira Hayes' and these other songs," Dick Weissman explains. "I know that a lot of people into Johnny Cash weren't into that. They wanted a 'Ballad of Teenage Queen' not 'Ballad of Ira Hayes.' They wanted 'Folsom Prison.' They didn't want songs about how Americans mistreated Indians."

Confused and angry, Cash needed to do something to get "Ira Hayes" out there. So he turned for help to Johnny Western, the man who'd bailed him out so many times before. "When 'Ira Hayes' came along, I had a partnership deal with a friend of mine named Pat Shields in Hollywood," Western says. "It was a production company that was actually a promotion company, and we had that song under contract with John to promote. We only had two or three clients. The biggest client we ever had was John. It was not going anywhere and we realized that radio was not going to play that song."

As the storm over "Ira Hayes" grew, Cash insisted on having the last word. The campaign was under way to censor the record. He had received plenty of hate mail from angry fans in his day, but when radio stations and DJs attempted to censor him, there was no way Cash was going to stand for it. He sat down and wrote a letter addressed to the entire record industry and paid *Billboard* to publish the letter as a full-page ad. Cash explained, "I talked about them wanting to wallow in meaninglessness" and noted their "lack of vision for our music." He went on, "Predictably enough, it got me off the air in more places than it got me on."

According to Charles Wolfe, another slight that had not been lost on Cash was the fact that *Billboard* magazine had refused to review the record.

Cash felt a deep kinship with Ira Hayes. Both men had served in the military as a way to escape lives of rural poverty and to create new opportunities. Plus both suffered from addiction problems: Cash had his pills and Hayes battled with alcohol. "When John was attacked for 'Ira Hayes' and then *Bitter Tears*, it just ripped him apart," Grant says. "Hayes was forced to drink by the abuse and treatment of white people who used and abandoned him. To us, it meant Hayes was being tortured and that's the story we told and it's true." Cash made sure to point this fact out by opening the *Billboard* letter with a searing statement about Hayes: "It is an astounding experience, the power that touches everyone who walks around the gigantic statue of the WWII flag raising based on that classic picture of Iwo Jima. There are five marines and one navy corpsman depicted in that bronze giant at Arlington national cemetery. I 'chilled' like that recently, then went to Columbia records and recorded 'Ballad of Ira Hayes.'"

Cash certainly let those in radio and the record industry know exactly how he was feeling in the *Billboard* letter in support of his protest record. Just a year before the same DJs and radio stations eagerly played "I Walk the Line" in heavy rotation but now refused to play "Ira Hayes." "I know many of you 'Top 40,' 'Top 50' [DJs and radio station managers] or what have you. So . . . a few of you can disregard this 'protest' ['Ira Hayes'] and that is what it is." Western explains, "We worked on that letter together and decided that the industry in general needed to know, in other words, 'You're cowards for not playing this record.' Then Pat Shields and I followed it up by mailing out all these copies to every disc jockey we could think of with a personal note from John saying, 'C'mon on, you guys; give this a shot.' That was the payoff: the *Billboard* letter and all the work we did from that little office on Western Avenue in Hollywood." Western and Shields contacted every radio station in the country they could. They asked Columbia for copies of the song, and Cash paid for about a thousand of them. "We shipped those babies out by hand with ten-inch little notes from John to major guys," Western recalls.

In the *Billboard* letter, Cash angrily writes, "Classify me, categorize me—STIFLE me, but it won't work. I am fighting no particular cause. If I did, it would soon make me a sluggard. For as times change, I change. This song is not of an unsung hero. The name of Ira Hayes has been used and abused in every bar across the nation." Cash praises Peter La Farge and proudly declares, "These lyrics, I realize, take us back to the truth . . . as written by his cousin Peter La Farge—I'm not afraid to sing the hard, bitter lines that the son of Oliver La Farge wrote." Cash spares no one, unafraid to challenge the record industry for its cowardice. He acknowledges that record sales are important but "another word for it is 'success.'" He continues, "Regardless of the trade charts—the categorizing, classifying and restrictions of air play—this not a country song, not as it is being sold. It is a fine reason though for the *gutless* (Cash's emphasis) to give it a thumbs down." Cash ends the letter leaving no doubt as to where he stands: "I had to fight back when I realized that so many stations are afraid of Ira Hayes. Just one question: WHY???" He continues, "'Ira Hayes' is strong medicine . . . So is Rochester, Harlem, Birmingham and Vietnam." Cash is referring, of course, to the race riots in U.S. cities where thousands of Blacks were being beaten, sprayed with water cannons, attacked by police dogs, and taken to jail in Selma, Alabama, just for asking to be treated as citizens. He also included the Vietnam War in his letter, as he was beginning to see the folly of the war and to understand the point many Native people made that the war was another terrible example of violence against indigenous people.

When the country music community read the letter, the backlash turned nastier. Until then, employing a longstanding southern tradition, many had taken the polite approach and kept their feelings about Cash's new music to themselves. "White southerners then and now have demonstrated a knack for politely avoiding acknowledgement of stances that challenge their domination," according to Jordan Green of the Institute of Southern Studies. But the "polite" censorship gave way in the aftermath of Cash's very public statements, especially when he linked the problems of Native people to what blacks had faced in America, stating in the letter, "I'd sing more of this land, but all God's children ain't free." Although the folk music ballad had a long and healthy tradition in the South, such social commentary never made its way into the politically conservative—and ultra-patriotic—country music scene. Cash had connected with a new audience that consisted of longhaired, poetry-reading northern bohemians, intellectuals, students, and minorities, and for country music purists, never the two shall meet. Charles Wolfe later noted that *Bitter Tears* "shattered the uneasy truce between the activist, protest-oriented folksingers and the normally conservative, patriotic country music establishment." Wolfe explains, "An editor of a country music magazine demanded that Cash resign from the Country Music Association, insisting, 'You and your crowd are just too intelligent to associate with plain country folks, country artists and country DJs.'" These comments sparked Cash's ire and he made sure to address them in the letter as well: "In closing—at the Newport Folk Festival this month I visited with many, many 'folk' singers—Peter, Paul & Mary, Theodore Bikel, Joan Baez, Bob Dylan (to drop a few names) and Pete Seeger. I was given 20 minutes in their Saturday night show (thanks to Mr. John Hammond, pioneer for Columbia by way of A/R). Ballad of Ira Hayes stole my part of the show." Nearly everyone who had a hand in making the record agrees that hundreds of radio stations and DJs—many of whom who had been devout Cash supporters—were simply not playing the record. "The length of the song certainly didn't fit into the standard radio station format," Johnny Western says. "But, c'mon! The song regardless of the length deserved to be played. The fact that so many radio stations were refusing to do so while scores of music trade papers and other media didn't even write about it was terribly troubling."

Cash couldn't win for losing. He often caught the scorn of the country music establishment for his departures from country and forays into rock or concept records. But now he was catching something different from the folk revival: a near total indifference. Except for a handful of people, the folk revival musicians never listened to *Bitter Tears*. Folksinger Happy Traum offers the standard response: "I really never listened and didn't even really know about Peter's work with Johnny Cash and the *Bitter Tears* album they recorded." Although a few in the folk revival scene welcomed Cash with open arms, others looked on with suspicion, questioning his motives for making a folk record. "It was also intriguing to see how people like Johnny Cash were starting to pay attention to what was emerging from Greenwich Village," John Cohen recalls. Dick Weismann adds, "I was very intrigued that Johnny Cash picked up on this stuff."

From his vantage point, Cash considered himself first and foremost a folksinger, as evidenced by what he told *Time* magazine in 1959 when he said his ultimate musical aspiration was to create "authentic folk music." Norman Blake says, "I would agree that John was a folksinger even though he got known kinda there in the early beginning in the rockabilly world. But in his heart of hearts he was a folksinger. I always said that he appreciated good songs. He wrote good songs and was always looking for good material and he liked anything old and traditional, but he was also in the more contemporary folk scene like the Paxtons, and the La Farges, and people like that."

Figure 2.11. Folksinger Tom Paxton (left) and Peter La Farge (right) backstage following their performance at Town Hall, circa 1962–1963. *Jim Marshall.*

FROM NASHVILLE to Newport to the 1964 Summer Olympics, which were held in Tokyo. William Mervin "Billy" Mills had qualified to compete in the 10,000-meter competition, an event that the United States had never won. Mills was a member of the Oglala Sioux and had grown up on the Pine Ridge Reservation in Pine Ridge, South Dakota. He had seemingly come from nowhere and therefore none of the runners gave him a second thought. After all, his time in the pre-liminaries was a full minute slower than Australia's Ron Clarke, who held the world record and was the odds-on favorite. There was also the defending champion, Pyotr Bolotnikov, of the Soviet Union, and Murray Halberg of New Zealand, who had won the 5000 meters in 1960. Billy Mills was just lucky to be there. At least that was the conventional thinking.

It seemed from the outset that Ron Clarke would win the race easily. His strategy and pacing pulled him quickly in front of all the runners. Pumping his arms and breathing steadily, Clarke left the entire field behind. Only four runners were in striking distance of him, and Billy Mills was one of them. Soon, Japan's Kokicki Tsuburaya faded, as did Ethiopia's Mamo Wolde, leaving Mills running stride for stride with Mohammed Gammoudi of Tunisia. No one could beat the world record holder at this stage of the race, as the announcers kept pointing out.

In an instant, the three runners were bunched together. Mills and Clarke were running so close that their arms kept scraping together. Gammoudi was close behind, his toes nearly butting into the dropping heels of the other two runners. Heading into the final lap, Clarke and Mills jockeyed for position. As they came upon the pack of runners they had left behind long before in the race, Clarke couldn't break free of them, and sensing that Mills had the better angle, he knew he had to do something. He pushed Mills once to free himself and then a second time. Nothing. The race was slipping away from Clarke. As Mills and Clarke battled for position, they lost track of Gammoudi, still very much in the race at just a millisecond behind them. Gammoudi seized the opportunity to bolt forward, elbowing Mills and Clarke out of his way, and taking the lead for the first time. It seemed the race was over for Mills, who appeared to fall back as Gammoudi and Clarke rounded the final curve. Realizing he had one final push left, Mills kicked his legs, brought his arms closer into his heaving chest, and sprinted for the finish line. Later he would tell Clarke that he felt a calmness descend over him, which relaxed him enough so he could dash forward. Mills's surge propelled him across the finish line and to a new Olympic record with a winning time of 28:24.4.

According to the *New York Times*, Mills was a "complete dark horse who barely sneaked onto the United States squad." Mills's victory placed him alongside Jim Thorpe as the only Native Americans to win Olympic medals. Even more, Mills was the first and only American to win the 10,000-meter run. When U.S. newspapers reported his historic triumph on October 14, 1964, many emphasized Mills's time as a former "Marine" who overcame "long odds" to win the daunting race. On the final sprint that led him to victory, he told the press, "I felt the spark and spring coming back into my legs." The fact that Mills was Native American was an afterthought. While the Sioux were rightfully proud of his unbelievable accomplishment and spread the news to other tribes around the country, many feared he would be received like other Native people before him who had achieved something significant. Ira Hayes's name came up often. Leona Gray, wife of the chairman for the Coeur d'Alenes of Idaho, summed up the response of many to Mills's victory: "After all, up here in Idaho, Sioux have to run far, fast, and often if they mean to stay alive." On the same day that Billy Mills made his historic run, Martin Luther King Jr. was making history of his own. The Nobel Prize committee announced that the civil rights leader had won the Nobel Peace Prize.

During the month in which Mills won his gold medal and King earned a Nobel Prize, Columbia finally released Johnny Cash's *Bitter Tears*. The controversy was far from over. Columbia, not at all pleased with the record, showed Cash what they thought about it when they barely promoted it. "Columbia only advertised it along with a dozen other innocuous releases," music scholar Charles Wolfe wrote. But as he had done so many times before, the *New York Times'* Robert Shelton stepped in to help. Following its release, Shelton listed the album as one of the best folk records of the year, placing it alongside the work of Woody Guthrie, Joan Baez, Bob Dylan, and Pete Seeger. The list was "designed to represent the best of the current folk revival," Wolfe explained. "Cash's was the only LP from a country artist to make the list." Robert Shelton was then put in the position to respond to critics like Gene Lee, who dismissed topical or protest folk music as "a music that rarely if ever exceeds the esthetic level of children's chants," and that is filled with "egomania and pomposity that abound in today's ersatz music." Lee argued further, "When art is chained to temporary social problems, it can only be temporary art—its value persists only as long as the problem persists." Shelton countered, "Is the problem of our treatment of the American Indian as posited in the songs of Miss Buffy Sainte-Marie, Johnny Cash or Peter La Farge temporary?"

BARRY GOLDWATER and the budding right-wing movement received a significant celebrity boost from actor Ronald Reagan when he took up the cause by championing Goldwater's candidacy. Reagan, who at the time was starring in the feature film *The Killers,* based on an Ernest Hemingway story, was later named co-chair of California Citizens for Goldwater-Miller. Musician Tex Ritter, who had joined the Goldwater campaign as well, approached his friend Johnny Cash about publicly supporting the Republican for president. Cash declined. But Reagan worked tirelessly on Goldwater's behalf to help topple the onetime GOP front-runner, New York governor Nelson Rockefeller. It was a political moment that the former head of the Screen Actors Guild seized ferociously. At the height of the bitter battle between Goldwater and Rockefeller, Reagan made it plain that Rockefeller's liberalism should be vehemently turned back. "A handful of people in the Republican party will not change the principles of my party to those of the opposition party if I have anything to say about it," Reagan avowed. His work for the Goldwater campaign elevated not only his public profile but also his growing personal political ambitions. Writing about Marlon Brando and the actor's loathing for Reagan, David Thomson presents a succinct description of the HUAC informant turned Republican leader: "Reagan was a hack to Brando . . . an actor and politician who does not bother to care . . . he steps out of one fake light into another, and seems able to call them both sunshine."

On October 27, 1964, Ronald Reagan appeared on national television in a spot sponsored by Goldwater-Miller on behalf of Barry Goldwater for president. He opened the prerecorded speech: "I have spent most of my life as a Democrat. I recently have seen fit to follow another course. I believe that the issues confronting us cross party lines. Now, one side in this campaign has been telling us that the issues of this election are the maintenance of peace and prosperity. The line has been used, 'We've never had it so good.'" He then responded to the charges of extremism and racism leveled at Goldwater by explaining, "Anytime you and I question the schemes of the do-gooders, we are denounced as being against their humanitarian goals. They say we are always 'against' things, never 'for' anything. Well, the trouble with our liberal friends is not that they are ignorant, but that they know so much that isn't so. We are for a provision that destitution should not follow unemployment by reason of old age, and to that end we have accepted Social Security as a step toward meeting the problem."

Despite Reagan's intervention and President Johnson's worsening political troubles—in Vietnam and at home—the country made what seemed like the more comfortable choice. With more than 60 percent of the popular vote, Johnson crushed Goldwater in the 1964 election. The president promised much, a Great Society, but many doubted that he could deliver. Ninety-five years after the passage of the Fifteenth Amendment, which guaranteed the right to vote, many in the country still didn't have it. The numbers in Selma, Alabama, a typical small southern town, proved the case: of 14,000 whites, 9,300 were registered; of 15,000 blacks, just 325 were registered. For this reason, Martin Luther King and civil rights activists had marched through Selma, Alabama, to demand that right. After all, when the civil rights bill was finally signed into law in July 1964, it bore little resemblance to what Johnson and civil rights leaders had originally sought, thanks to a southern filibuster that took eight months to overcome.

IT WAS time for the Seneca to receive the compensation promised by the federal government for the land that had been flooded to make way for the Kinzua Dam. Johnny Cash, Buffy Sainte-Marie, and scores of other musicians had performed at various benefit concerts, including one in Buffalo, New York, that caught the public's attention in the hope of halting the flooding of Seneca land and preventing the dam. These same musicians were now trying to build public support in an effort to hold the government accountable for the promised compensation. "Johnny Cash's *Bitter Tears* album and his efforts on behalf of the Seneca and the American Indian were held in high regard,"

Rovena Abrams of the Seneca Nation says. "He performed at benefits and did his best to shed light on our situation." Scholar and activist Larry Hauptman adds, "Because he could have an effect on molding public opinion, I think Cash did this work on behalf of Native issues because he rejected the individual and focused on the community. He was all about the community." Native activist Dennis Banks adds, "Cash's music was seen as very, very positive and convinced us that we were on target. We need support from the music and art circles because there are not that many Native people left in this country to create some kind of political clout. We don't have that huge voting block that could effect political change. A lot of people run roughshod on Native American issues in Congress because they can get away with it, just like they did with the Seneca and Tuscarora. Thanks to Cash, now we knew that a lot more people were actively involved in raising the consciousness of America on behalf of Native people. He did *Bitter Tears* in such a clever way that people were drawn into it without noticing that they were raising their shackles with us." Grateful for and proud of Cash's efforts on their behalf, the Seneca named him "Ha-Gao-Ta," meaning Story Teller.

However, before the Seneca could get their judgment bill honored, the Senate presented a final demand: termination. "Just another betrayal in the long line of betrayals," Larry Hauptman says. In section 18 of the agreement, the Senate had slipped in a termination rider that required the Seneca to develop a plan for termination within three years. If they did not comply, they would not receive the agreed upon compensation. Having stripped them of their land, the Senate seemed intent on leaving the Seneca with nothing. "The Senate was determined to punish the tribe for having the temerity to ask for compensation for land which the United States had illegally taken," Clyde Warrior wrote.

Although Native people, Blacks, and other excluded groups were finding the path to justice strewn with obstacles in the United States, their cause appeared to be finding sympathetic support on the international front, particularly after Martin Luther King Jr. was awarded the Nobel Peace Prize. When King traveled to Oslo to accept the prize, his speech surprised many in the United States. His stance was more forceful than ever before. With the world listening, he sent a clear message to America's political leaders that patience was running out: "What the main sections of the civil rights movement in the United States are saying is that the demand for dignity, equality, jobs, and citizenship will not be abandoned or diluted or postponed," King declared. "If that means resistance and conflict, we shall not flinch. We shall not be cowed." The day after King's speech, Sam Cooke was murdered in a California motel. His own protest song of hope, "A Change Is Gonna Come," was released a few weeks later. It quickly became an anthem for the black communities throughout the country, breaking into the *Billboard* top ten by year's end.

On September 24, 1964, Moe Asch sent a memo to Columbia Record's Edith Sommers requesting permission to reissue La Farge's performance of "Ira Hayes." Asch explained, "It is a necessary document in the fight of the American Indian for their rights in the sun in our country." With the year coming to a close, Johnny Cash's version of "Ira Hayes" had landed on the *Billboard* charts. "We had worked so hard to get that song out there for people to hear," Johnny Western says. "When it hit the charts, it was one of the proudest days of my life." Western and Cash had a right to be proud. Together they had mailed out over a thousand records to DJs and record stations around the country. Stuffed inside was Cash's heartfelt but scathing indictment of the record industry's act of censorship. When Western joined Cash for a concert in Des Moines, he couldn't wait to share the news of the success of "Ira Hayes." When he saw Cash backstage he said, "We did it, we got that baby out there." Visibly moved, Cash took the Apache tear from around his neck and hung it around Western's neck. Western thought to himself, "As long as I live, I'll never take this off."

Grabbing the Air for
Something to Hold On To

PRESIDENT JOHNSON WAS looking forward to 1965 in the hope
that by pushing through the Civil Rights Act in 1964, he had
weathered the worst of the racial discord and countercultural backlash. He had also managed to assist Native people through the War on
Poverty Office of Economic Opportunity (OEO). For a brief moment
in the deeply scarred history between the United States and Native
people, a federal government program opened the door to a measure
of tribal sovereignty. With the OEO, a key component of Johnson's
Great Society program, Native people successfully lobbied for passage
of a law that granted them funds directly rather than through state or
federal agencies. "The great society programs were the first major instance in which tribal governments had money and were not beholden
to the Bureau of Indian Affairs," Philip A. Deloria explained. "This
created an enormous change in the balance of power on reservations
and in Washington . . . These things altered the nature of the BIA and
the relationship between tribes and the federal government. They
changed the face of Indian affairs in a way that will never completely
be reversed."

With a renewed sense of purpose and stronger resolve, Johnson
used the State of the Union address on January 4, 1965, to officially
unveil the Great Society program, which he felt was the most ambitious

social program since the New Deal and which he believed would increase the public's trust in his administration and cement his legacy. "We worked for two centuries to climb this peak of prosperity," Johnson told the country, "but we are only at the beginning of the road to the Great Society. Ahead now is a summit where freedom from the wants of the body can help fulfill the needs of the spirit. We built this Nation to serve its people. We want to grow and build and create, but we want progress to be the servant and not the master of man. We do not intend to live in the midst of abundance, isolated from neighbors and nature, confined by blighted cities and bleak suburbs, stunted by a poverty of learning and an emptiness of leisure. The Great Society asks not how much, but how good; not only how to create wealth but how to use it; not only how fast we are going, but where we are headed."

But Johnson did little to address the criticism leveled at his justice department for its continued inability to act swiftly in protecting civil rights activists from harm, particularly in the South. Following a violent clash set off by two hundred Alabama state troopers when they attacked some six hundred civil rights protestors in Selma on March 7, Johnson could no longer drag his feet. The clash became known as "Bloody Sunday" and pushed civil rights leaders like Martin Luther King Jr. to intensify their efforts while increasing the pressure on the Johnson administration to use everything in their power to protect the activists. Clearly, Johnson's continuation of Kennedy's approach to "protection"—filing lawsuits—was not working.

"After the passage of the Civil Rights Act and with the defeat of Barry Goldwater, there was widespread expectation that barriers would disintegrate with swift inevitability," King wrote in his annual article for *The Nation*. "This easy optimism could not survive the first test. In the hardcore states of the South, while some few were disposed to accommodate, the walls remained erect and reinforced. Those who expected a cheap victory in a climate of complacency were shocked into reality by Selma and Marion, Alabama. In Selma, the position was implacable resistance. At one point, ten times as many Negroes were in jail as were on the registration rolls." Something needed to be done or hundreds of similar scenes would erupt throughout the South. The hope with which Johnson began the year was draining away, in large part because of his decision to send the first set of combat troops to South Vietnam the day after Bloody Sunday.

Although Johnson managed to push through the Voting Rights Act in 1965—expanding and strengthening the Fifteenth Amendment— and signed an Indian jobs bill authorizing $15 million a year to "train Indians in institutions, on the job and in apprenticeship programs," little real progress had been made in dealing with issues of poverty, healthcare, and education for Native people. Treaty rights were still wantonly disregarded and reservation life was still dismal. Activist groups like the National Congress of American Indians and the Tribal Land Rights Association had scored a victory against discrimination by forcing Calvert Distillers Company to remove racist whisky ads (the ads depicted a war bonneted Sioux brave raising a glass of whisky over the tagline: "If the Sioux had soft whisky, they would have never called it firewater. Why do you think they were yelping all time?"), but real systematic change on issues affecting the Native people's day-to-day reality had yet to materialize.

In many ways, Washington State was the battleground for Native people throughout 1965 as Senator "Scoop" Jackson continued his push to terminate the Coleville Reservation. Vine Deloria Jr., now serving as the executive director of the National Congress of American Indians, appeared before the Senate Indian Affairs subcommittee to challenge the government. Deloria argued that the "educational level of the Colevilles was so low that they did not have the perspective to decide between continued federal supervision and the proposed sale of their $100 million forest to the government." Supporting Deloria's testimony were Eagle Sellastee, chairman of the Yakima Tribal Council, and Oswald C. George, vice chairman of the Coeur d'Alene Tribal Council, both of whom agreed that the government's efforts were a shameless land grab. Lucy Covington, granddaughter of the Colevilles' Chief Moses, was among the most vocal leaders of the resistance to termination. She took her case directly to the public, traveling around the country and to the nation's capital to prevent Senator Jackson from taking the reservation. Referring to the symbol of tribal membership, Covington often said, "Termination is like giving your eagle feather away."

JOHNSON WAS not the only one to start 1965 on shaky ground. Peter La Farge and Johnny Cash were on parallel courses toward self-destruction. The musicians met at a moment in time when they were both retreating into themselves and away from everyone around them. La Farge's troubled mind burned white hot, lit first by a broken childhood and stoked further by the tragic naval accident that scarred him both physically and mentally. His unstable sense of himself only deepened as he devoted his energies to speaking out on behalf of Native people. La Farge remained haunted by the naval explosion and the screams of his burning shipmates, and he seemed condemned to repeatedly drag his demons up a steep mountain only to tumble to the bottom again. His was a lifetime punctuated by short bursts of clarity and peace set against an eternity of storms. When Albert Camus wrote, "The struggle itself towards the heights is enough to fill a man's heart," his words seemed to describe the life of Peter La Farge.

As people and artists, Cash and La Farge embraced this vision of existence and responded, as Camus contends in his essay, not by shrinking away from the absurdly impossible but by marching headlong into the struggle, supported only by a dream that can and must be made real. Despite the sense of purpose, the love of music, and the hope for something better that each musician possessed, they both fell victim to their frailties as they dangled on the edge of sanity and survival. When Cash broke big in 1957, he started swallowing pills to help him move from show to show, town to town. To meet the increasing pressures from a red hot career, including a tour schedule with well over two hundred shows a year and a record company that didn't want the hits to stop coming, Cash followed the path of countless other artists and befriended billy whizz (amphetamines) to help him cope. By the time he recorded *Bitter Tears*, he was taking nearly one hundred pills a day. The amphetamines gave him the burst he needed, allowing him to soar, and tranquilizers made him feel soft and safe, returning his feet to the ground. Compared to La Farge, who was forever climbing and falling from peaks, Cash's struggle suggests a rocket flight straight into the blinding sun; he never stopped trying to soar as high as he could in pursuit of what he believed, even if it meant being engulfed by the intensity of the heat.

For La Farge, the zeitgeist of the folk revival had seemingly passed him by as he failed to tap into it as Dylan had. If there was a moment for La Farge, it was his collaboration with Cash. He tried to build on that momentum, hoping to land on a path paved with gold; instead, he found himself on the road leading to New York's Bellevue Hospital for psychiatric care. It was becoming harder and harder to keep himself straight. Over the past few years, La Farge's fragile mental state—further degraded by drugs and alcohol—had led to frequent stays in various mental institutions. As La Farge battled mental illness, he began reaching out to his sister Povy in Santa Fe, New Mexico. "During this period, Pete went to Bellevue Hospital a couple times," Povy says. "My mother went to New York from Colorado to take care of him for one bad stretch. He had a lot of mental problems."

La Farge was not helped any when he met singer Inger Neilson, who recorded an album of Danish folksongs for Folkways but more significantly suffered from mental illness herself. In La Farge's personal notes, he mentions sending a care package to Inger when she was in Tower 10 of the mental ward at New York's Roosevelt Hospital. In 1965, La Farge's half brother came to stay with him in New York on his way to visit other relatives. John Pen La Farge, only thirteen years old at the time, remembers finding his older brother "charming and gregarious" and "living with a beautiful blonde woman." Peter was sharing a garden apartment with Inger near the United Nations, and John Pen recalls that his brother "affected cowboy boots, a blue velveteen shirt, and a cape . . . he stood out as much as he possibly could from the ordinary rung of mankind. Also what made quite an impression on me was that he had a stack of *Playboys*. When you're thirteen, that is quite impressive. I found it so impressive that Pete said he would get me a subscription for my birthday."

Until John Pen's visit, the two brothers had not had a chance to get to know each other. Peter's thorny relationship with his father meant that they only met when Peter managed to visit Santa Fe. "They had a difficult relationship," John Pen says of his father and Peter. "The relationship was quite distant and difficult, never mind whatever mental problems Pete had. He was rebellious. I think he felt lost and a need to measure up to my father's legacy." La Farge's friend Seymour Krim wrote, "When Pete in his confused late teens [and after] sought him [Oliver] out in Santa Fe, there was a competition and spite between them, with the degraded Indians as the prize, because the son insisted on getting deliberately close . . . Oliver La Farge kicked his son out of his house and told him to keep away." Indeed, Peter had tried his best to measure up to his father by trying to build on Oliver's work on behalf of Native people. "Pete found my father's interest in Indian affairs to be an opportunity. Also because he carried the name, he found an opportunity that he could exploit," John Pen explains. "I think he had a real feeling for it in as much that the folk revival was cause oriented. The Indian cause was not taken up before the way Pete had in the folk scene. Pete did have a real feeling for it."

Still, John Pen noticed that his brother was "quite delicate mentally," adding, "As charming as he was—and he was quite charming and quite bright—he was definitely a square peg in a round hole." Peter's "delicate" state of mind could not have prepared him for the news that Inger was expecting a child by year's end. "I was pretty worried about Inger taking care of the baby and what was going to happen," Povy says.

La Farge felt stuck in two worlds: he wanted to keep trying his hand at music, refining his guitar playing and expanding his songwriting, but he also felt the pull to move back to the Southwest. Even with a child on the way, he felt alone and without any support to help him through. He needed his family, and Povy and her husband, John, were happy to encourage him to return to New Mexico. They would provide that missing sense of family that seemed to elude La Farge for most of his life. "Pete was calling me often," Povy recalls. "He thought I did a much better thing with my life and thought he would like to come out to Santa Fe. Start fresh." Oscar Brand adds, "There were a lot of guys that would be with him because they were into 'the stuff' [drugs]. But when it was over they would leave him out in the street. They had some place to go and he didn't." Being on the outside looking in must have been too much for La Farge to handle. "He was as emotionally frail as a sheet of the thinnest glass," is how Seymour Krim described La Farge's mental state at the time. "You could imagine [his mind] popping under sudden heat."

In spite of everything, La Farge kept getting up on stage every chance he could, and his performances had an added sense of urgency. As the country focused its attention on the standoff between the state and civil rights activists in Selma, Alabama, La Farge continued to shine a spotlight on justice for Native people while offering continued support for other social issues. He had become a regular performer at various benefits organized by *Broadside* including a hootenanny for the United Mine Workers in 1965. On February 25, 1965, he agreed to perform at a benefit at the Village Gate for the Downtown Community School Scholarship Fund. The impressive slate of performers included the jazz great Charles Mingus, the South African singer and civil rights activist Miriam Makeba, actress Estelle Parsons, and folk musician John Cohen of the New Lost City Ramblers. For the performance, La Farge teamed up with his friend and fellow folksinger Len Chandler. Chandler's impact on the folk scene included Bob Dylan's use of one of Chandler's tunes for his protest ballad "The Death of Emmett Till."

The next night at Town Hall in New York, La Farge performed at a second benefit for the Oliver La Farge American Indian Fund. The benefit show marked the third time in two years that La Farge headlined a Town Hall performance. "The program was a testament to Mr. La Farge's inexorable belief in justice for the American Indian and to

Figure 2.12. From left, Gil Turner, Thom Parrott, Pete Seeger, unknown, unknown, unknown, Eric Andersen, and Peter La Farge (far right) performing at a 1965 Hootenanny for *Broadside* magazine in New York City, one of La Farge's final performances. *Photo by Diana Davies, courtesy of the Ralph Rinzler Folklife Archives and Collections, Smithsonian Institution.*

his equally inexorable faith in his own creative abilities," the *New York Times* reported. Over three hundred people turned out for the event, witnessing the progress La Farge had made as both a musician and an entertainer. Music critic Robert Shelton, who had followed La Farge from the very beginning of his career, wrote, "Mr. La Farge is growing as a musician. His songs, which he produces prolifically, attack the Indian situation from every angle in moods of humor, ridicule, narrative, or educational pleas." At the show, La Farge debuted "Hey, Mr. President, We're Going to Charge You Rent," a humorous spin on the title song from The Almanac Singers' 1942 record, *Dear Mr. President.* La Farge's tune offers a tongue-in-cheek alternative to the government's seizure of Native land: "Hey, Mr. President, we're going to charge you rent / For every treaty broken and every treaty bent / We are making reservations that will be just for whites / We're going to be the tourists; we'll come to see you dance."

THREE YEARS after his first appearance at Carnegie Hall in 1962, Johnny Cash headed back to New York to perform once again at the great recital hall. During the intervening years, he had traveled thousands of miles, crisscrossing the country and parts of the world on his synchronized ascension to superstardom and descent into addiction. Yet on that summer night in 1965 the music star came full circle, taking the stage not in a Dexedrine delirium as he had in 1962, but seizing the moment to write a new chapter with a set of performances that left the disastrous debut a distant memory. "We were scheduled to perform at the New York Folk Festival in June," Grant says. "We were all hoping to not repeat what happened the first time at Carnegie Hall." This time there would be no collapse, no letdown. The four-day festival included over sixty performers participating in a series of nine concerts and two seminars from Thursday, June 17, through Sunday, June 20. The program that opened the festival was called "The Evolution of Funk"— arranged by gregarious folksong revival stalwart Dave von Ronk and narrated by Sam Charters. Performers included Son House, Muddy Waters, Chuck Berry, and Mance Lipscomb.

The New York Folk Festival boasted a lineup of performers who were the luminaries, legends, and virtuosos of the moment. "It was a pretty special and important few days for music," Archie Green explains. "Johnny Cash was right in the middle of it all. Peter La Farge's performance was memorable. This is the only time I met Peter, at this beautiful venue and big concert with a lot of big stars." Green, a prominent folklorist and professor at the University of Chicago, shared narrating duties for the festival along with disc jockey Hugh Cherry, who had penned the liner notes for *Bitter Tears* one year earlier. Johnny Western recalls, "This was a great show and good way to put that first Carnegie Hall show behind us. Cash just knocked it out of the park."

In all, Cash performed four shows and participated in the "Contemporary Singer Composers" program on Friday, June 18, with Buffy Sainte-Marie, Billy Edd Wheeler, Mississippi John Hurt, and Chuck Berry; and the "Grassroots to Bluegrass to Nashville" program with the New Lost City Ramblers, Statler Brothers, Doc Watson, and the

Blue Sky Boys. June Carter joined Cash for all of his performances. Cash returned on Saturday, June 19, for the second part of the Contemporary Singer Composers program, which was narrated by Jerry White. He found himself among folksingers like Phil Ochs and Patrick Sky and musicians he admired including The Staple Singers, who had recently released "March Up Freedom's Highway," a freedom song in support of the Selma march, and Muddy Waters, the father of Chicago Blues. The final musician in the program was Peter La Farge, and Cash was thrilled to see him again. The two shared a bond strengthened by the *Bitter Tears* alliance and further solidified by the ensuing fight against the record's censoring.

Following the fallout over *Bitter Tears* that began 1964 and continued into 1965, La Farge praised Cash in the May 1965 issue of *Sing Out!* for his courage to fight back against attempts to keep "Ira Hayes" and *Bitter Tears* off U.S. airwaves. Written in an affecting and cutting tone, La Farge described why Cash was drawn to the Native cause and folk music. La Farge writes, "Driven, complicated, and expert, Johnny Cash is a great American voice. He's hated himself for the success he earned. He hasn't sung just trash, witness 'Five Feet High and Rising,' his flood song, or the songs he's sung, 'Folsom Prison Blues' and, as a matter of fact, 'I Walk the Line.' Johnny wanted more than the hillbilly jangle; he was hungry for the depth and truth heard only in the folk field (until Johnny came along, anyway). The secret is simple, Johnny has the heart of a folksinger in the purest sense, and he has a very lovely soul. He is capable of anything he puts his soul and his Band-Aid heart to, and he is capable of being a folksinger in the very essence of folk truth. He would love to be out from the heavy legend that binds him to hillbilly heaven." La Farge points out that when Cash set out to make a folk record, he didn't choose "a catchy love song" but "a protest song about some drunken Indian." La Farge declares his love for Cash as a "blood brother" who "hates the lies of publicity and selfish grabbing of the crowd. Look at him everyone, he's different, Johnny Cash cares."

Cash and La Farge found the best parts of themselves performing at the New York Folk Festival. Cash stole the spotlight in each of the concert series he participated in. He had come back to Carnegie Hall and found redemption. "Johnny Cash brought high excitement to each of his performances," wrote Robert Shelton of the *New York Times*. "The lean Arkansas songwriter is one of the most arresting performers in folk and country music. Mr. Cash's stage manner, one of constant movement, is reminiscent of a graceful matador in the ring and keeps his performances crackling with visual interest." When La Farge's turn came on the night of Saturday, June 19, he too delivered. "I cannot even begin to tell you how well received Peter La Farge was on that show," Green says. "He performed 'Ballad of Ira Hayes' and it just brought the house down. They gave him such an ovation that it made it impossible for him to leave the stage. Of course, I had to make him leave the stage; we had a schedule we had to keep, but his performance and the crowd's reaction was unforgettable." On June 23, *Variety* singled out La Farge's performance at the festival for his "spirited, bitter 'Ballad of Ira Hayes.'" Brand adds, "He did well as a singer. He had a fine feeling, a reality about his songs, and made something of the music." The entertainment sheet went on to describe Cash as "a winsome, forthright performer" and the "Sinatra of the swampland." "Every musician had ten or fifteen minutes," Green says. "It was obvious to me that Peter was wildly popular with a big following in New York. When he played 'Ira Hayes,' which I think was his best song, it resonated. It was ironic. Here was this hero of Iwo Jima come back to a desert country, drowned in this ditch with very little water. Whether it actually happened as the song portrayed is questionable, but he [com]posed a good song probably [based] on newspaper accounts."

Both men desperately needed what the New York Folk Festival offered them. Earlier in the month Cash had been arrested after a camper he was using caught fire and caused the devastation of five hundred acres of California's Los Padres National Forest. The fire also killed forty-nine of the refuge's fifty-three endangered condors. Whether or not the tragedy was due to Cash's carelessness, as he explained to the judge presiding over the case, "I didn't do it, my truck did, and it's dead, so you can't question it." At the time he took the stage at Carnegie Hall, the federal government was suing him for $125,172 in damages caused by the fire.

CASH WAS not going to attend the next Newport Folk Festival, but many of the usual performers were scheduled to perform: Dylan, Baez, Seeger, Josh White, Mark Spoelstra, Odetta, Oscar Brand, and the New Lost City Ramblers. The festival's promoter, George Wein, was confident that the 1965 event was going to be the biggest, most successful one yet. "We were excited because 1964 had gone so well," Wein explains. "In my opinion, what happened on the Newport stage reflected and in no small affected the rest of the world." Wein's eagerness for the upcoming '65 festival was indeed in tune with the times, as folk music was at its peak in terms of popularity. The turnout—more than 76,000 people attended the festival—proved the iconic promoter right. Each of the prior festivals had broken the previous year's attendance record and collectively they had left the Newport Folk Foundation with a $200,000 surplus. Still, when Wein reported that the "unity of the Newport Folk Festival board was stronger than ever," Robert Shelton countered by reporting that he saw "growing rips in the canvas that covers the three-ring circus of American folk music." At his Sunday night performance, the largest rip was unexpectedly and unintentionally made by Bob Dylan.

In the two years since the 1963 festival, Dylan had achieved superstardom. He was twenty-five years old, and yet many people put the weight of the world's problems on his slight shoulders and asked him to lead them to salvation. Dylan just wanted to play music. In debates over Dylan's success, it was as if people split Greenwich Village's Bleecker Street down the middle with each taking a side for or against him: Stand on the north side of the street if you think Dylan deserves his success. Move to the south side of the street if you believe that Dylan has committed heresy against the sanctity and purity of the folk movement by selling out. "Bob Dylan seems unable to sneeze without causing controversy," Robert Shelton wrote.

When he took the Newport stage looking every bit like an eighteenth-century trouvère, he was followed by guitarist Mike Bloomfield, drummer Sam Lay, and bassist Jerome Arnold of the Paul Butterfield Blues Band, along with Dylan secession musician Al Kooper and piano player Barry Goldberg. He was slotted between two traditional folk acts, Cousin Emmy and the Sea Island Singers. Dylan walked on stage without the benefit of a sound check. As the crowd sat quiet, anxiously awaiting their protest poet-in-residence, Dylan and his backing band nervously tuned their instruments. Even before he strummed the first chord of the tune, however, controversy was already roiling around him.

In November 1964's *Sing Out!* Irwin Silber wrote an "Open Letter to Bob Dylan." With a mix of fatherly lecturing and holier-than-thou scorn, Silber expressed distress that Dylan was "in a different kind of bag now," traveling with an entourage that "will never challenge you to face everyone's reality." Silber criticized Dylan's move away from topical songs: "Well, okay, call it anything you want. But any songwriter who tries to deal honestly with reality in this world is bound to write 'protest songs.' How can he help himself?" For Dylan, the folk revival scene had become the establishment; a pop culture fad listened to by mainstream America on one side and guarded by pedantic journalists, dogmatic folk musicians, and high and mighty folk followers on the other. Silber's reaction goes a long way in explaining why the music star must have felt alienated by the gatekeepers of the folk scene: "You seem to be relating to a handful of cronies behind the scenes now rather than to the rest of us . . . you're a different Bob Dylan from the one we knew. The old one never wasted our precious time."

Only a few years earlier, Cash had come to Dylan's defense when the executives at Columbia labeled Dylan "Hammond's folly." Now he was moved to action by a letter Dylan published in an early 1964 edition of *Broadside,* in which the young folksinger spoke with a vulnerable, honest voice about the struggle not to lose himself while trying to maintain creative freedom in the face of exceedingly unrealistic fan expectations. Cash wrote a letter to *Broadside* in support of

Dylan's plea to be left alone and it was published in May, a few months before the two met at 1964's Newport Folk Festival. He was touched by Dylan's poetic letter: "Away away be gone all you demons / An' just let me be / human me / ruthless me / wild me / gentle me / all kinds of me." Cash responded in kind, adding his own playful, even audacious tone: "I got hung, but I didn't choke / Bob Dylan slung his rope / I sat down and listened quick . . . Gravy from that brain is thick . . . / Don't bad mouth him till you hear him / Let him start by continuing / He's almost brand new / SHUT UP! . . . AND LET HIM SING!" Cash's letter uplifted Dylan. "This was before I even met him," Dylan said later. "The letter meant the world to me. I've kept the magazine to this day."

Tired, frustrated, and bored with expectations of him as a "voice for the people" playing "finger-pointing songs," Dylan was eager to break free, move in another direction, and stretch creatively. The success that people were condemning him for had made Dylan more introspective and a bit jaded but also enormously determined. Cash could relate to everything Dylan was going through. He had left Sun Records when they blocked his efforts to move in different musical directions, had felt the scorn of those who disliked his concept albums or forays into rock, and was still battling his current label to record at a prison. With the *Bitter Tears* controversy still fresh, Cash knew all too well the pitfalls of success and the towering expectations of fans. In one moment, people look to you as a new musical messiah, and in the next, they condemn you as a false prophet. Cash was keenly aware of this stark reality, and the roots of his empathy for Dylan are evident in his defiant words to those who criticized him: "I haven't changed my style of music. I do the only thing I know how to do, the kind of music I've always done." Dylan should be afforded the right to do the same, Cash publicly argued.

As Dylan and his makeshift band began playing "Maggie's Farm," the festival audience responded, some with hostility, others with confusion, and very few with polite applause. After their third song, Dylan told the band to stop and they left the stage. The crowd had turned on Dylan, leaving the young musician confused and shaken. Perhaps unintentionally, it seemed that Dylan was serving notice that no matter what his faithful followers wanted or the custodians of the folk flame demanded, he was going his own way. Dylan's choice to start the electric set with "Maggie's Farm" was itself a powerful cry for independence as the song's metaphorical lyrics summed up the historical moment: "No, I ain't gonna work on Maggie's farm no more / Well, I try my best / To be just like I am / But everybody wants you / To be just like them / They sing while you slave and I just get bored." Johnny Cash could relate to every word of the song while sensing how low Dylan must have felt scuttling off the stage after failing to meet the unreasonable expectations of the crowd.

Robert Shelton later compared the Newport crowd and backstage reaction to Dylan's plugged-in performance to the May 29, 1913, premiere of Stravinsky's "The Rite of Spring" at the Théâtre des Champs-Elysées. On that night in Paris, many in the crowd nearly rioted, shouting down the composer's work as "a blasphemous attempt to destroy music as an art." Perhaps, as Dylan stood backstage feeling confused and shaken, he recalled Cash's letter to summon his courage as people came at him from every direction demanding to know "why" and pleading for him "to get back out there before a riot breaks out."

Standing backstage, Dylan was fed stories that Pete Seeger had tried to cut the power with an ax (Seeger denies this). "I was standing right there on stage when Dylan went on," Wein says. "There were axes around because prisoners from Texas were singing folksongs while they chopped wood. I know Pete went out to a car because he couldn't stand the noise. Somebody said, 'You better go see Pete. He's very upset.' Pete told me, 'You got to do something about that sound.' I said, 'Pete, it's too late, man, it's on there now.' The crowd was booing. Many more were booing than cheering. Dylan didn't want to go back, but I said, 'You have to go back because there will be a riot.' He went back out and sang, 'It's All Over Now Baby Blue.'"

Billboard, which had refused to review Cash's *Bitter Tears,* labeled Dylan's performance "folk rock" and "nose thumbing sounds like

you're looking down on what is fantastic, great music." A less outraged take was offered by Jim Rooney in *Sing Out!*:

> It was disturbing to the Old Guard. Bob is no longer a neo–Woody
> Guthrie. . . . The highway he travels now is unfamiliar to those
> who bummed around . . . during the Depression. He travels by
> plane . . . the mountains and valleys he knows are those of the
> mind—a mind extremely aware of the violence of the inner and
> outer world. The people so loved by Pete Seeger are "the mob" so
> hated by Dylan. . . . They seemed to understand that night for the
> first time what Dylan has been trying to say for over a year—that
> he is not theirs or anyone else's—and they didn't like what they
> heard and booed. . . . Can there be no songs as violent as the age?
> Must a folksong be of mountains, valleys, and love between my
> brother and my sister all over this land? Do we allow for despair
> only in the blues? . . . The only one in the entire festival who ques-
> tioned our position was Bob Dylan. Maybe he didn't put it in the
> best way. Maybe he was rude. But he shook us. And that is why we
> have poets and artists.

Cash's pill addiction had reached new levels by 1964 and it was on
full display during the *Bitter Tears* recording session; he was skin and
bones, erratic, and as unpredictable as a loose wire carrying one thousand volts of electricity. "He was extremely committed to *Bitter Tears*,"
Marshall Grant says. "And somehow in the midst of his own down-
ward spiral, he summoned the energy and spirit to do this album."

The making of *Bitter Tears* introduced a different Johnny Cash
from the one the record industry, his fans, and everyone else who knew
him had come to expect. It started with the album's cover. "You can
see it all in that cover," Grant says. "Look it at closely. Look at his
face, skin, bones, his elbow; that's what we were dealing with." The
image of Cash is at once striking and startling. Taken from the shoulders up, the photograph shows Cash's gaunt, leathery face framed by
close-cropped hair ringed by a red headband. His sunken eyes stare

out through the cover, past the viewer, gazing back and forth in time. The album's stark cover image warned potential listeners that Cash's mind and heart were heavy with serious questions of human rights, equality, and justice for Native people while he was physically harming himself in pursuit of his beliefs. As he later explained, "These were things I was thinking about. But that ad in *Billboard*? It took about 100 milligrams of amphetamines to do that."

Even as Cash was dealing with the *Bitter Tears* controversy, he closed out 1964 by putting the finishing touches on his twentieth record, *Orange Blossom Special*. The album is among the finest recordings of Cash's career to that point and reveals that the musician had no intention of stifling his musical curiosity. It includes covers of country crooner Lefty Frizzell's 1959 hit song "Long Black Veil" and The Carter Family's classic "Wildwood Flower." Yet the record's main appeal stems from Cash's vision to include three Bob Dylan songs: "It Ain't Me, Babe," recorded with June Carter; "Mama, You've Been on My Mind"; and "Don't Think Twice, It's All Right." The lyrics of this last song—"Ain't no use in turnin' on your light, babe / I'm on the dark side of the road"—seemed to capture Cash's state of mind at the time. He broke into the top 5 of the *Billboard* country charts with "It Ain't Me, Babe" in 1964. The following year, the record hit number 3 on the country charts and broke into the top 50 on *Billboard*'s pop charts. In promoting the record's release, *Sing Out!* displayed a Columbia advertisement that described Cash as one of America's leading contemporary folksingers: "There are few who sing more eloquently than Johnny Cash," and "Few have his ability to share a vivid emotion."

Cash followed the success of *Orange Blossom Special* with another Americana concept album, *Johnny Cash Sings the Ballads of the True West*. A double album with different traditional ballads of the American West, the tracks included "Streets of Laredo," "I Ride an Old Paint," and "Bury Me Not on the Lone Prairie." In addition, Cash presented new songs from Carl Perkins's "The Ballad of Boot Hill," Shel Silverstein's "Twenty-Five Minutes to Go," and the album's single, "Mr. Garfield," Ramblin' Jack Elliott's tale of America's grief following the assassination of President James Garfield. Cash also recorded a cover of Peter La Farge's tune called "Stampede." The song's comic and intrepid spirit must have resonated with Cash: "Be proud that you're an Indian / and give the ladies hell . . . Now some admire headstones / but I think he'd like this best / He ain't fancy in his livin' / He ain't fancy in his rest."

Cash found the strength to record his twentieth album, but the rest of his life was severely out of tune. His wife, Vivian, had had enough and asked him to leave her and the couple's four daughters. He found an apartment on the outskirts of Nashville that was less a home than a pharmacy, a drug gallery where he stashed bags of painkillers, amphetamines, and barbiturates. Cash decided to invite a young musician named Waylon Jennings to stay with him at the Fontaine Bleu apartments. The *New York Times* described Jennings as a "tall, scrawny, beat-up Texan who got his start as Buddy Holly's bass player and has been putting a hard edge of rhythm into country music, living on the mean side of life and singing about it." "I was on dope," Jennings recalled. "John and I were big dummies. We were going through a time when we felt uncommonly sorry for ourselves in the process of trying to get rid of one wife while trying to hang on to another woman, and neither one of them understood us." Individually, the two men were a mess; as a pair, they were a calamity. "There was a carpenter who we kept working a lot," Jennings said. "Putting hinges back on our door because we were always locking each other out. Kicking the door in."

Cash's temper was getting the worst of him, and people started to wonder if he was going to make it through the year. The Carter Family witnessed Cash's rapid physical decline firsthand. "They'd seen what happened to Hank Williams and I don't think they wanted it to happen to me," Cash explained. They told him he could stay at their house anytime, and he readily accepted. Cash hoped to curry favor with June's father, Eck "Pop" Carter, as he wished to build a relationship with the legendary musician's daughter June. Mother Maybelle had seen Cash kick in doors and pry open windows trying to get into her house because he often lost his key. "He always fixed everything he tore up," Mother Maybelle later said. "You know when he'd come to the house, he'd come starved. I'd always see he got something to eat, and if his clothes needed washing, I'd see to that, because John did a lot for me. We had to stick by him. His people weren't here. He was alone." Cash was fortunate and he knew it. "I was always sick and Maybelle was always trying to take care of me. She saw me at my very worst and never pointed it out to me except to say loving things like, 'I hope you'll take care of yourself because we really need you.'"

"We had a show at the Grand Ole Opry set for the fall of 1965," Marshall Grant recalls. "John was losing his family, living in a bad state and we were seeing him messed up on those damn pills more often than not." When the Opry show finally rolled around and John showed up, Grant knew the night was going to go badly. "You could see it just like that Carnegie Hall show," Grant says. "He was gone. Just out of it." Something in Cash just snapped, and before Grant looked up, he began smashing all the stage lights with his microphone stand. "The band kicked off a song, and I tried to take the microphone off the stand," Cash later explained. "In my nervous frenzy, I couldn't get it off. That was enough to make me explode in a fit of anger. I took the mike stand, threw it down, then dragged it along the edge of the stage. There were fifty-two lights, and I wanted to break all fifty-two, which I did." Incensed, the Opry manager went looking for Cash after he had disappeared backstage. "You don't have to come back anymore. We can't use you," the manager told Grant. Cash was no longer welcome at the venue that had played a key role in establishing his myth and legend when he debuted there in 1957, dressed for the first time entirely in black. It was during a performance at the Opry's Ryman Auditorium earlier in 1965 that Cash had impressed a young former Rhodes Scholar named Kris Kristofferson who had gone on to join the army. Kristofferson liked *Bitter Tears* and some of Cash's other folk forays. "I went to Nashville, and I shook hands with Johnny Cash backstage at the Opry when I was on leave in June of 1965," he said. "He was electrifying. It was one of the big reasons I decided I was going to get out of the army and come back. I loved everything about his voice, the strength of it, the dark power of it. As much as that was what he was singing. When Cash sang 'Big River,' it was the most powerful folk music going on at the time." Cash had recorded the tune the same day he recorded "Ira Hayes."

Cash continued pouring pills down his throat like water. Soon there were car accidents, missed performances, and cancelled shows, until one day in October when the situation turned even more serious. Returning from a trip to Juarez, Mexico, Cash was stopped and searched by U.S. Customs agents at the El Paso International Airport on suspicion of smuggling heroin. Stuffed inside his guitar case were hundreds of pills and tranquilizers. Placed in the county jail for the night, Cash pled guilty to a misdemeanor count, paid a $1,000 fine, and received a thirty-day suspended sentence. His arrest made national news when photographers snapped photos of a visibly shaken Cash leaving the courthouse with his wife. When the photos of Cash and Vivian hit the newsstands, some mistook Vivian—who was of Italian descent—for a light-skinned black woman. In response, the National States Rights Party in Birmingham, Alabama, launched a campaign to boycott Cash's shows and records, writing in their publication, *Thunderbolt*: "Money from the sale of [Cash's] records goes to scum like Johnny Cash to keep them supplied with dope and Negro women."

As CASH dealt with the fallout from his arrest, Peter La Farge lingered in New York, trying to get well and preparing himself for the birth of his child and the possibility of making a clean break by moving to the Southwest. He also found some hope in addressing his mental illness. Since the start of the decade, there had been a number of breakthroughs in the treatment of mental illness, some of them effective and some still in experimental stages. Eager to get well, La Farge agreed to undergo experimental treatments. "He said to me there was a number of experimental drugs for people with schizophrenia and other mental problems," Povy La Farge recalls. "One of these drugs was cobra venom. He agreed to it and started treatments." During this time, La Farge called his sister often to discuss his plans for the future. "I kept telling him he could come to stay, and he was saying he wanted to come," she says of their phone calls.

On October 27, Inger came home to the apartment she shared with La Farge on East Fiftieth Street and discovered the musician unconscious. By the time the ambulance and police arrived, La Farge was dead. News of the folksinger's death spread throughout New York City. Rumors started to circulate that La Farge had killed himself or died of a stroke, heart attack, or drug overdose. Even more were the outlandish stories that the FBI was somehow involved in his death—from ransacking his apartment to trying to place him in Bellevue in order to thwart his activities on behalf of Native people. Another wild tale had folk musician Liam Clancy finding La Farge in his apartment after he had committed suicide. None of these was true according to La Farge's sister. "I do not think he ever committed suicide," she says. "Just before he died, he was on the phone with me making plans for the future. It was all the forward planning all of it." There is plenty of evidence to support Povy's claims in La Farge's personal letters and correspondence. In a letter to Moe Asch dated March 4, 1965, La Farge sounds bright and hopeful: "Thank you very much for sending over records for the Town Hall concert. We finally got through Shelton's defenses. Things are looking up for the coming season, with a possible concert tour coming up next fall. Love to you all."

On October 29, 1965, two days after La Farge's death, the *New York Times* reported, "Peter La Farge, a folksong writer and performer who championed the American Indian, was found dead." The article indicated that, according to the police, "Several empty medicine bottles and a hypodermic syringe were near Mr. La Farge's body." It also mentioned Peter's father, from whom he "inherited his deep concern for the Indian," adding that "some of his friends thought he was part Indian, although his lineage could be traced back to Benjamin Franklin." The obit that followed in the *Times* was just a few short lines. Many of La Farge's friends and fellow musicians felt saddened by what they perceived as a callous dismissal of his life by the press and the city's authorities. "I learned of Peter's death through a nasty little one-paragraph obit in the *Times*," writer Josh Dunson explains. "I wrote a letter to the *Times* saying that this was a terrible thing to say or imply that he died of a heroin or drug overdose. It missed the whole point. It was wrong. The journalist wrote me back and said, 'We have all the evidence and that's what happened.' He missed the main point, which was that he didn't understand: Peter La Farge was not just the son of Oliver La Farge. He was a very important creative person in his own right."

When Povy La Farge traveled to New York with her family to deal with her brother's death, she discovered, as John Pen had only a few months earlier, just how popular her brother had been. "His friends started lining in the halls to pay their respects," Povy says. "There were hundreds of people. I tried to get coffee pots and other stuff for all these people. Just hundreds. And the radio station was playing his music all night. All night." After seeing La Farge's body, Povy was certain that her brother did not commit suicide. "When I saw the body, he looked so peaceful. He even had a knee up with a smile on his face and his ankle crossed over it like he was about to read something," she says. "And that's how Inger found him. I feel that in his attempt to deal with his mental illness, he took another dose of cobra venom and it hit his heart and paralyzed it. That's how he died." The family took the body back to Colorado for burial and, based on their Baha'i religious beliefs, did not request an autopsy, so the death remains shrouded in mystery. "I think he died accidentally but I can't prove it," Povy says. "People think that's naïve." Tom Paxton adds, "His death was a terrible shock. To this day, none of us know if it was accidental or intentional or a combination of the two. I don't know." Pete Seeger, who recorded his own version of "Ira Hayes" just a few weeks before La Farge died, says, "La Farge came up to my house in Beacon, New York, and built a fireplace. There's just something significant about that moment for me. I also had included his song "Coyote, My Little Brother" in my repertoire of songs. The song is profound and beautiful."

A number of La Farge's fellow musicians agree with his sister's view of his death and expressed as much in moving tributes that appeared in *Broadside* and *Sing Out!* On November 15, 1965, a smiling, handsome, guitar-strumming La Farge graced the cover of *Broadside* no. 64. Inside the magazine, Len Chandler and Gil Turner contributed eulogies. The editor's note supports the view that La Farge was indeed making plans for the future, which included writing a book about his Korean War experience and an autobiography. (In an earlier interview in *Broadside*, La Farge had lamented the war and its aftermath, calling it a "stupid war that should have never been fought in the first place." He felt it created an entire generation of disillusioned and embittered young Americans, himself included.) Chandler also wrote that La Farge "had gone back to painting, was working well at it, and had recently sold his first new painting." Gil Turner's "October Song to an Indian Summer One-Time Man" praises La Farge: "Your time of life that flows no more . . . too soon . . . so close behind that I cannot sing *of* you . . . only still *to* you."

The magazine was able to point out that before he died, La Farge had been spending countless hours on the phone talking with friends; he was full of hope and ideas for the future. Len Chandler was one of those friends. Shortly before learning of La Farge's death, Chandler had composed a poem based on his conversations with La Farge. He called it "I Would Be a Painter Most of All (for Peter La Farge)," and the poem is a moving sketch of his friend's life. "I think best upside out and inside down," Chandler writes. "The day I started going blind / I know it to be / The day I discovered it was easier not to see / But now I dare see clearly as a child / And now I even almost understand / Now I would be a painter most of all." Writer and musician Julius Lester, who had just appeared and performed with La Farge on Bob Fass's WBAI-FM radio show, defends his friend's life and memory in *Sing Out!* describing the folksinger as "a man who wrote songs and poems protesting and celebrating the multifaceted human condition." Lester's portrait of La Farge takes aim at his detractors and those who were quick to dismiss and criticize the musician's lack of success or troubled mind: "He is beyond the audiences that never quite under-stood him, and the friends who pitied him. None of them can hurt him anymore. Those who used his face for a mirror and those, filled with the wisdom of their press notices, who thought his lack of suc-cess was a reflection of his mettle, just as they thought their own ac-quisition of success was a reflection of theirs. Their tongues and pens can no longer hurt one who was too gentle to retaliate and not strong enough to resist." "He is a seldom man," Lester writes, borrowing from La Farge's poem "Epitaph" that Peter wrote for his father. Lester concludes with La Farge's poem for Cisco Houston: "But he's gone away / and the morning rises / on the people who stay."

According to Marshall Grant, when Cash learned of La Farge's death, "He was deeply saddened." It must have brought his own struggles into sharper contrast while serving as a warning of where he could be headed. "All I can say is that it made John all the more proud of *Bitter Tears* and of his relationship with Peter," Johnny Western says. Grant adds, "We all were just terribly sad to learn about Peter, especially John, of course. We were now playing 'Ira Hayes' at almost every show, so it just made it all the more tragic in a way." Indeed, it's difficult not to link the story of Ira Hayes to that of La Farge. Both died in their thirties and both struggled with in-ternal demons, stoked by the horrors of war, that they tried to quiet with alcohol or drugs. "After Peter's death, I saw 'Ira Hayes' as a personal song," folklorist Archie Green says. "He identified with Ira Hayes, a war hero who died because whites discriminated against In-dians. It was a completely biographical song and it would have had the same ending because Peter was anticipating his own death—he didn't die because people were discriminating against him, of course—he died because of the demons within that he could never conquer." John Cohen of the New Lost City Ramblers adds, "Peter was intense, troubled, a bit of a self-styled hero, and a solitary char-acter, who needed the support of the music scene, and desired to see himself as part of all that was happening in New York at that time. He had strong stories to tell. He brought his personal experience to us, and seemed to need recognition. It was an adventurous time."

Posthumously La Farge offered a final "Indian" song called "Crimson Parson," which was published in *Broadside* no. 64 and appears on his Folkways record *Peter La Farge on the Warpath*. The song tells the story of the Sand Creek massacre in Colorado's Kiowa County. On November 29, 1864, Reverend Colonel John Chivington led eight hundred troops from the First Colorado Cavalry, the Third Colorado Cavalry, and a company of First New Mexico Volunteers in an attack against the Cheyenne. The Cheyenne had brokered a peace accord with the federal government, which told Chief Black Kettle to raise an American flag if trouble arose, a gesture they were assured would keep them safe from any potential U.S. attack. Chivington ordered his soldiers, who were in a frenzy, to ignore both the American flag and later the white flag that Chief Black Kettle flew. In one of the most brutal and horrific acts of violence against Indians in history, Chivington's soldiers slaughtered nearly everyone they encountered. Later, Chivington boasted that he'd killed between five and six hundred Cheyenne. The killing, in fact, was not the worst part but rather what the soldiers did after the attack. They plundered and looted, and as they started to leave, some of the troops returned to kill the wounded and scalp the dead. The soldiers then adorned themselves with the scalps and other body parts, which allegedly included genitalia, and their weapons were festooned with bloody fetuses. At a congressional hearing, an interpreter who witnessed the massacre testified, "They were scalped, their brains knocked out; the men used their knives, ripped open women, clubbed little children and knocked them in the head with their rifle butts, beat their brains out, mutilated their bodies in every sense of the word."

La Farge's song vividly captures the scene: "They called him Crimson Parson, the Reverend Chivington / History don't recommend him for the trouble he begun / Kill and scalp all Indians big and little, was his cry / Nits make lice, kill babies too / Let every Indian die." La Farge exposed the hypocrisy of piety and patriotism that Chivington tried to hide behind: "Oh, the Reverend Colonel Chivington with his bible by his side / Oh, the Reverend Colonel Chivington he took a bloody ride / And when he'd done ridin' from hell's belly, hate was tore / Oh, the Reverend Colonel Chivington started up a mighty war." La Farge shows how Chivington's actions led to the so-called "Indian Wars" when word of the massacre spread and many tribes decided to fight back against U.S. aggression: "All the way up to Sitting Bull they told their bloody tale / and warpaths smoked as they hadn't smoked since they cut the Oregon trail / Indian war for just twelve years scattered all about the land / and the Reverend Colonel Chivington did it with his little band."

Drawing a parallel to the unfolding tragedy in Vietnam, the *Broadside* editor printed a note alongside La Farge's song that said: with "scientific warfare advances . . . 1965 Americans turn Vietnamese women and their children into burned and mangled flesh by pushing buttons in bomber and fighter planes" while claiming a "glorious victory for their country by killing undernourished 12-year-old Vietnamese boys in hand-to-hand combat." La Farge crafted a powerful metaphor for what was happening in Vietnam through the story of the Cheyenne massacre in 1864 at Sand Creek while tapping into a growing mood of anger in the Native community. As Hank Adams had done in 1964, many Native people were beginning to speak out about Vietnam and refusing to go off to fight people they felt were victims of a colonial injustice similar to their own. Many Native people believed the "Native people" of Vietnam were receiving a similar treatment at the hands of the United States to what they had endured when their land was first colonized. "Indians raised the question of the American past," Vine Deloria Jr. later wrote. "Since this bloody past was then being revived in search-and-destroy missions in Vietnam . . . it was apparent that few people in the government heeded the lessons of history." As historian and author Howard Zinn says, the antiwar movement "had a powerful, stimulating effect on the Native American movement. An Indian from Oklahoma connected the plight of Indians with that of the

Vietnamese people, who were being exploited and invaded like Indian land had been."

Native people continued to face very real and threatening problems from termination and the relentless encroachment on their land resulting from the government's denial of treaty rights. In the Northwest, the battle over fishing treaty rights turned violent. Exactly two weeks before La Farge died, forty-five armed government agents of Washington State attacked a group of nineteen Native women and children at Frank's Landing on the Nisqually River. After that, a group of fifty Native people had staged a series of protest fish-ins, and over the previous months some twenty-three Native fishermen were arrested for attempting to exercise their rights to fish. Similar to strategies used by the civil rights movement, Native people were using civil disobedience to fill up jails and tie up the court system in an effort to demand immediate attention for their issues.

During the 1964 presidential campaign, Johnson had pledged not to escalate the war in Vietnam: "We are not about to send American boys nine or ten thousand miles away from home to do what Asian boys ought to be doing for themselves." Not even a month after he spoke these words, the Johnson administration sent bombers into North Vietnam in what they called "Operation Rolling Thunder." When he took office after Kennedy's assassination, there were 16,000 advisors—not combatants—in Vietnam. But by the end of 1965, over 200,000 combat troops were in-country and had begun offensive ground operations. Even though Johnson had pushed through the Civil Rights Act of 1964, the Voting Rights Act of 1965, and rolled out the Great Society program, protestors gathered outside the White House on a daily basis for the remainder of 1965. The civil rights movement and antiwar movement had blended together by this point. Where protestors had once stood in front of the White House singing "We Shall Overcome," they now chanted, "We shall live in peace." In nearby Lafayette Park, protestors flew the North Vietnamese flag accompanied by chants of "Ho, Ho, Ho Chi Minh . . . the NLF is gonna win." A rising tide of disgust was building toward Johnson's Vietnam

War efforts. As Robert Caro writes, at the start of 1965, "LBJ had been a reluctant ally; now he was the enemy."

IN ONE last sad, curious development in a time of many, on May 4, 1965 archeologists discovered a 1,900-year-old irrigation system in Arizona. It was the system developed by the Pima Indians, Ira Hayes's ancestors, and later destroyed by the United State Army Corps of Engineers. "The irrigation system antedates by 500 to 700 years the oldest previously known hydraulics works in the United States," the *New York Times* reported. "This bolsters the theory that carriers of this civilization came northward from Mexico and Central America. It took a lot of organization to maintain an irrigation system, keep the canals cleared out, and maintain agreement on division of water among the users. We have trouble doing that today." The lyrics of "Ira Hayes" were eerily prescient:

A proud and noble band,
Who farmed the Phoenix valley in Arizona land,
Down the ditches for a thousand years.
The water grew Ira's peoples' crops
Till the white man stole the water rights,
And the sparklin' water stopped.

"When I hear 'Ira Hayes' and a lot of Peter's work," says Native activist Dennis Banks, "I see an artist way in front of everybody, especially when I compare him to other artists of the time. Cash was like that too." Oscar Brand agrees: "La Farge's work is important because it is a connection between the La Farge family and the Guthrie family. He was in between, and he was the real one who'd been spoiled and wrecked."

As 1965 came to a close, the rips and tears of the previous four years split the fabric of America in two. The country was at odds with itself, with conflicts raging between the political and cultural, foreign and domestic, young and old, white and black, citizen and immigrant,

Figure 2.13. Johnny Cash touring Wounded Knee in December
1964 with descendants of the survivors of the 1890 massacre.
He performed songs from *Bitter Tears* at a benefit show for the
tribe the day before. *Courtesy of John L. Smith.*

worker and professional, and Native and non-Native. The counterculture tried to seize the day, pushing against a postwar vision of the
world that seemed outdated, shaped by those who were emotionally
numb and held firm by those who were living in an old America that
was dying on the vine or only ever existed as a sentimental Hollywood
fable. Soon, Johnson's war in Vietnam turned to folly, opening the

door to a new era of reactionary American politics. The Nixon and Reagan years followed.

As Cash stumbled through the next few years, stepping out of the darkness and into the light, his consciousness and concern for the world around him continued to grow more acute. Four years after *Bitter Tears*, Cash performed at Wounded Knee, where Peter La Farge's songs took on new resonance. "When Cash sang 'Ira Hayes' on the Sioux Reservation, I thought it was kinda interesting because the Pima Indians were very different than the Sioux Indians in terms of appearance and culture," Archie Green says. "In that sense it signified that the song had become a national rallying point for Indians." After Cash's performance of "Ira Hayes," one of the Native chiefs seated in the front row approached the musician, who now looked vastly different than he had when he recorded the song in 1964. "I had a dream that you would come here and sing this song for us," the chief told Cash. Looking every bit like an eighteenth-century highwayman dressed in a long black coat, crisp white shirt, and taut black vest, the musician was visibly moved by the chief's words.

On their way to the airport after his time at Wounded Knee, Cash sat in the front seat next to John L. Smith. With June Carter, whom he had recently married, asleep in the back seat, Cash started asking Smith about the 1890 Wounded Knee massacre. After each of Smith's responses, Cash quietly wrote in a notebook, pausing for a moment, and then asking another question. This went on until they reached the airport. By then, Cash had composed the song "Big Foot" in tribute to the chief of the Miniconjou Lakota Sioux who was killed during the massacre. "Big chief Big Foot / It's good that you can't see / Revenge is being wrought / By Custer's 7th Cavalry . . . But the white flag is still waving / Today at Wounded Knee."

It's hard not to imagine that at that moment, standing among the descendants of the survivors of Wounded Knee, Cash wasn't thinking of his friend Peter La Farge. Perhaps composing "Big Foot" after his profound experience at Wounded Knee was Cash's attempt to honor La Farge and continue their legacy with a new "Indian" song. (Later, when *Bitter Tears* was slated for re-release, "Big Foot" was added to the record.) "We just never stopped playing songs off of *Bitter Tears*," Marshall Grant says. "John never forgot." Johnny Western adds, "Peter La Farge and that experience had a long, profound effect on Cash." Through one short but lasting encounter, La Farge and Cash had come together, allied as men searching for themselves and musicians hoping to connect with the world outside. "As far as our generation goes," says John Trudell, "to my knowledge, La Farge was the first one to address grave Native issues as an artist, musically speaking. He became that first so-called protest songwriter for Native people, but his writing became that voice. He wasn't limited to that; he also did things like 'Radioactive Eskimo,' in addition to the music people are more familiar with like 'Ira Hayes' and 'As Long as the Grass Shall Grow.'" Oscar Brand believes that La Farge and Cash developed a special kinship because they were "the outsiders . . . the guys that would never put an anklet on, a bracelet—I'm talking about the steel stuff. They would never bend so someone can put a rope around their neck. No one would ever get a leash on 'em."

"For Pete, his life was like trying to be on a trapeze," says Povy La Farge. "He was jumping up in the air and trying to get his hands around it and just couldn't hold on." While it's true that La Farge occasionally walked on the dark side of the road, the same could be said for Cash, who also lived life jumping in the air, trying to go higher and reach farther. Yet instead of an empty hand, he always found something and someone to grab on to, whether it was his family, The Carter Family, his music, or his vision of a new and better world. With *Bitter Tears*, Cash went back to move forward. In remembrance of the past, he sought the light of redemption in the present and the freedom that the future promises.

AFTER

When the World's on Fire

On November 3, 1969, the night that Richard Nixon delivered what would become famous as his "Silent Majority" speech, John Trudell, a Santee Sioux born in Omaha, Nebraska, was in the midst of the largest Native protest to occur in the twentieth century. Trudell had served in the U.S. Navy, as La Farge had, but he did so during the early years in Vietnam. After leaving the navy he became active in the Native movement, joining the newly established Red Power group, the American Indian Movement. AIM was formed in Minneapolis in 1968 during a particular historical moment. The Black civil rights movement, following the loss of Martin Luther King Jr., was starting to whither. Borrowing some its fiery rhetoric from Stokely Carmichael's call for "Black Power," the emerging Red Power movement found its early roots in the 1961 formation of the National Indian Youth Council. According to Dennis Banks, one of the cofounders of AIM, "The NIYC was very active, stepping up and setting the tone. AIM was formed in '68, so we took a lot of our cues from NIYC. A lot of our actions were generated by what was going on previously with those organizations. Their early statements were essential."

AIM had its sights set on grabbing the world's attention. In what the *New York Times* described as a "pre-dawn invasion" on November 20, 1968, eighty-nine Native people occupied Alcatraz Island, the former federal prison in San Francisco Bay that had been shut down in

1963. As they had in 1964—and using nearly word for word the same language—the activists declared the island theirs "by right of discovery." Banks remembers, "Early that morning I got the phone call from AIM founder George Mitchell. He told me to turn on the news. They were talking about something happening on Alcatraz with our people. I said we got to get on this, go there and support these people. So we got there five days after and stayed there for two weeks. We left three people there who stayed for the eighteen-month-long occupation."

John Trudell, of course, was one of the eighty-nine.

A few days later, the group of activists, now consisting of members from one hundred tribes, celebrated Thanksgiving in their own way. "It will be our first Thanksgiving of multi-tribal type," Mohawk Richard Oakes said. "If they try to remove us we will barricade ourselves or hide out."

Later, Trudell says, "Alcatraz came and just basically grabbed the world's attention. I think all of us played a role. What happened with our generation in regards to Alcatraz was that electronic communication had spread enough that everything could be worldwide instantaneously or at least by the next day. For our generation the thing that was beneficial for us was that a civil rights movement was going on, a youth movement was going on in the form of anti-war, environment, free speech, women's rights—those things going on simultaneously allowed us to merge in the way that we did."

The political moment spawned a cultural renaissance for Native people. Longtime Native activist leader Vine Deloria Jr. published *Custer Died for Your Sins* in 1970. (In tribute to Deloria's book, Sioux Floyd Crow Westerman used the title for his 1970 album.) The title alone is enough to notify the reader that Deloria didn't pull any punches; he meant to punch back—hard. Then Dee Brown published *Bury My Heart at Wounded Knee*, also in 1970. "This was when we began to see the emergence of a number of things coming out, including Indian literature, *Bury My Heart at Wounded Knee*, *Custer Died for Your Sins*, etc. Indian scholars and activists began publishing a great deal of powerful material," Howard Zinn says. "Indian newspapers like the one out of New York's Mohawk Valley, *Akwesasne Notes*, was being born. I used a lot of these notes when writing *A People's History of the United States*. They are remarkable materials."

The increasing level of activism generated by the Alcatraz takeover and the birth of a new Native literature and scholarship was just another in a long line of political and cultural events that President Nixon couldn't stomach. Seeking reelection in 1972, Nixon instructed members of his staff to compile an "enemies list." A memorandum from White House Counsel John Dean described the list as "address[ing] the matter of how we can maximize the fact of our incumbency in dealing with persons known to be active in their opposition to our Administration; stated a bit more bluntly—how we can use the available federal machinery to screw our political enemies." Actor Paul Newman, a vocal opponent of the war and Nixon's policies, was number 19 on the list. "A person without character has no enemies," Newman presciently told the *New York Times Magazine* in 1966. Later, friends said Newman, who died in 2008, was very happy about making the list, stating that it made him cooler in the eyes of his children.

Still, censorship of artists was a very real and long-standing problem, particularly as the Vietnam War became a hopeless quagmire. Pete Seeger, Buffy Sainte-Marie, Tom Paxton, and even Arlo Guthrie, whose antiwar song "Alice's Restaurant" struck a nerve, continued to endure threats of censorship.

After Cash's experience in the 1950s when Sam Phillips denied him the opportunity to record Americana and gospel—or a live prison album—and more painfully when radio stations refused to play the single "Ira Hayes" and other songs from *Bitter Tears* in 1964, Cash had come to know a thing or two about the danger of trying to suppress the artist's voice. It troubled him deeply, particularly in a society that valued freedom of expression. "Cash left Sun because he felt he was essentially being censored, not allowed to do what he wanted to do like recording a live album in a prison," says Bob Johnston, producer of *Johnny Cash at Folsom Prison*. "When he got to Columbia, where he thought he would be allowed to do these records, he encountered the same thing.

None of what Cash did or what we did was done without record executives threatening to fire us, sue us, or ruin our careers. Nothing."

In July 1972, Cash went to the White House to speak with Richard Nixon on behalf of prison reform. The president invited Cash to perform, requesting that the musician play Merle Haggard's "Okie from Muskogee" and Guy Drake's "Welfare Cadillac." The latter is a controversial song for what some call its discriminatory representation of welfare recipients, and the former is about people who hate war protestors. Cash told Nixon that he wasn't familiar with the songs and therefore wouldn't be able play either. Instead Cash chose to perform songs that were more truthful and universal. The first tune he played was "Ballad of Ira Hayes," followed by two of his own songs, "What Is Truth?" and "Man in Black." Offering no political argument for or against Nixon's request, Cash later repeated that he just didn't know those other tunes. Yet of the hundreds of songs Cash recorded, he chose to perform three of the most socially conscious and politically sharp compositions in his repertoire, all of which in their own way condemn war.

Cash debuted the song "Man in Black" in 1970 on his hit television program, The Johnny Cash Show. Following each weekly broadcast, Cash would stay and take questions from the audience. People always asked why he dressed in black. For some reason, one day the question stayed with him. Between shows, Cash composed "Man in Black" and performed it the next week. The day Cash performed it at the White House must have been a dark moment for Richard Nixon, particularly when the music star sang the passage directed against the Vietnam War: "I wear the black in mournin' for the lives that could have been / Each week we lose a hundred fine young men." One couldn't help but wonder that Cash's music must have shaken Nixon with rage while giving the president's opponents a brief moment of pleasure.

Cash repeatedly used his show as a platform for inviting the very artists Nixon and his followers despised. "It all came to a silent stop when Lyndon Johnson and Richard Nixon did their blacklisting," Buffy Sainte-Marie says. "But I was so busy—and so naïve—I didn't even notice that I was dead in the United States. I never expected to last more than a summer, and my joy hasn't been within the music business; it's been the fun and education I've gotten on the road." So Sainte-Marie, Seeger, Guthrie, and Odetta, as well as Dylan and Ramblin' Jack Elliott all appeared on his show. "When you think of folk music, many of these artists you think are protesters or are hippies, who country music fans hated," observes Doug Yeager, who managed Odetta, Ed McCurdy, Tom Paxton, and Oscar Brand. "Johnny Cash was able to pull this off because he had integrity, and in the end he had the character to do it." Arlo Guthrie says, "When I was on his show, I was not the performer I am today. It was also very controversial to have me—a long-haired hippie peacenik—on. My voice was high, his was low, but we managed to perform my father's song 'Oklahoma Hills.' Johnny paid tribute to my dad before we started and then Mother Maybelle and the Carter sisters joined us on 'Valley to Pray.'" Buffy Sainte-Marie went on the show as well and performed La Farge's "Custer."

ABC executives tried to stop him from bringing these performers on, but Cash never backed down, even when it seemed that the network wouldn't relent. Pete Seeger was a case in point; he was still under the microscope because of his past blacklisting, and he was receiving additional scrutiny because of a fresh controversy that was swirling around his antiwar song "Big Muddy." Always one step ahead, Cash decided to have Seeger on anyway and before the two performed together, Cash spoke to the legendary folk musician in his dressing room on camera. For more than seventeen years, Seeger had been blacklisted from television. In their dressing-room meeting, Cash defends Seeger by describing the folksinger and banjo player as one of the world's most important musicians. If anyone wanted to argue the point because of Seeger's politics, Cash welcomed the debate because he believed Seeger to be one of the country's "greatest Americans" and foremost "patriots." Good friends for some time, Seeger and Cash greatly admired each other. When Seeger appeared on the show, Cash gave him a one-hundred-year-old fretless banjo, a gift he presented on behalf of Bob Johnson, Norman Blake's old friend. Together, they performed The Carter Family's "Worried Man Blues," encouraging the audience to join them in a sing-along.

A few years earlier, in 1966, a very stoned Cash and a quiet June performed on Seeger's PBS show, *Rainbow Quest*, paying tribute to Peter La Farge with renditions of "Coyote, My Little Brother" and "As Long as the Grass Shall Grow." Cash told Seeger, "Ya know in '57 I wrote 'Old Apache Squaw' and then I forgot the so-called protest song for a while. No one else seemed to speak up for the Indian with any volume or voice." A discussion ensued about Cash's song "The Talking Leaves," which had appeared on *Bitter Tears*. Seeger then asked Cash to talk about La Farge: "Yes, Peter La Farge was an Indian who loved his heritage, his country, and his music. He used it, not as a vicious tool, but as a great voice for the American Indian. We were very proud that he came down from New York City and brought us five songs to do on this *Bitter Tears* album of protest songs for the American Indian, which I think was long overdue." Together, Cash, Carter, and Seeger performed "As Long as the Grass Shall Grow."

Cash's television show, while popular, was cancelled in 1971, after fewer than two years on the air, and Native people were again in the headlines not long after. Again it was the Pine Ridge reservation in South Dakota. Where Big Foot and his people were once slaughtered by the Seventh Cavalry in the dead of winter eighty-three years prior, a few hundred Oglalas, with the support of the American Indian Movement, staged a large protest at Wounded Knee by occupying the old trading post and the church on February 28, 1973. The protestors demanded that the Senate Foreign Relations Committee hold hearings on broken treaties and also start a full investigation into government treatment of Native people, including the squalid living conditions and inadequate healthcare rampant on reservations. Federal marshals fired on the protestors, claiming that they held ten to twelve people hostage. Carter Camp, a spokesman for the protestors, explained, "We will occupy this town until the government sees fit to deal with Indian people, particularly the Oglala Sioux Tribe in South Dakota.

We want a true Indian nation, not one made up of Bureau of Indian Affairs puppets."

Soon the area was surrounded by hundreds of federal agents. Calvin Kentfield, reporting for the *New York Times,* wrote, "A Rapid [City] businessman came to me . . . He said, 'The only thing to do is wipe them 'em all out; go out there and wipe 'em all out." A standoff ensued, lasting seventy-one days. Nixon pledged to send White House representatives to listen to AIM's grievances. Harlington Wood Jr., assistant attorney general for the civil division of the U.S. Justice Department, was the first government representative granted access to Wounded Knee to negotiate with the protestors with the intention of ending the occupation without any violence. By May 5 AIM agreed to disarm, and evacuated Wounded Knee three days later. On July 4, the church that housed the protestors burned to the ground. No one was hurt in the fire.

One of the AIM leaders arrested following the showdown at Wounded Knee with the FBI was Dennis Banks. After posting bond, Banks disappeared. On September 26, 1973, a warrant for his arrest was issued. But actor Marlon Brando, who had remained involved in the Native movement since his participation in the fish-ins in 1964, helped Banks flee. "Brando stayed connected all the way through," says Jose Barriero, of the Smithsonian's National Museum of the American Indian.

It's true. After the fish-ins on the Nisqually River in 1964, Brando's commitment to Native issues deepened, showing a thoughtfulness and sincerity that not only touched Native activists such as Dennis Banks and Hank Adams but helped them to continue pressing their case before the American people. Just a few months removed from his arrest in Washington, Brando was in New York, where he offered himself to the nation's entertainment press in a marathon all-day press blitz to promote the upcoming World War II thriller *Morituri.* He was far from thrilled to sit for hours answering banal questions: "It's a wonderful show," one reporter says about the film. "Did you see it?" Brando asks. "No, I haven't seen it yet." Amazed, the actor responds,

"Then how do you know?" So instead, Brando mocked, charmed, and engaged the reporters.

On March 4, 2009, I traveled to a production studio in Harlem to spend an afternoon watching the film made in 1965 of Marlon Brando's farcical press junket called *Meet Marlon Brando*. The film was shot by the pioneering filmmakers Albert and David Maysles who, with their ever-present camera, showed Brando moving quickly from one facet of his character to another, one moment a mischievously reluctant movie star and the next an intensely thoughtful citizen-artist speaking out on civil rights and justice for Native people. Standing in front of Central Park across the street from New York's Hampshire Hotel, where the interviews were conducted, Brando, speaking in fluent French, tells the French interviewer, "We all have an obligation, we are all responsible . . . you are responsible for France as an individual . . . you give much responsibility to General de Gaulle, but you personally are responsible and so am I."

Next, Brando stops a young black woman who is walking by, hand in hand with a child, and asks, "Do you think the American government is responsible for the progress of the American Negro?" The woman answers, "No, I don't, not at all. What's been done and what's going to be done, [Negroes] are going to have to do it." For Brando, this tied in directly with the Native drive for self-determination and self-rule, free of the interference of U.S. government. When a reporter later asks Brando about his work with Native people, Brando turns serious and says, "We're having a lot of fun here and this is something that I can't be flippant about. It's not something that I could really go into here . . . but I've found when I talk about the American Indian to people, I've been amazed about how little anybody knows about them." With head bowed, a reflective Brando continues, "For instance, nobody knows that the mortality rate of Indian children is five-to-one in comparison to any other minority group here in America. I think it would be important for all of us to realize what the American Indian is, what his position is. I hope to make a film of the subject." Watching the outtakes three decades later with one of the film's directors, Albert Maysles (we laughed hysterically at Brando's antics, which included comparing his popularity to the hula hoop fad), revealed even more moments in which Brando discusses the Native cause, at one time telling the ten or so reporters that one of the finest films made about any issue, not just the Native issue, was *The Exiles,* released in 1961.

Barriero explains that "Brando got himself in trouble with financing Dennis Banks when he was on the run during Wounded Knee II in the early '70s." And Banks comments that "when he showed up to my trial, it just made our cause more visible. I ended up staying at his house off and on for a period of three years. I relied on him to help me out on issues when we needed attention." Eventually Dennis Banks and Russell Means, another AIM leader, were acquitted of all charges. "The trial was nine months long," Banks recalls. "It was filled with corruption, deceit, and deceiving the court—and those are the judge's words. You have to remember Wounded Knee is on Indian land. It's not, like, off Indian land. We were occupying our own land." Indeed, Judge Nichol thrashed the FBI and the government's handling of the case: "The U.S. Attorney may strike hard blows, but he is not at liberty to strike foul ones . . . I am forced to conclude that prosecution acted in bad faith at various times throughout the course of this trial . . . The fact that incidents of misconduct formed a pattern throughout leads me to believe that this case was not prosecuted in good faith . . . *The waters of justice have been polluted* [judge's emphasis] . . . Dismissal, I believe, is the appropriate cure for the pollution in this case. It is hard for me to believe that the FBI, which I have revered for so long, has stooped so low." According to a Gallup poll taken during the trial, 72 percent of Americans agreed that the Native people's actions were justified. "The mood, the gut feelings were on our side," Banks says. "It was a right time in history." Later it came to light that FBI regional director Joseph Trimbach, who helped orchestrate a broad military siege with scores of U.S. Marshals, F-4 Phantom jets, FBI, state and local law enforcement, armored personnel carriers, and the formation of a vigilante group of Pine Ridge reservation natives

called the Guardians of the Oglala Nation, or GOONs, perjured himself during the trial of Banks and Means.

Then, on June 26, 1975, two FBI agents were killed on the Pine
Ridge reservation. Sixteen people connected to AIM were suspected.
On April 18, 1977, Leonard Peltier was found guilty of first-degree
murder in the killing of two FBI agents. Many questioned the government's case against Peltier. Fours years later, the world-renowned
human rights group Amnesty International condemned Peltier's trial
and imprisonment in a report asserting that the FBI "fabricated evidence and used other means to put leaders of black, Indian, and
other minority groups behind bars." The group, which won the
Nobel Peace Prize in 1977, singled out Peltier's case, revealing that the
FBI targeted AIM with a crackdown filled with "misconduct" and
"abuses." The human rights organization also learned that a key witness against Peltier, Myrtle Poor Bear, "was threatened with death by
the FBI if she didn't testify against the dissidents." Former head of
Amnesty International Jack Healey tells me: "Peltier got a bad, a very
bad trial. I spoke out a lot about it. Just another bad American story
in thievery and a long line of abuse, neglect, and land grabs." The
"takeover" of the church and trading post on the Oglala reservation
and the subsequent hostile conflict between the FBI and AIM from
1973 to 1976 have become known as Wounded Knee II and what the
Oglala people call "the reign of terror," during which time more than
sixty murders of Native people occurred and none investigated by the
agency which had jurisdiction, the FBI.

In 1980 Johnny Cash told a reporter: "We went to Wounded Knee
before Wounded Knee II to do a show to raise money to build a school
on the Rosebud Indian Reservation and do a movie for Public Broad-
casting System called *Trail of Tears*." After Wounded Knee II, Cash
joined fellow musicians Robbie Robertson, Kris Kristofferson, and
Willie Nelson, among many others, in calling for the release of AIM
activist Leonard Peltier. Soon, other entertainers, including Steve
Earle, Carlos Santana, and even Tony Bennett lent their voices in support of Native people. Bookending the Wounded Knee II period, the

Native movement orchestrated two ambitious campaigns. The first, the "Trail of Broken Treaties," took place in 1972 and sought to bring attention to Native living conditions and treaty rights. In all, eight Native groups organized the Trail of Broken Treaties, including the American Indian Movement, the National Indian Youth Council, and the National American Indian Council. Russell Means and Dennis Banks of AIM were instrumental in planning the campaign, which included creating the "Twenty Points" paper. When AIM leaders realized that the organizers were unable to secure housing for everyone in Washington, D.C., they marched over to the Bureau of Indian Affairs. After an angry confrontation between AIM representatives and building guards, the demonstration turned violent. Five hundred Native activists took control of the building, piling up office furniture in an effort to block the entrances and demanding amnesty and the government's assurance to honor the "Twenty Points" paper. The occupation lasted for six days and ended only after White House aides agreed to review the activists' grievances as well as consider "proposed solutions to century-old treaty rights, self-determination, and economic opportunities." The aides also agreed to assemble a special federal body led by the White House to present recommendations directly to President Nixon by June 1, 1973. As they left the building on November 8, 1972, Native activists hauled out at least two truckloads of materials they described as "incriminating" documents that they would make public if the government did not honor the agreement.

The second event was the "Longest Walk," a 2,700-mile walk from San Francisco to Washington, D.C. Also organized by AIM, 2,800 people participated in the walk, which protested eleven bills before Congress that would have altered or broken Native treaties that dealt with further restrictions on Native hunting and fishing rights, or sought to cut federal support for Native resources such as education and healthcare and weaken tribal governments. "We didn't think they would pass," Jose Barriero says. "But the fact that they were being debated was not a good thing for Native people." Clyde Bellecourt, one of the AIM leaders and organizers, spoke at a rally on July 15, 1978, and summed up the situation: "We are here to stop one of the most massive, criminal assaults ever to take place against our people—the move in Congress to take 60 percent of this country's energy resources that lie under Indian lands." The few thousand Native protestors participating ended up setting up makeshift camps in parks in Baltimore and Greenbelt, Maryland, before establishing an encampment on the grounds of the Washington Monument.

Brando was in Washington to offer support, as was Muhammad Ali, who had been introduced to the movement years earlier by comedian Dick Gregory, who also was still very active. AIM's Jose Barriero, the press secretary for the walk, remembers Ali coming into Brando's room to clown around with the actor. "I had to deliver some papers over to Brando. When I knocked on his hotel room door he invited me in, and he was just hanging out there, naked. He was in no rush to put on his clothes and very leisurely walked over and put on his robe." Soon after, Ali appeared with a couple of his sparring partners. "Ali came in and just started to rag on Brando," Barriero says. "It was all pretty funny and good-natured. Then I left with Ali and took the elevator down to the street with him and his sparring partners. This was an old, classy hotel with those small elevators. It was a very small space, and of course they are huge guys compared to me. They start throwing each other around [and] punching each other. They weren't mad, just joking around. But they nearly crushed me to death. With all this incredible energy it was like being in an elevator with a buffalo."

Later both men spoke at the Washington Monument camp. "Even though Brando was a very quirky guy, he consistently supported Native causes," Barriero says. "He spoke at the Longest Walk gathering in Washington and stayed in D.C. for several days on that issue." Barriero remembers Ali mixing with Native people in the camp. "Ali asked if there was anybody who wanted to spar with him. Some Indian guy from California jumped up and said, 'I'll take you on.' Ali said, 'I didn't know Indian guys were that dumb.'" The campaign prompted the passage of the American Indian Religious Freedom Act in August 1978. A few smaller campaigns took place during the twelve years that Ronald Reagan and George H. W. Bush were in the White House, but they were not as fervent, and the times were not as fertile for the Native movement—or any movement for that matter—as the 1960s and '70s were.

ON JULY 29, 2008, I found myself in the Woody Guthrie Archives sitting with Guthrie's daughter Nora, who took a film crew on an impromptu tour of the archives while I was researching various Guthrie materials. While searching through Guthrie's correspondence, photos, and related artifacts, I learned that the archives had recently added the great musician's personal record collection. Old, beat-up, and in a state of such fragility that I had to wear white gloves to handle them, I came across a collection of The Carter Family albums. One record grabbed my attention, in large part because Guthrie had written hundreds of words on the dust jacket. In precise, small handwriting, Guthrie had written beautiful prose-style notes all over Asch Records' *American Folksay Ballads and Dances,* perhaps offering his own version of liner notes. Dated January 16, 1945, these notes provide eloquent glimpses into his sharp, creative mind and suggest the intensity of his admiration for the power of folk music.

I had just come across these annotations when Nora stepped into the archives with a BBC documentary film crew in tow. With cameras rolling, Nora, standing over my right shoulder, asked me to read a passage for the film crew. I started to read, and then Nora read aloud with me: " . . . Union will grow watered on this music because this is union music, work music, fight and study, yell and run music. Folks will say it is real music. Folks say. Folksay. This is the music of what folks say. And the name of this album of records is the voice of you thinking and talking, it is called Folksay. It is Folk say."

These words haunted me throughout my research and writing. They brought to mind then-candidate Barack Obama's grand appeal "to continue the long march of those who came before us, a march for a more just, more equal, more free, more caring and more prosperous America" in his A More Perfect Union speech, delivered at

Philadelphia's Constitution Center on March 18, 2008. The union, the unity that Obama asked the country to consider only grows more vital, and it reminds me of the unity Woody Guthrie sought hopping on and off railroad cars, singing his way through factories during the Great Depression, and busking from the Dust Bowl to the streets of New York City. "It is folk say" because in the purest, simplest sense, what we need as a people is each other—an indivisible but diverse community.

Johnny Cash felt this and acted on it most profoundly with *Bitter Tears*. "That's what John believed in—a world that was more open," Norman Blake says. "Music can be the champion of the downtrodden and represent the story of poor and working people. John and I shared this view." That's why *Bitter Tears* is not just an album of "Indian" songs but a noble chapter in the unbound book that is the human experiment, which depends on art and culture to nourish and sustain its health and survival. "When Johnny Cash did *Bitter Tears*, he got it more airplay, so to speak, so people could hear La Farge's Native songs," John Trudell says. "If I'd call that record a spear, I'm going to look at the original La Farge work as the spearhead. I think that the original records that Peter made as an artist and an individual are the spearheads. Cash came along and made a larger spear out of it. Cash was the shaft and La Farge the spearhead of that movement in many ways. I appreciate what Johnny Cash did by acknowledging Native people and specifically acknowledging Peter La Farge."

This year marks the forty-fifth anniversary of the recording of *Bitter Tears: Ballads of the American Indian*. So many of the people that led Cash to that moment are gone, including Ed McCurdy, the ribald musician who introduced Cash to La Farge. Others, like the great Floyd Red Crow Westerman, Vine Deloria, and Clyde Warrior all have passed on as well. Still, artist-activists like John Trudell continue the work that many of these people started with thrilling records like *Original AKA Graffiti Man*, which Bob Dylan called "the best album of 1986." His other albums include *Blue Indians* and *Bone Days*. The vital voices of *Bitter Tears* continue to circulate in American popular culture because many of the problems Cash sang about in 1964 still exist today. "Julius Lester once said of the civil rights movement that he realized at some point, once you tear down one wall, there's another and another, until one day, you realize you can't see past the walls," Josh Dunson says. "But it was important for me—and many of us—to keep struggling and organizing."

In the end, for Cash, accepting the status quo—which keeps us locked into a worldview that is lost in another time and place, dead to the real world that exists—was never an option. Nor was it for the thousands of activists in the Native, civil rights, and antiwar movements who helped breathe life into Cash's *Bitter Tears* recording. The more skepticism and cynicism Cash ran into, the more he rebelled. During the controversy surrounding *Bitter Tears*, he lashed out at those who censored him because he was offering a critical view of the United States' long history of mistreatment and injustice. In the *Billboard* letter, he wrote, "I'd sing more of this land, but all God's children ain't free."

WHILE I was wandering through the streets of Washington, D.C., the night before Barack Obama's inauguration, accompanied by a film crew, I came across a concert taking place at the foot of the Lincoln Memorial in honor of the new president. The sound of Woody Guthrie's "This Land Is Your Land" faintly drifted overhead. I thought of Odetta, called "the queen of American folk music" by Martin Luther King Jr. She had died on December 2, 2008, just before I could speak with her. In the 1963 March on Washington for Jobs and Freedom, Odetta sang a stirring rendition of "O Freedom." She told the *New York Times* in 2007: "They were liberation songs. You're walking down life's road, society's foot is on your throat, every which way you turn you can't get from under that foot. And you reach a fork in the road and you can either lie down and die, or insist upon your life."

Cash insisted upon life with *Bitter Tears*, pushing out songs while a movement was finding itself. Indigenous rights were not a passing cause célèbre for Cash; he remained a strong advocate for rights and reconciliation until the end of his life. "What he did was and is still respected,"

Jose Barriero says. "Johnny Cash remains deeply respected in Indian country." AIM cofounder Dennis Banks agrees: "Cash was way out in front. He did *Bitter Tears* in such a clever way that people were drawn into our movement."

At that Lincoln Memorial concert, Bruce Springsteen joined Pete Seeger for "This Land Is Your Land." The musicians performed the entire song, the way Guthrie intended it to be sung, which included long-excluded verses about the struggles brought on by the Great Depression including home loss, hunger, and poverty—issues exceedingly relevant at this time in our country's (and the world's) history. As the two legendary musicians rousingly sang Guthrie's tune for everyone everywhere to hear, the music floated in the air carrying with it a feeling of optimism and hope. Certainly, one cannot ignore the momentous historical moment underway in the United States. "We feel Obama is a positive for us," Dennis Banks says. "We see him visiting Native people, being involved with some of our programs, the expansion of the Higher Education Act, etc. He is placing more Native people in his administration than anytime before." (Obama has appointed Standing Rock Sioux Jody Gillette as the deputy associate director of the Office of Intergovernmental Affairs.) The *Native American Times* agrees with Banks: "Obama has started to aggressively reach out to Native Americans in word and deed. In his words he has put together a policy which truly addresses Native problems. In his deeds he has actually gone to Indian reservations to seek our votes. He is also the cosponsor of the all important Indian Health Care Improvement Act." Obama also promised to not interfere with Native jurisdiction as tribes all across the land attempt to deal with problems: from "meth use to domestic violence to murder, the problems on Indian land should be the providence of Indian governments."

In May 2008, Obama visited Crow Agency in Montana, promising Native people that he would create a new department on Native American affairs run by a special policy czar who would report directly to him, which he promptly created in February 2009. On March 3, 2009, he authorized millions of dollars in federal aid to provide drinking water to rural areas, repair water infrastructure, and rebuild schools on Indian reservations.

Yet there is much, much more that needs to be done. For example, in 2006 the U.S. Supreme Court reauthorized the 1965 Voting Rights Act, and in doing so expanded its protections to include western states that have historically discriminated against Native voters. The Voting Rights Act is slated for reauthorization in 2009, and leading progressive legal, civil and voting rights groups, and activists, fear that the new, highly conservative court may undo many of the gains.

On a positive note, however, Banks senses that one enduring legal nightmare will come to an end: Leonard Peltier will finally be released during Obama's presidency. "If Obama pardons him or not, he will have served his time," Banks says. "He will have done it all by the end of Obama's first term. Leonard will get out and continue to be a great leader for us."

Watching this new era celebrated with the music of what "folk say," the song "This Land Is Your Land," its melody borrowed from The Carter Family, caused me to reflect on the partnership of Peter La Farge and Johnny Cash with an added sense of joy and optimism. The words written by Guthrie sixty years ago, the tune strummed by Mother Maybelle Carter's hand a year before that, this song was brought to full glory on the steps of the Lincoln Memorial by a folk legend and a rock superstar. The Carter Family, Seeger, La Farge, Cash, and Springsteen remain tied together by the power of music, a timeless connection that knows no borders and flows to the very soul of a people.

Cash's legacy is matchless and unquestionable. The effects of the recording of *Bitter Tears* and the controversy surrounding the album, and the influence of La Farge in the folk revival and on Cash had been obscured over time, but there are many who stumbled upon the music and discovered its transformative power. The influence is most richly seen and heard on Springsteen's 1980 album, *Nebraska*, to me a direct descendant of La Farge and Cash's *Bitter Tears*. On September 20, 1982, the *Boston Globe*'s Steve Morse wrote: "What makes *Nebraska* such an achievement . . . is that . . . Springsteen does not fall into nervous, slavish imitation. He expands from [Hank] Williams' legacy, showing he has also listened to artists as diverse as Townes Van Zandt and Peter La Farge, while never letting his own soul be submerged." According to Springsteen, "*Nebraska* was a reaction to what I was singing and writing about and what I was feeling—what I felt the role of a musician should be, what an artist should be." It's the exact same sentiment that pushed Cash to record *Bitter Tears*: "I dove into primary and secondary sources, immersing myself in the tragic stories of the Cherokee and the Apache, among others, until I was almost as raw as Peter. By the time I actually recorded the album I carried a heavy load of sadness and outrage."

The list of the people who came together to create this lasting protest record, but are no longer with us, is long: producers Don Law and Frank James, Cash's guitarist Luther Perkins, Merle Travis, Peter La Farge, June Carter Cash, and Johnny Cash himself. But the music, of course, remains, and La Farge's "Ira Hayes" has continued to be recorded by scores of artists since he first wrote it in 1960. The ballad appears on more than forty Johnny Cash collections. Kris Kristofferson, Townes Van Zandt, Hazel Dickens, Kinky Friedman, Patrick Sky, and Charley Pride are just a few of the musicians who have covered the song. In my conversations with Cash's son, John Carter, he often referred to *Bitter Tears* as his "favorite album by my father." Through his Bear Family Records, Richard Weize put together a comprehensive four-CD box set titled *Come Along and Ride This Train*. Released first in 1991, the set includes seven of Cash's concept albums, including *Bitter Tears*, *Ride This Train*, and *Blood, Sweat and Tears*. "I think Peter La Farge was far better [than Cash]," Weize says. "La Farge's folk music remains impressive. To me, the Cash recordings don't have the depth to [them] like La Farge's recordings. But *Bitter Tears* is a very important record in Cash's career because it made people aware of the subject. Since he was in the limelight and Peter La Farge would never be, Cash gave something and did something to the songs. People would never have noticed if it was just Peter La Farge." In January

2009, the *Nation* magazine selected "Ballad of Ira Hayes" as one of the ten best progressive anthems of all time.

As I listened to Springsteen and Seeger's performance of "This Land Is Your Land," another Carter Family song came to mind. "When the World's on Fire," a tune also known to have inspired Guthrie and beloved by Cash, carries the line, "I'm going to heaven when the world's on fire." These words lead me to imagine a moment when La Farge and Cash may once again find themselves together, now free from the struggles of this world, living in eternal peace in the next. In the end, politicians—even those carrying such a sense of urgency and hope as Barack Obama—cannot save us when the world is burning with war, hate, and injustice. Here is where art and culture can and do point the way to a system more honest, and a society more just and fair. "Music creates life," Albert Camus believed. Cash agreed; his belief in the power of music may have been the truest principle underlying the faith he held so dearly. For Cash, what was right had more to do with producing music that didn't "wallow in meaninglessness" than with formal politics, as he said in defense of *Bitter Tears*. With his low voice, straightforward lyrical style, and ever-present Martin guitar, Cash fashioned an individuality that made it impossible to lock him down politically or creatively. Right or left. Country, rock, folk, or pop. These labels meant nothing more than an attempt to control and marginalize anything that shakes up the system both within and outside the music industry. Cash rings true because he carried an authenticity rooted in his own early rural, poverty-filled life. Appearing on the American popular cultural scene rich with constant change, Cash's own career marks time with the United States' meteoric transformation from the 1950s to the dawn of the new millennium. His life story is the story of the real America, ever expanding and constricting, close to disintegrating and then suddenly finding new life. "Even though he's a kaleidoscope of a thousand different ideas, he's a straight line," Cash's friend Merle Travis once said. "There's ain't no twilight and there ain't no dusk to Johnny Cash. He's like a sunny day, or he's completely dark."

JOHNNY CASH left us on September 12, 2003, at the age of seventy-one. Yet his age doesn't adequately indicate the many lives Cash lived. Cash was more sinner than saint, more Native than cowboy, more rebel than outlaw, more peacemaker than soldier. The redemption he forever sought is the fulcrum that balances his long music career and life. Ultimately, what *Bitter Tears* represents is the ability of music to be a social and spiritual force, allowing us to forge a bond with people who come from entirely different places yet who have the same purpose in their minds and hearts. "Right now there is a huge lawsuit concerning billions of dollars ripped off from Indian country," Banks says, "but no one is going to jail for that. You don't see anyone being indicted for that—it's business as usual. So we need the Cashes of the world who can get the people to listen and maybe help." Acclaimed Cayuga and Wolf Clan actor Gary Farmer agrees: "Cash with his music but also other artists with film, etc., can establish a vital voice for human rights and the Native cause." Farmer has done just that with both his music and his acting. Farmer starred along with Johnny Depp in Jim Jarmusch's 1995 film, *Dead Man*, a film that I view as a visual counterpart to Johnny Cash's *Bitter Tears*. Shot in austere black and white and accompanied by a jagged, rough score by Neil Young, *Dead Man* has the visceral and emotional protest power of *Bitter Tears*. And just as La Farge's haunting lyrics made Cash's record both raw and beautiful, Farmer's portrayal of the Native character named "Nobody" carries the same spirit and energy. The character's name is a clever metaphor for how Native people are ignored, unseen in American society. In the hands of a lesser actor, the performance may have come across as heavy-handed, a cinematic stereotype in a long line of many. Instead, Farmer's mesmerizing performance is imbued with a humanism and defiance similar to Cash's approach in his recording of *Bitter Tears*.

Cash was the eternal seeker motivated by innate instincts, rather than the predictable opportunism of celebrity. In the late 1970s and the 1980s, country music turned its back on Cash, and after twenty-five years of recording, Columbia dropped him. Once again broken and battling drug addiction, Cash emerged with a series of moving songs known as *American Recordings*. His newfound success showed Cash as he truly was: a man whose home was the world, in which he lived openly and painfully, devoid of pretense and full of humanity. In the end, he still refused to be cowed, speaking out until the day he died against the Iraq war, telling his daughter Roseanne Cash, herself a musician, "to convey his opposition to the impending invasion to audiences at her concerts." The sense of justice he believed in was a fundamental principle. Cash was a "holy terror . . . a dark and dangerous force of nature that also stood for mercy and justice for his fellow human beings," Kris Kristofferson, who famously played with Cash at the 1969 Newport Folk Festival, said at his funeral. His path was distinctive but universal. Consigned to a footnote in his career, Cash's album *Bitter Tears* and his work with Peter La Farge evoke writer Anatole France's eulogy of novelist Emile Zola: "Let us envy him: he has honored his country and the world with an immense body of work and a noble act. . . . His destiny and his heart endowed him with the greatest of fate of all: he was a moment in the conscience of humanity."

ACKNOWLEDGMENTS

I never considered Johnny Cash an archetype of "country music" because it was obvious from just a brief listen that Cash's creativity was entirely distinctive. Timing is everything, and Cash, beginning in 1955, had the benefit of standing at the crossroads of a new era of American popular music. This, together with his musical passion, which encompassed every sound that floated into his ears—gospel, blues, country, folk, rock, hillbilly—allowed Cash to transcend the music industry's narrow marketing categories. Yet it isn't the fact that he effortlessly moved between musical styles that makes Cash an important figure in music, it's the fact that he grew beyond the various influences. By internalizing, not imitating, Cash made everything he brought into the studio wholly his own. The result was pure Johnny Cash. All important artists share this quality: the almost innate ability to soak in what's outside, blend it with what's in their hearts, their minds, and produce work that's altogether their own. Duke Ellington, Bob Dylan, and The Clash are a few others that were capable of creating work that rises above simple classification. It's this quality that establishes Cash's work as timeless—more spiritual than any religion and truer than any rule of law.

For this reason, as I look back at my life, one so profoundly informed and transformed by music, I see the artist Johnny Cash first through the eyes of my father, Lorenzo. My father was a bricklayer who immigrated to West Philadelphia in the late 1960s from Colli Al Volturno, a small mountain village in the Province of Isernia, part of the Molise region of Italy. He loved Italian football, of course, but he also loved country music. When I was a kid, I was often left scratching my head when I tried to wrap my mind around how the two disparate passions were connected.

Despite speaking very little English, with delight my father crooned along with the local country music station. I witnessed this scene most often, starting from the age of seven years old, when he enlisted me as his laborer for weekend masonry jobs. Until he died, when I was fifteen, I helped him dig foundations, mix cement, carry bricks, and clean up work sites. I loved every minute of it. I learned more in that time than I did in twenty plus years of schooling. Working alongside my father, uncles, cousins—all immigrants from the same small town in Italy—taught me the fundamentals of life: honor, respect, and integrity. Not much has come close to matching those shared moments. Pushing wheelbarrows full of cement and unloading pallets of bricks on long, hot days—that wasn't tough. But his country music "singing," that was tough.

It was on these Saturdays, mostly, when, after stopping for our usual eggs-over-easy with rye toast and hash browns breakfast at the Red Robin Diner on Frankford Avenue in Philadelphia, we'd jump into his big blue Ford dump truck—nicknamed "the jet" by my father—and ride over to our next job to build a fireplace, lay a driveway, or construct a patio or stone retaining wall. It was honorable work done by men who were looked at as simple but who simply worked hard whether it was bitterly cold or blazing hot. They never complained. Ever. My respect for them ran deep. I looked at these people as the true architects of democracy because they built this country on their knees, with their hands and hearts, receiving very little in the way of thanks or acknowledgment. So I, too, tried never to complain, that is, until we got back into the truck and headed home. After putting "the jet" into gear and moving slowly along with the Philadelphia traffic, my father would click on the radio, which was always set to his favorite country station, 92.5 WXTU. Next, the "singing" began. In me, he had a captive audience, and he just wailed away to whatever country tune moved him. Every once in a while he would glance over at me with a wide smile and a wink as if to say, "Isn't this just great?!" "Not really," I thought pressing my head against the window of the passenger door, praying for the drive to end quickly.

In those countless hours spent traveling from job to job, I heard all of the greats of country music, but I was too young and too rigid in my love of rock, punk, and rap to listen to them. But in a strange, full-circle kind of way, I lost those stubborn, narrow views and came to see that without this music I wouldn't have the music I love. When work of any kind is worthwhile, it captures those unknowable, untranslatable qualities that define the human experience: love, honor, respect, compassion. I suddenly saw the connections that had once been invisible lying clearly in front of me: the historical thread that links all music, as each generation and every sound influences and inspires the next. It was a revelation to discover these connections. The music of The Carter Family was as significant—maybe even more so—as the music of The Kinks. The musical greats that moved my father—Hank Williams, Ernest Tubb, and the Singing Brakeman, Jimmie Rodgers, Lefty Frizzell, Roy Acuff, Merle Travis—they were all there in the truck, singing to me too. I heard it all twenty years later when my father once again clicked on the radio through his spirit, now found in my memories.

Now, I think I see the affinity my father felt with a musician like Johnny Cash. He could feel in Cash's music the deep sense of struggle, the will to stand up, the strength to fight for something better, and the unbreakable refusal to give in. The courage leads to a place less painful and creates a space more peaceful. Music can give this to us but only through the stewardship of citizen-artists who straddle two worlds: the artistic one in their minds and the compassionate one in their hearts. Cash did this for more than four decades, embodying Albert Camus's belief that "music is . . . the most perfect of the arts. I should like to know what there is in common between a melodic phrase and everyday life. Nothing is more ideal than this art: there is no tangible shape, as in painting and sculpture. And yet each musical work has its own individuality. Music expresses the perfect in a manner fluid enough for no effort to be necessary. Thus music is the most perfect art. Better than any other, it has shown us *Art* soaring above life."

As I attempt to do the nearly impossible—thank all those who generously stepped forward to help me realize the dream that is now this book—I look back on a time when I formed new friendships, learned much about a world obscured from view, and ultimately grew in incalculable ways as a person and writer. My debt of gratitude could well be a book unto itself.

First let me thank my thoughtful editor and friend Carl Bromley of Nation Books, who has believed in my vision and work since we first met at the *Nation* magazine over a decade ago. His enthusiasm for and commitment to this project is immeasurable. I also would like to offer deep appreciation to Johnny Cash's longtime manager Lou Robin, who was the very first to offer support, generously providing me a long contact list of people connected to Cash. Johnny Cash's son John Carter Cash was also supportive throughout and does much to carry on his father's significant legacy. Next, are two people to whom I owe much, because their guidance and counsel were unwavering and profound: Cash's official discographer, John L. Smith, and the folk scholar Ronald Cohen. Sadly, John L. Smith died on May 4, 2009, after a battle with cancer. This book owes much to John's generous spirit and never-ending support. I offer my most heartfelt sympathy to his family. As his wife Charlene (Charlie, as John called her) wrote me: "He won't be able to accompany you once the book is released but you know he will be with you." I will miss him. Longtime Cash emcee Johnny Western and great Tennessee Two (and later Three) bass player Marshall Grant provided me with deeply moving, rich stories that made this narrative come alive. Likewise, the legendary musician Norman Blake was generous with his time and exceedingly eloquent in discussing his creative collaboration with Johnny Cash.

I wish to thank writer and filmmaker Sandra Schulman, who was one of the very first to speak to me about the mysterious folksinger Peter La Farge. Her passion for La Farge's story made her insights all the more enlightening. Povy La Farge, Peter La Farge's sister, provided me with an account of her brother's life that was equal measures charming, witty, and heartbreaking. A wonderful storyteller with an obliging spirit, Povy's contribution was invaluable. Likewise, Peter La Farge's half brother, John Pen La Farge, spoke about his brother and his family's life in an engagingly intelligent and sophisticated manner that also went a long way in helping me. I thank them and the entire La Farge family.

The scholars, archivists, curators, producers, and folklorists who keep the folk flame burning were also unfailingly helpful. Jeff Place of the Smithsonian Folkways Recordings and Todd Harvey of the Alan Lomax Collection at the Library of Congress supplied key research materials and always made themselves available to me as I seemingly contacted them daily. The inimitable Archie Green, considered by many to be the dean of American folklore, invited me to his house on a number of occasions to speak at length about my book and its subject. Producer Greg Geller, who worked on recent Johnny Cash box sets for Sony-Legacy Recordings, always assisted in meeting my various requests for recording session notes and other crucial historical recording-related materials for both Cash and La Farge.

From the Native community there are so many who spoke to me openly and honestly that I am left with a lasting feeling of immense pride in the story that their words played a significant role in crafting. In particular, John Trudell and Dennis Banks of the American Indian Movement contributed a unique insiders' depiction of two of the most momentous Native actions in American history as well as the Native movement in general. They supplied an authoritative assessment of the influence of *Bitter Tears*—and specifically Johnny Cash and Peter La Farge's music—on the Native movement. Jose Barriero of the National Museum of the American Indian in Washington, D.C., added not only historical weight to the narrative but also humor in regard to some its characters, including Marlon Brando and Muhammad Ali. I must offer much thanks to Mary Ahenakew of the Native Information Network, who met my myriad requests for books, papers, and other hard-to-find Native research materials with a kindness and consideration that made my research work less a task and more a joyous journey of discovery.

I am indebted to the countless musicians who showed me much patience and generosity in addressing my many queries. The great folksinger Tom Paxton was one of the first to speak to me about Peter La Farge and the folk revival movement. Paxton's eloquence opened a door for my book for which I will be forever grateful. The immensely talented and courageous Buffy Sainte-Marie shared her memories and moving experiences. They are priceless. Of course I must mention Pete Seeger, who even in brief conversations provided lasting insights. George Wein, the remarkable jazz impresario and founder of both the Newport Jazz and Newport Folk Festivals, welcomed me into his home and regaled me with rich stories of a history he had a big hand in shaping. Arlo Guthrie, who is connected to both Cash and La Farge, spoke so powerfully about his time as a young musician among these larger-than-life artists that his words made me weep.

A special note of thanks to my agent, William Clark, a resolute and dedicated champion of both this book and my work. Likewise, it has been a great pleasure to work with Basic Books publisher John Scherer. I thank him for offering me such an incredible opportunity to tell the extraordinary story of Johnny Cash's *Bitter Tears* record. I am deeply grateful to Gregory Rossi, who eagerly volunteered to read through a draft of this book, affording me the advantage of a sharp pair of eyes and an even sharper mind, while demonstrating the true depth of his friendship. His sincere reflection made passages of this book more refined. I am eternally thankful to Shepard Fairey, a friend and collaborator whose passion for this book is found in the artwork that graces the cover. From our first conversation, he grasped the book's spirit and created an iconic design beautifully evoking the force of the words found inside. Special thanks to the Nation Investigative Fund for its research support. I would also like to thank the Nation Institute for its ongoing support. A note of appreciation to Charles Soule of Cohen & Gressner for his expert legal services in helping me research a myriad of federal documents. Both the Nation Investigative Fund and Cohen & Gressner were vital in my investigative research. Many thanks to the indomitable photographer Jim Marshall, who contributes never-before-published photos of Peter La Farge, Bob Dylan, Tom Paxton, and Odetta, among others. I am proud to include them here. I also offer this book as a special tribute to the late Freddy "Frogs" Toscano, a special person who lived every moment to the absolute fullest and Archie Green, both of whom died just after I completed this book. You both will be missed but never forgotten.

Finally, I composed this book in various San Francisco neighborhoods, throughout the borough of Brooklyn and upstate New York, and many places in between. I thank all those who opened their doors to me, offering a comfortable place to write. In particular, I am grateful to the San Francisco Public Library, Brooklyn Public Library, and New York Public Library, especially the Performing Arts Library. Once again the people at these institutions and the libraries themselves prove how vital a social service the public library is in our society. In a time when they are underfunded and facing the threat of closure, these bastions of democracy, thought, and culture must be protected and expanded. As always, special thanks to all my friends spread throughout the world, my family in Italia and the United States, and the many people in and around La Lutta NMC. You all played a vital role not only in this book but also in my life: you kept my spirits high during moments when they threatened to slip down low. For that, I am forever grateful.

A BIBLIOGRAPHICAL NOTE

A Heartbeat and a Guitar came to life through hundreds of hours of interviews, research, travel, and listening sessions. There are quite a few good books written about Johnny Cash's life and career, and countless others on the history of folk music, civil rights, and to a lesser degree the Native movement. I tried to immerse myself in each world as deeply as possible, while remaining true to my vision and to the spirit of crafting a work that presents a unique and engaging portrait of a transformative historical moment that fed Cash's artistry, allowing him to produce what I believe is a timeless record in both the musical and the historical sense. There is much overlap among the various narrative threads that form the overarching story found in this book, particularly among the respective interviews; but in the interest of clarity I've tried to keep each section as specific as possible.

With these notes I hope to offer further thanks and praise to those gifted writers, artists, scholars, journalists, musicians, archivists, curators, producers, and activists whose work served such a vital role in helping unlock the story embedded in my head and heart. Much of the newspaper coverage, particularly of the folk music revival, comes from Robert Shelton's tireless reporting for the *New York Times* during the time frame covered in this book. For this reason, I include the biographical note here.

Finally, there are many musicians who appear throughout this book. I listened quite extensively to each of their music catalogues. These are quite large, so it would be almost impossible to mention all of the individual records I listened to beyond those of Cash, La Farge, and a few others.

CASH

For me, learning about Johnny Cash begins and ends with listening, because his music provides the best chronicle of his life. I listened daily for over a year to the album *Bitter Tears: Ballads of the American Indian*, wanting the record to become such a necessary part of my life that I took to studying the music by learning how to perform it, understanding each note as the blood of the body of Cash/La Farge's music and the lyrics as its heartbeat. I first listened to the original Columbia released record and the reissued album by Bear Family Records at Bowling Green State University's Music Library and Sound Recordings Archives. After assembling the materials from the archives, I contacted Richard Weize of Bear Family Records in Germany to discuss his role in reissuing the record, which included Hugh Cherry's essay, the August 24, 1964, *Billboard* ad (Cash's letter), Cash discographer John L. Smith's photos of Cash's visit to Wounded Knee in December 1968, Cash's own story of each song, La Farge's take on working with Cash, and Charles Wolfe's liner notes. I spoke extensively with producer Greg Geller, who continues to work closely with Sony-Legacy Recordings on various releases of Cash's music. Geller supplied me with incredible archival materials, including the session reports of Peter La Farge's Columbia recording *"Ira Hayes" and Other Ballads*. In addition to *Bitter Tears* I listened to all of Cash's Americana explorations to get a feel for what Cash was attempting to do creatively. These albums, recorded between 1960 and 1963, include *Ride This Train, The Lure of the Grand Canyon*, and *Blood, Sweat and Tears*. I also spent time listening to *Orange Blossom Special* and *Johnny Cash Sings the Ballads of the True West*. I recommend visiting the Bear Family Records website, www.bear-family.de, where you can obtain the masterful box set *Come Along and Ride This Train*, which contains all of these records.

There are key Johnny Cash biographies that I found not only enlightening but also especially enjoyable. They include Christopher S. Wrens's *Winners Got Scars Too: The Life and Legends of Johnny Cash* (Dial Press, 1971), Michael Streissguth's *Johnny Cash: The Biography* (Da Capo Press, 2007), and *Ring of Fire: The Johnny Cash Reader* (Da Capo Press, 2003), Peter Lewry's *A Johnny Cash Chronicle: I've Been Everywhere* (Helter Skelter Publishing, 2001), and *Johnny Cash: The Life of an American Icon* (Omnibus, 2003). Cash's own book, *Cash: The Autobiog-*

raphy (HarperOne, 2003), written with Patrick Starr, has these qualities as well, of course. All of these are terrific reads in their own way, providing constructive insight to Cash's remarkable life. Michael Streissguth also graciously spoke to me at length about his work that centers around Cash's career. I would also like to point you to Peter Lewry's website, www.johnnycashfanzine.com, which is full of amazing information on all things related to Johnny Cash. Colin Escott and Martin Hawkins's *Good Rockin' Tonight: Sun Records and the Birth of Rock 'n' Roll* (St. Martin's Griffin, 1992) provided important context.

Incredibly significant is the work of John L. Smith, Cash's official discographer. Smith's *The Johnny Cash Discography* (Greenwood Press, 1985), with a foreword by Johnny Cash and Johnny Western, is meticulously detailed and makes an astonishing contribution to the field of music scholarship. Smith also provided me with his personal correspondence with Cash, newspaper clippings of the Wounded Knee visit, personal photos he took of Cash at Wounded Knee, and innumerable details that made this particular story come to life. Smith's *Another Song to Sing: The Recorded Repertoire of Johnny Cash* (Scarecrow Press, 1989) is an extraordinary compilation of all things related to Cash's music, including dates of sessions, personnel, composers, recording locations, producers, and release dates for LPs, EPs, singles, and CDs. His *Waylon Jennings Discography* (Greenwood Press, 1995) is worth a look as well. With regard to identifying Cash's music as a creative force in democracy, I examined a number of engaging works, including Albert Camus's *Youthful Writings* (Vintage Books, 1977), William Blake's *The Complete Prose and Poetry of William Blake* (University of California Press, 2008), André Gide's *If It Die . . . : An Autobiography* (Vintage, 2001), and Cervantes' *Don Quixote* (Harper Perennial, 2005).

For my account of Johnny Cash's first Carnegie Hall show, I drew on interviews with Carnegie Hall representatives, references from Cash's autobiography, interviews with Johnny Western and Marshall Grant, and newspaper coverage, most notably that of Robert Shelton of the *New York Times*. Carnegie Hall's Rob Hudson was invaluable; he gave me access to the building itself to help with my effort to re-create how the day may have unfolded on Cash's first visit in 1962. Hudson supplied me with key archival materials, including the famous Carnegie Hall ledger, the Cash program guide, relevant newspaper articles, archival photos of Carnegie Hall, and countless hours of support and thoughtful feedback. I am indebted to him. I wish to thank Nithya Rajederan for first helping me contact Carnegie Hall's archivist Gino Francesconi, who was also supportive.

For my discussion of Jimmie Rodgers, I looked at Nolan Porterfield's *Jimmie Rodgers: The Life and Times of America's Blue Yodeler* (University Press of Mississippi, 2007), Mary E. Davis's *Waiting for a Train: Jimmie Rodgers's America* (Rounder Books, 2008), and Carrie Rodgers's *My Husband, Jimmie Rodgers* (Vanderbilt University Press, 1995). Archie Green, the dean of American folklore, shared his recollections not only of Jimmie Rodgers and Johnny Cash but also of Merle Travis. Specifically, Green's *Only a Miner: Studies in Recorded Coal Mining Songs* (University of Illinois Press, 1972) is an excellent resource. Also, "Merle Travis on Home Ground" (*Sing Out!* 25:1, January 1976), "The Saga of Sixteen Tons" (*United Mine Workers Journal*, 10:4, December 1, 1955), and Pat Travis Eatherly's *In Search of My Father* (Broadman Press, 1987) were all helpful.

Similarly, my descriptions of Cash's meeting with Ed McCurdy and later Peter La Farge are based on interviews with Johnny Western, Cash's own statements, and La Farge's story, which is found in his personal notes and in *Sing Out!*, the folk magazine. McCurdy's most recent manager, Doug Yeager, recalled the details of Cash's friendship with McCurdy. Unfortunately, many of the people involved with the recording of *Bitter Tears* are no longer with us, so for my depiction of the *Bitter Tears* recording sessions, I relied on interviews with two key musicians who were there, Norman Blake and Marshall Grant. Blake is one of the finest musicians of that or any era, and his insight into Cash's music and career were both touching and decidedly educational. Producer Bob Johnston offered a colorful analysis of *Bitter Tears* and the significance of Cash as an incomparable music visionary. There were many who offered opinions and perspectives on the controversy surrounding *Bitter Tears*, but none had as intimate a connection as Johnny Western, who worked hand-in-hand with Cash to fight back against the censoring of the song. Hugh Cherry's essay, included with the reissue of *Bitter Tears*, was also helpful in crafting this story. In further piecing together the "polite" censoring of Cash's *Bitter Tears*, William H. Chafe's *Civilities and Civil Rights: Greensboro, North Carolina, and the Black Struggle for Freedom* (Oxford University Press,

1981) and discussions with Jordan Green of the Institute of Southern Studies in Durham, North Carolina, were extremely illuminating.

For my portrayal of Cash's connection to The Carter Family, I drew on a number of critical writings about the first family of folk, including Mark Zwonitzer and Charles Hirshberg's magnificent biography, *Will You Miss Me When I'm Gone?: The Carter Family and Their Legacy in American Music* (Simon & Schuster, 2004). Others include Lee Smith's novel *The Devil's Dream* (based on The Carter Family; Ballantine Books, 1993), Fred Soklov's *The Carter Family Collection* (Hal Leonard Corporation, 1999) and *The Original Carter Family: With a Biography by Johnny Cash* (Hal Leonard Corporation, 1999), and Kathy Conkwright's 2005 PBS American Experience documentary *The Carter Family: Will the Circle Be Unbroken*. Also informative was Ed Badeaux's "The Carters of Rye Cove," (*Sing Out!* 11, no. 2, April/May 1961). Several films involving Cash deserve a mention. The first, and one of the finest, is Robert Elfstrom's 2003 documentary, *Johnny Cash: The Man, His World, His Music*. Elfstrom won the Albert Maysles Award for this captivating portrait of Cash. Cash's 1965 appearance on Pete Seeger's PBS show, *Rainbow Quest*, as well as various episodes of his own program, *The Johnny Cash Show*, prove just how powerful he was as a performer and how committed he was to social issues like the Native cause. Cash also starred as the chief of the Cherokee Nation in the 1969 film *The Trail of Tears*. The film tells the story of the forced relocation of the Cherokee, and the long journey during which 4,000 of the 15,000 Cherokees died.

Finally, I also spoke with Dick Boak of the Martin Guitar Company, who worked closely with the musician in building the perfect D-28 Martin that Cash loved so dearly. His recollections served to bring a lively element to Cash's work.

LA FARGE

As I did with Cash, I began assembling what I could on Peter La Farge by listening to his music, including his first Columbia record, *"Ira Hayes" and Other Ballads*, produced by John Hammond. But the story of Peter La Farge became alive for me when I spoke with Sandra Schulman, who has dedicated her filmmaking and writing talents to rightfully transforming Peter La Farge's life from an asterisk in folk music history into a focal point among the genre's most important performers. Specifically, Schulman and Delores Smith's thirty-two-minute documentary film on La Farge titled *The Ballad of Peter La Farge* (Slink Productions/One Woman Works, 2007) was informative, skillfully presenting an overview of La Farge's all-too-brief life.

I had the good fortune to spend time at the Smithsonian Folkways Archive in Washington, D.C., which contains most of what there is about La Farge. There I was able to begin knitting together some of the worn threads of La Farge's long-forgotten story. Liner notes written for La Farge's Folkways records—including *Peter La Farge Sings Cowboy Songs* (1963), *Woman's Blues* (1965), *As Long as the Grass Shall Grow* (1965), and *Peter La Farge on the Warpath* (1965)—and notes by Oliver La Farge for Peter's Columbia recording *"Ira Hayes" and Other Ballads* were enormously helpful. Also, the acerbic Seymour Krim's essay on La Farge, "Son of Laughing Boy," found in *What's This Cat's Story? The Best of Seymour Krim* (Paragon House, 1991) was enriching as well as humorous. Moreover, I am deeply indebted to Visual Materials Archivist Stephanie Smith of the Smithsonian's Center for Folklife and Cultural Heritage for helping me track down nearly one-third of the photos related to La Farge and the folk revival that appear in this book. For my description of La Farge's relationship with Folkways' Moe Asch, I drew from many memos, letters, and other correspondence found in La Farge's Smithsonian Folkways Archive file. I also found *Making People's Music: Moe Asch and Folkways Records* (Smithsonian Institution Press, 1998) by Peter D. Goldsmith and *Folkways Records: Moses Asch and His Encyclopedia of Sound* (Routledge, 2003) by Tony Olmstead to be extremely valuable. For details on his relationship with prominent folk artist manager Harold Leventhal, I relied on Michael Kleff, who is currently working on a biography of Leventhal. I also questioned everyone I spoke to about Leventhal and his relationship to the musicians he managed.

A number of people who knew La Farge during his time on the folk scene spoke to me eloquently about the musician's life. Through a lengthy correspondence with Buffy Sainte-Marie, I learned more about La Farge's troubles, but also just how isolated each one was in the folk scene as, essentially, the only musicians tackling Native issues. My sketch of La Farge's relationship with Bob Dylan was deeply informed by my interview with Arlo Guthrie. Also enlightening was my discussion with Suzie Rotolo. Rotolo's *A Freewheelin' Time: A Memoir of Greenwich Village in the Sixties* (Broadway, 2008) is an engaging chronicle of her time with Dylan and living in Greenwich Village in the 1960s. Julius Lester, now at the University of Massachusetts, Amherst, provided me with a key interview early on. Former *Sing Out!* writer Josh Dunson recalled many important moments that found their way into this book. Of note are Dunson's own books, *Freedom in the Air: Song Movements of the Sixties* (Greenwood Press, 1980) and *Anthology of American Folk Music* (a songbook; Oak Publications, 1973), co-edited with Ethel Raim.

Musician Tom Russell's first-rate article in the January 18, 1985, *Goldmine* magazine was especially beneficial. I also interviewed Russell, who imparted major insight to La Farge's story. I culled some great details from interviews with Robert Cohen, Ramblin' Jack Elliott, Arlo Guthrie, Dick Weissman, Happy Traum, John Cohen, Julius Lester, Oscar Brand, George Wein, Guy Carawan, Jim Marshall, and numerous others. For my sketch of La Farge's participation in the performance of *Dark of the Moon*, I read the play by Howard Richardson and William Berney (Theatre Arts Books, 1985). Carnegie Hall's Rob Hudson supplied me with the program guide of the play, which was staged by Temple Productions at Carnegie Hall Playhouse on February 26, 1958; it lists Peter La Farge as Burt Atkins.

In painting a portrait of La Farge's life, his sister, Povy Bigbee, and his half brother, John Pen La Farge, were extremely gracious and exceedingly obliging in providing the missing details of the one-time bronc rider turned folksinger. In particular, Povy's depiction really helped me understand La Farge's struggle with mental illness. Her openness informed my telling of the naval accident that deeply scarred Peter and allowed for answers to the questions lingering around his untimely death. John also met with me in Santa Fe, New Mexico, where he shared his precious family photo album. Here I discovered photos of Peter riding in a rodeo and as a young boy in Colorado, as well as his naval portrait. All of these photos appear in this book. For my account of La Farge's moving performance of the "Ballad of Ira Hayes" in Alan Lomax's apartment, I am indebted to Todd Harvey of the Library of Congress's Alan Lomax Collection. Harvey set me up with an audiotape that captured the entire gathering of musicians at the folk impressario's New York City apartment. The unedited recording was rich with details that pushed this book to a higher level. La Farge's performance will appear on film sometime soon in *Ballads, Blues, and Bluegrass*. In addition to Povy's version of La Farge's death, I relied on interviews with La Farge's contemporaries, including Oscar Brand and Tom Paxton, as well as articles, editorials, and essays found in *Broadside* no. 64 (November 15, 1965) and *Sing Out!* magazine from that same month.

For my snapshot of Oliver La Farge, I found it most beneficial to read Oliver La Farge's 1930 Pulitzer Prize–winning novel, *Laughing Boy: A Navajo Love Story* (Mariner Books, 2004). Other Oliver La Farge books I explored include *A Pictorial History of the American Indian* (Crown, 1956), *Behind the Mountains* (Riverside Press, 1956), and *The Changing Indian* (from a symposium arranged by the American Association on Indian Affairs, 1942). I also read many of the essays, articles, and editorials he wrote for various publications, including the *New Yorker*, the *New York Times*, and the *Washington Post*, among many others.

NATIVE MOVEMENT

I tried my best to investigate as many materials as possible and to contact their respective authors, as well as the key Native activists discussed. The late Vine Deloria Jr.'s work was essential to my understanding of the Native movement, especially his *Custer Died for Your Sins: An Indian Manifesto* (University of Oklahoma Press, 1988), which is a blisteringly powerful read. I also examined Deloria's *Spirit and Reason: The Vine Deloria Reader* (Fulcrum, 2006), *Aggressions of Civilization: Federal Indian Policy Since the 1880s* (Temple University Press, 1984), *American Indian Policy in the Twentieth Century* (University of Oklahoma Press, 1985), *A Brief History of the Federal Responsibility to the American Indian* (Washington Department of Health, Education, and Welfare, 1979), and *The Nations Within: The Past and Future of American Indian Sovereignty* (Pantheon, 1984). The materials produced by the National Youth Council are quite extraordinary and inspiring to read. The University of New Mexico, University Libraries, Center for Southwest Research houses the National Indian Youth Council's records. The NIYC's Clyde Warrior's writings, including two influential essays, "Which One Are You? Five Types of Young Indians" and "We Are Not Free," were stirring. The latter can be found in *Red Power: The American Indians' Fight for Freedom*, edited by Alvin M. Josephy Jr. (University of Nebraska Press, 1971). The former appears in Stan Steiner's *The New Indians* (Harper & Row, 1968). I re-read *Bury My Heart at Wounded Knee* (Holt Paperbacks, 2001) by Dee Brown. With each successive reading, the book's power and pain only grow. D'Arcy McNickle's amazing *The Surrounded* (University of New Mexico Press, 1978) led me to understand how it stirred so many, including the actor Marlon Brando, to join the Native cause. Other McNickle books that I investigated include *They Came Here First: The Epic of the American Indian* (Harper & Row, 1975), *The Indian in American Society* (National Congress of American Indians, 1955), *An Historical Review of Federal-Indian Relationships* (American Indian Policy Review Commission, 1975), and *Indian Man: A Life of Oliver La Farge* (Indiana University, 1971). The last title provided much-needed insight into a key figure found in this book. Howard Zinn pointed me to *Akwesasne Notes*, describing the magazine as "remarkable." It is—as is the work of *Akwesasne Notes* editor John Mohawk, whose *Basic Call to Consciousness* (Native Voices, 2005) is an outstanding example of this groundbreaking work.

In crafting the Tuscarora standoff with Robert Moses, I drew upon many sources, but none more searing and compelling than Chief Clinton Rickard's *Fighting Tuscarora: The Autobiography of Chief Clinton Rickard* (Syracuse University Press, 1994), edited by Barbara Graymont. I examined *Tuscarora Nation* (Arcadia Publishing, 2007) by Bryan Printup and Neil Patterson Jr. and *The Six Nations of New York: The 1892 United States Extra Census Bulletin* (Cornell University Press, 1996) by Robert W. Venables. In examining Robert Moses, I reviewed the extensive *New York Times* coverage as well as Robert Caro's exceptional *The Power Broker: The Rise and Fall of Robert Moses* (Vintage, 1975).

For my description of the Allegany Seneca–Kinzua Dam situation I tapped a number of informative sources. Joy A. Bilharz's *The Allegany Seneca and Kinzua Dam: Forced Relocation through Two Generations* (University of Nebraska Press, 2002) is a definitive work on the subject. Thomas S. Alber's *Cornplanter: Chief Warrior of the Allegany Senecas* (Syracuse University Press, 2007) proved beneficial as well. Other key sources that helped shape both the Tuscarora and Seneca stories include Douglas M. George-Kanentiio's *Iroquois on Fire: A Voice from the Mohawk Nation* (University of Nebraska Press, 2008), with a forward by

Vine Deloria, and *Iroquois Culture and Commentary* (Clear Light Publishers, 2005), and Laurence M. Hauptman's *Conspiracy of Interests: Iroquois Dispossession and the Rise of New York State* (Syracuse University Press, 2001) and *Seven Generations of Iroquois Leadership: The Six Nations Since 1800* (Syracuse University Press, 2008), which is excellent. I interviewed both authors as well. I am also deeply grateful for the assistance and guidance of Distant Eagle (James David Audin), who connected me to the author-activists listed above. Distant Eagle's own extraordinary book *Circle of Life: Traditional Teachings of Native American Elders* (Clear Light Publishers, 2004) was inspiring.

I reviewed Edmund Wilson's original 1959 "Reporter at Large" articles for the *New Yorker*, which appeared as a four-part series that later became the book *Apologies to the Iroquois* (Syracuse University Press, 1992), which I also read. Gore Vidal's essay "Edmund Wilson: Nineteenth-Century Man," found in *Virgin Islands: Essays 1992–1997* (Andre Deutsch, 1997), proved useful. Brooks Atkinson's "Critics-at-Large" column for the *New York Times*, in which he featured the Seneca plight from 1961 to 1965, furnished significant information as well.

For my account of the Ira Hayes story, I explored a number of materials. James Bradley's *Flags of Our Fathers: Heroes of Iwo Jima* (Bantam, 2006) is a compelling rendering of the flag raising and its aftermath. In 2006, Clint Eastwood directed a feature film based on Bradley's book with actor Adam Beach presenting a sympathetic portrayal of Hayes. Delbert Mann's 1961 film *The Outsider* and Tony Curtis's portrayal of Hayes also provided an interesting perspective on the former Marine's tragic life. Tony Curtis's memoir, *American Prince* (Harmony, 2008), proved useful. Catching a glimpse of the real Ira Hayes in the 1949 *Sands of Iwo Jima* was worthwhile for me as well. I also did a rigorous analysis of nationwide newspaper stories about Hayes, finding the most notable coverage in papers based in Chicago. I found James LaGrand's *Indian Metropolis: Native Americans in Chicago, 1945–75* (University of Illinois Press, 2005) educational in regard to the forced relocation of Native people to urban areas. Likewise, Kent Mackenzie's 1961 film *The Exiles* is an astonishing work that I highly recommend.

For my discussion of the Native Pima, I contacted the Gila River Indian Community. Information can be found through their website, www.gilariver.org. I found *An Oasis Remembered—An Indian Agency Sacaton, Arizona: A Pictorial and Historical Review About the Place and Its People* (Trafford Publishing, 2006) by Robert E. Ramsey, *A Pima Remembers* (University of Arizona Press, 1959) by George Webb, *The Pima-Maricopa* (Chelsea House Publishing, 1989) by Henry F. Dobyns, *The Papago (Tohono O'odham) and Pima Indians of Arizona* (Filer Press, 2000) by Ruth M. Underhill, and *The Pima Indians* (Government Printing Office, 1908; reprinted by Kessinger Publishing in 2006) by Frank Russell, all very helpful.

For my profile of the Lumbee Indians, I reviewed *The Only Land I Know: A History of the Lumbee Indians* (Syracuse University Press, 1996) by Adolph L. Dial and David K. Eliades, *Living Indian Histories: The Lumbee and Tuscarora People in North Carolina* (University of North Carolina Press, 2006) by Gerald Snider, and *The Lumbee Problem: The Making of an American Indian People* (University of Nebraska Press, 2001) by Karen I. Blu. For my discussion on the fish-in movement, I relied on details from northwest regional newspapers. More significantly, Charles Wilkerson's *Messages from Franks Landing: A Story of Salmon, Treaties, and the Indian Way* (University of Washington Press, 2006) was a fascinating resource.

For my sketch of the American Indian Movement I spoke to a number of former and current members. In particular, AIM cofounder Dennis Banks provided a compelling and thoughtful recollection of his time in the Native movement. There are really no words to describe Banks's moving book *Ojibwa Warrior: Dennis Banks and the Rise of the American Indian Movement* (University of Oklahoma Press, 2002). Native activist and artist John Trudell provided me with some of the most emotional details about Peter La Farge and the rise of the Native movement. I've been familiar with Trudell's work for some time and found it most useful in shaping my own thinking around this book. His book *Lines from a Mined Mind: The Words of John Trudell* (Fulcrum, 2008), with a foreword by Louise Erdrich, and the beautiful record *AKA Graffiti Man* (Rykodisc, 1992) were especially bountiful. The 2005 documentary film directed by Heather Rae called *Trudell* is worth attention. Another noteworthy film I screened is *Incident at Oglala: The Leonard Peltier Story* (1992), directed by Michael Apted and produced by Robert Redford. Apted also directed a feature film produced by Robert De Niro called

Thunderheart starring Trudell and including an appearance by Dennis Banks, and this one is worth a look too.

Likewise, Paul Chaat Smith and Robert Warrior's *Like a Hurricane: The Indian Movement from Alcatraz to Wounded Knee* (New Press, 1997) was of assistance. Paul Chaat Smith also spoke to me about the Native movement, Oliver and Peter La Farge, and Johnny Cash. I investigated Troy Johnson's authoritative *The American Indian Occupation of Alcatraz Island: Red Power and Self-Determination* (University of Nebraska Press, 2008) as well as his *You Are on Indian Land: Alcatraz Island, 1969–1971* (University of California, 1995) and *Red Power: The Native American Civil Rights Movement* (Chelsea House Publications, 2007). I later interviewed Johnson, who presented me with important insights about the Native movement as well as *Bitter Tears*. John William Sayer's *Ghost Dancing the Law: The Wounded Knee Trials* (Harvard University Press, 1997) is also worthwhile. Finally, there is an exhaustive list of books that I scoured during my research, particularly at New York's Museum of the American Indian. Charles Wilkerson's *Blood Struggle: The Rise of Modern Indian Nations* (W. W. Norton, 2006) is a thorough study that I relied upon. I enjoyed as well Clifford E. Trafzer's *As Long as the Grass Shall Grow and Rivers Flow: A History of Native Americans* (Wadsworth, 1999). Additionally, Jose Barriero, formerly of the American Indian Movement and currently of the National Museum of the American Indian in Washington, D.C., was extremely helpful, as was Rovena Abrams of the Seneca Nation.

I screened the twenty-nine-minute 1965 film *Meet Marlon Brando* and its outtakes with the film's director, Albert Maysles. The film offers a glimpse of Brando's profound feeling for the Native cause. I also reviewed Brando's FBI file, which was quite extensive. Additionally, I relied on Lawrence Grobel's *Conversations with Brando* (Cooper Square Press, 1999), *Marlon Brando: Actor and Activist* (Biographiq, 2008), Stefan Kanfer's *Somebody: The Reckless Life and Remarkable Career of Marlon Brando* (Knopf, 2008), and Marlon Brando's *Brando: Songs My Mother Taught Me*, written with Robert Lindsey (Random House, 1994). For Dick Gregory, I culled reporting from across the country, including articles from New York, Washington, D.C., and Chicago dailies. Gregory's *Callus on My Soul*, is a captivating memoir of his life and his commitment to the Native cause. For Muhammad Ali, I reviewed Mike Marqusee's gripping *Redemption Song: Muhammad Ali and the Spirit of the Sixties* (Verso, 2005). I also spent time at the Institute of American Indian Arts Museum in Santa Fe, New Mexico, where I found the exhibit Fritz Scholder: An Intimate Look helpful in creatively contextualizing my own consciousness in regards to the reality of life for Native people in the United States. Also worthwhile is Fritz Scholder: Indian/Not Indian, an excellent exhibit presented by the National Museum of the American Indian. I urge everyone to view Scholder's beautiful and transformative work, particularly *Drunk Indian #2* (1972) and *Dead Indian in Gallup* (1973). While in Santa Fe, I met with actor Gary Farmer, a Canadian Cayuga, and we discussed his work as a musician, actor, and activist. Farmer provided many amusing and interesting anecdotes about Marlon Brando as well. I strongly recommend screening Jim Jarmusch's *Dead Man* (1995) specifically for Farmer's magnificent performance. Other exceptional Farmer performances are found in *Powwow Highway* (1989) and *Smoke Signals* (1998). His music with the band Gary Farmer and the Troublemakers is worth a listen as well. Finally, the University of New Mexico has assembled an impressive collection of materials related to the Native movement, in particular the National Indian Youth Council. The university's Inventory of the National Indian Youth Council Photograph Collection, 1962–1995, part of the Rocky Mountain Online Archive, is an outstanding resource. Here, thanks to the thoughtful assistance of Kari L. Schleher and Laura Katharine York, I was able to track down hard to find photos of the NIYC—in particular, the 1961 photo of the NIYC from collection 000-703 National Indian Youth Council Photograph Collection of the Center for Southwest Research, University Libraries, University of New Mexico.

FOLKSONG
My folksong education began with the highly engaging work of folk scholar Ronald D. Cohen. Cohen's *Rainbow Quest: The Folk Music Revival and American Society, 1940–1970* (University of Massachusetts Press, 2002) is a wonderful portrait of the folk music revival; it is thoroughly researched, filled with detailed notes, and offers a helpful bibliography. The book led me to Cohen himself, and countless meetings and discussions ensued. Cohen also edited *Broadside* magazine's Sis Cunningham and Gordon Friesen's joint biography *Red Dust and Broadsides* (University of Massachusetts

Press, 1999), which contains an introduction by Pete Seeger. In many ways, Cohen served as my all-knowing guide, connecting me to a diverse group of the most significant people in the folk world. Jeff Place of Smithsonian Institute's Folkways remained a consistent resource throughout. Place opened the archives' doors for me, and there I thoroughly researched the music of Peter La Farge, Buffy Sainte-Marie, Pat Skye, Pete Seeger, and a host of other folk stalwarts. I also spent time researching the Folkways collection of *Sing Out!* and *Broadside* magazines that cover the early to mid-sixties. I gathered together numerous articles on folksong, La Farge, Cash, Bob Dylan, Cisco Houston, and Seeger, as well as the numerous others involved in folksong who appear throughout this book. Also noteworthy was Place and Cohen's *The Best of* Broadside *1962–1968: Anthems of the American Underground from the Pages of Broadside Magazine* (Smithsonian Folkways, 2000), which is an excellent compilation from the publication (which at one time was mimeographed) that asserted such a strong presence in the folk community.

For my history of Guy Carawan and the Highlander Research and Education Center, I first interviewed Carawan at length. I then relied on Carawan's music and his fine books, written with his wife, Candie, which include *Sing for Freedom: The Story of the Civil Rights Movement through Its Songs* (NewSouth Books, 2008), *We Shall Overcome! Songs of the Southern Freedom Movement* (Oak Publications, 1963), and *Ain't You Got a Right to the Tree of Life? The People of Johns Island, South Carolina; Their Faces, Their Words, and Their Songs* (University of Georgia Press, 1994). E. B. White's "Moment of History" in the *New Yorker* (March 25, 1965) was also useful.

As for my sketch of Woody Guthrie, I began with a trip to the Woody Guthrie Archives in New York, where I sifted through the folksinger's letters and other correspondence while listening to many hours of interviews with notable figures from his life. I spoke with his daughter Nora and son Arlo, as well as with numerous musicians from Tom Paxton to Norman Blake, Dick Weissman and Buffy Sainte-Marie to Oscar Brand, John Trudell, and Tom Paxton about Guthrie. Of course, Guthrie's book *Bound for Glory* (Peter Smith Publisher, 1985) is a must-read. I also enjoyed Joe Klein's *Woody Guthrie: A Life* (Delta, 2009) and Ed Cray and Studs Terkel's *Ramblin' Man: The Life and Times of Woody Guthrie* (W. W. Norton, 2006). The Woody Guthrie quotation found in the "After" section of this book comes from the musician's own annotations contained within the jacket of *American Folksay Ballads and Dances* (Ash Records) found in the Woody Guthrie Archives (Accession # 2008–100).

For my discussion of Pete Seeger I examined the legendary musician's impressive body of work, including his voluminous records and his writings, such as *Carry It On* (Hal Leonard Corporation, 1991) and *The Incomplete Folksinger* (Simon & Schuster, 1973). I examined *Reprints from the People's Song Bulletin 1946–1949* (Oak Publications, 1961), with a foreword by Pete Seeger, and also looked at David King Dunaway's *How Can I Keep from Singing? The Ballad of Pete Seeger* (Da Capo Press, 1980) and *"Sing Out, Warning! Sing Out, Love!": The Writings of Lee Hays* (University of Massachusetts Press, 2004), edited by Robert S. Koppelman. A few films by filmmaker Jim Brown were also useful: *Pete Seeger: The Power of Song* (2007), *The Weavers: Wasn't That a Time?* (1982) and *Isn't This a Time: A Tribute to Harold Leventhal* (2004). Of special note are Bruce Springsteen's thrilling record of Seeger songs titled *We Shall Overcome: The Seeger Sessions* (Sony, 2006) and his 1982 record *Nebraska* (Columbia). The latter bears a huge debt to Cash's *Bitter Tears* record. My discussion of Bruce Springsteen was informed by June Skinner Sawyers and Martin Scorsese's *Racing in the Street: The Bruce Springsteen Reader* (Penguin, 2004), Dave Marsh's *Bruce Springsteen: The Definitive Biography, 1972–2003* (Routledge, 2003), and Robert Coles's *Bruce Springsteen's America: The People Listening, A Poet Singing* (Random House, 2004).

For my depiction of Johnny Cash and Peter La Farge's performance at the New York Folk Festival, I relied on Robert Shelton's reporting in the *New York Times*. Archie Green, who served as one of the emcees/moderators of the festival, provided essential details about both La Farge and Cash. Once again, Rob Hudson provided some important pieces of information that helped me tell this part of the story, supplying me with the festival's program guide and related newspaper stories.

The writings on Dylan are so vast that perhaps only Jesus has been the subject of more books. For this reason I relied on a handful of materials that include discussions of folk, La Farge, and Cash in relation to Dylan. The resources I discovered to be beneficial for my purposes were Anthony Scaduto's *Bob Dylan: An Intimate Biography* (Signet Books, 1973), Benjamin Hedin's *Studio A: The Bob Dylan Reader* (W. W. Norton,

2005), Howard Sounses's *Down the Highway: The Life of Bob Dylan* (Grove Press, 2002), and the aforementioned Rotolo and Dylan memoirs. Of special note are Robert Shelton's *No Direction Home: The Life and Music of Bob Dylan* (Da Capo Press, 2003) and *The Formative Dylan: Transmission and Stylistic Influences, 1961–1963* (Scarecrow Press, 2001). Of course, Dylan's own *Chronicles: Volume One* (Simon & Schuster, 2005) is quite interesting; it helped me with not only his story but those of Peter La Farge and Johnny Cash. Martin Scorsese's 2005 documentary, *No Direction Home*, is worth a look as well.

For my portrait of John Hammond, the more notable titles I read include Dunstan Prial's *The Produce: John Hammond and the Soul of American Music* (Picador, 2007), John Hammond's own *John Hammond on Record: An Autobiography* (Penguin, 1981), and Gary Marmorstein's *The Label: The Story of Columbia Records* (Da Capo Press, 2007). In addition to my research at the Library of Congress's Alan Lomax Collection, my discussion of Alan Lomax was supported by his seemingly infinite recording and documentary work, including *The Land Where the Blues Began* (New Press, 2002), *American Ballads and Folk Songs* (Dover, 1994), written with John Lomax, *Hard Hitting Songs for Hard-Hit People* (Oak Publications, 1967), written with Woody Guthrie and Pete Seeger, and Ronald Cohen's excellent *Alan Lomax: Selected Writings, 1934–1997* (Routledge, 2005).

For my account of the Newport Folk Festival, my interview with George Wein was revelatory. The venerable producer added much weight to my stories of Dylan, La Farge, and Cash as well. Wein's autobiography, *Myself Among Others* (Da Capo Press, 2004), is a very enjoyable insider's take on significant cultural happenings from jazz to folk to civil rights. In his note to me inside the book, Wein wrote, "Keep searching—you will find it." With his help I certainly had a wonderful head start. Similarly, Studs Terkel's work went a long way in helping me weave together the various narrative threads found in this book. Unfortunately, Terkel died before I could speak to him, but his memoir, *Touch and Go* (The New Press, 2007), and the archival recordings of his show, *The Wax Museum*, were of great assistance. Also, I found the following two Murray Lerner documentaries revealing: *The Other Side of the Mirror: Bob Dylan Live at Newport Folk Festival 1963–1965* (2007) and *Festival!* (1967).

Other books of note include *Josh White: Society Blues* (Routledge, 2002) by Elijah Wald, *The Mayor of MacDougal Street: A Memoir* (Da Capo

Press, 2006) by Dave von Ronk with Elijah Wald, *Positively 4th Street: The Lives and Times of Joan Baez, Bob Dylan, Mimi Baez Fariña, and Richard Fariña* (North Point Press, 2002) by David Hadju, *Which Side Are You On? An Inside History of the Folk Music Revival in America* (Continuum International, 2006) by Dick Weissman, *Folk Songs of the Southern Appalachians as Sung by Jean Ritchie* (University Press of Kentucky, 1997), and *900 Miles: The Ballads, Blues and Folksongs of Cisco Houston* (Oak Publications, 1967). I also interviewed David Hadju, who spoke to me at length and with great insight about the folk revival, Cash, and music overall. Dick Weissman, who was a member of the folk group The Journeymen, not only imparted a critical perspective on La Farge but also educated me on folk music.

CIVIL RIGHTS

If one were to combine all the books written on Cash, folksong, and the Native movement, they would comprise a ridiculously small percentage of the books published on civil rights. With this in mind, and for the purposes of this book, I once again read parts of the brilliant *Parting the Waters: America in the King Years, 1954–63* (Peter Smith Publisher, 2006) by Taylor Branch. I also reviewed Branch's *Pillar of Fire: America in the King Years, 1963–65* (Simon & Schuster, 1998) and *At Canaan's Edge: America in the King Years, 1965–68* (Simon & Schuster, 2006). There really is no finer work. Howard Zinn's *SNCC: The New Abolitionists* (South End Press, 2002) is a pioneering work, and his *A People's History of the United States: 1492–Present* (Perennial Classics, 2003) still crackles with the same counterculture spirit that fueled Cash's *Bitter Tears* recording.

Pete Seeger and Bob Reiser's *Everybody Says Freedom: A History of the Civil Rights Movement in Songs and Pictures* (W. W. Norton, 1989) is excellent. Kenneth T. Andrews's *Freedom Is a Constant Struggle* (University of Chicago Press, 2004) was also helpful. For my discussion of Freedom Summer I relied on interviews with Robert Cohen and books such as Doug McAdam's *Freedom Summer* (Oxford University Press, 1988). For my discussion of Bob Moses I read his book, *Radical Equations: Civil Rights from Mississippi to the Algebra Project* (Beacon Press, 2002), as well as Eric Bruner's *And Gently He Shall Lead Them: Robert Parris Moses and Civil Rights in Mississippi* (New York University Press, 1995). James Baldwin's 1962 "Letter from a Region in My Mind," which appeared in the *New*

Yorker and then later became the book *Fire Next Time* (Vintage, 1992), is a powerful manifesto. Again *Redemption Song: Muhammad Ali and the Spirit of the Sixties* (Verso, 2005) by Robert Marqusee was useful, as was *The Autobiography of Malcolm X: As Told to Alex Haley* (Ballantine Books, 1987). Other sources of note include Nicholas van Hoffman's *Mississippi Notebook* (David White Company, 1964) and Jack Mendelshon's *The Martyrs: 16 Who Gave Their Lives for Racial Justice* (Harper & Row, 1966).

A number of works were informative in my discussion of John F. Kennedy, including Gary Wills's *The Kennedy Imprisonment: A Meditation on Power* (Mariner, 2002), Robert Dallek's *An Unfinished Life: John F. Kennedy, 1917–1963* (Little, Brown, 2003), and David Talbot's *Brothers: The Hidden History of the Kennedy Years* (The Free Press, 2008). For my account of Lyndon B. Johnson, Robert A. Caro's studied biography *The Years of Lyndon Johnson: Means of Ascent* (Vintage, 1991) was exceedingly informative, as was Doris Kearns Goodwin's *Lyndon Johnson and the American Dream* (St. Martin's Griffin, 1991). For my discussion of the 1964 presidential election and Barry Goldwater's campaign, the following books were useful: Barry Goldwater's *Conscience of a Conservative* (Hillman Books, 1960) and *With No Apologies* (Berkeley, 1980), J. William Middendorf II's *A Glorious Disaster: Barry Goldwater's Presidential Campaign and the Origins of the Conservative Movement* (Basic Books, 2003), Lee Edwards's *Goldwater: The Man Who Made a Revolution* (Regnery Publishing, 1995), and Rick Perlstein's *Before the Storm: Barry Goldwater and the Unmaking of the American Consensus* (Nation Books, 2009). Perlstein's amazing *Nixonland: The Rise of a President and the Fracturing of America* (Scribner, 2008) went along way in helping me in my characterization of Richard Nixon. In discussing Ronald Reagan I found Lou Cannon's *President Reagan: The Role of a Lifetime* (PublicAffairs, 2000) highly engaging. I also spoke with Dan E. Molder and reviewed his investigative *Dark Victory: Ronald Reagan, MCA, and the Mob* (Viking Penguin, 1987). For background on the Vietnam War, I examined David Halberstam's *The Best and the Brightest* (Ballantine Books, 2003) and Tim O'Brien's *The Things They Carried* (Broadway, 1998) and Ron Kovic's beautiful "Born on the Fourth of July" (Akashic Books, 2005).

INDEX